FROM APPLE PIE
TO PAD THAI

Neighborhood Cooking North of Boston

LINDA BASSETT

Commonwealth Editions

Beverly, Massachusetts

Recipes in this book have been adapted by the author.
Any errors are her own.

Library of Congress Cataloging-in-Publication Data
Bassett, Linda, 1948–
From apple pie to pad Thai: neighborhood cooking
north of Boston / Linda Bassett.
p. cm.
Includes index.
ISBN 1-899833-38-X (pbk.)
1. Cookery, International.
2. Cookery—Massachusetts—Boston.
I. Title.
TX725.A1 B344 2002
641.59—dc21   2002029905

Cover and interior design by Joyce Weston.
Photos of Barbara Lazarides by Ralph P. Turcotte;
all other photos by Janet Knott.
Printed in Canada.

Published by Commonwealth Editions,
an imprint of Memoirs Unlimited, Inc.,
266 Cabot Street, Beverly, Massachusetts 01915.

Visit our Web site: www.commonwealtheditions.com.

For my husband, Tim,
and my children, Marisa and Timmy

CONTENTS

PREFACE

M Y NEIGHBORHOOD is Boston's North Shore, but don't ask me to draw a map. No one here agrees on where it begins or ends. Some say it begins at Chelsea or Revere, but others say Saugus. Some say it ends at Salisbury or Newburyport; others say Methuen or Haverhill or Topsfield. So, here is the consensus: starting on some hazy horizon north of Boston, the North Shore comprises small industrial cities, seaside towns, and cozy suburbs that cling to the sea, winding all the way through the Merrimack Valley to New Hampshire.

For centuries, diverse settlers found their way to our shorelines and schoolhouses, farms and factories. With only family traditions and sundry kitchen tools, they adapted available ingredients to their native recipes. The earliest English settlers, for example, merged English foodways with the Native American "three sisters"—corn, beans, and squash—substituting them for familiar foodstuffs. They even experimented with the Native American technique of cooking in a hole in the ground. Each succeeding group of settlers faced that challenge, right up to recent Asian immigrants, who sometimes use ketchup to season noodles. All these recipes, yanked from their roots and restructured, have created a hyphenated cuisine in the *tradition* of the original: no longer Italian but Italian-American, no longer Greek but Greek-American.

Although the North Shore's culinary pot bubbles with multicultural flavors, the wider perception is that everyone here eats "New England" food. Maybe it's because of our proximity to Plymouth Rock, or because of Norman Rockwell's depiction of family feasts. Certainly our Medford neighbor Fannie Farmer had a significant influence. In 1896, she documented recipes from the American home kitchen in the *Boston Cooking-School Cook Book,* a book that has been firmly planted on America's kitchen shelves for generations. When people who know the book travel to this historic sliver of New England, they seek out restaurants with the familiar dishes. As a result, they leave with the impression that we subsist on a diet of chowder, baked beans, and the occasional boiled lobster. The reality is quite different: we eat food from many traditions. Recipes tweaked by generations of cooks echo their countries of origin but incorporate new accents.

I decided to scribble down what goes on the table when those of us from many traditions gather to celebrate, give thanks, or close the day. As I collected recipes, I met the cooks, home and professional, living and legendary, shy and forthcoming, from descendants of the earliest English settlers to hopeful young faces from Southeast Asia. I found surprising people in unexpected places. In Salisbury, former Peace Corps volunteers Rita Wollmering and Brook Finn coax herbs and heirloom tomatoes from the soil of a saltwater farm. Harley-riding Bob Bolgonese, the owner of an auto body shop, bakes apple pies to relax. He seemed an original until I met burly biker Dan Roland from Groveland, who spends weekends cooking up vats of his Sicilian great-grandmother's tomato sauce. My breath caught at the sight of the house in Marblehead where children of freed slaves opened a bakery while the ink on the Constitution was barely dry. I found jewel-colored bottles of incendiary pepper sauce in Peabody where shopkeepers speak Portuguese, Jewish-American chopped liver in Swampscott, Yankee ship's crackers in Newburyport, and Polish-American cookies in Salem. The home cooks I spoke with carry on the traditions that provided comfort and familiarity to their ancestors. So I gathered recipes from cooks and their neighbors, tested and adapted them, and rewrote the instructions for present-day cooks. Many of them are concerned that no one will cook these dishes in the future—that their children or grandchildren will not be interested or will find the recipes too time consuming.

A small book can't possibly encompass an entire cuisine, so I've included mere tastes to pique your appetite. I've grouped the recipes into chapters based on ethnic traditions; the order of those chapters loosely reflects the chronology of arrival on the North Shore. The final chapter, "The Global Table," collects recipes from a variety of ethnic groups, some of whom have arrived only in the past decades. You'll also find two "mini-chapters" in the book, with recipes from country clubs and diners. Each in its own way reflects "neighborhood" cooking, having taken the dishes from Grandma's table and re-created the comforts of home in another environment.

To get a true flavor of each tradition, I interviewed professional and home cooks throughout the North Shore. Each chapter begins with a general discussion of a particular tradition, followed by a profile of a cook. In telling the cooks' stories, I hope to give a sense of how heirloom recipes have been passed along and adapted as time goes on—and a sense of family, neighborhood, and celebration. Those cooks and others on the North Shore have contributed recipes, which I've adapted after testing in home kitchens. Among the variety of recipes in each chapter—which include everything from appetizers to desserts—I've included some recipes for festive occasions—Hanukkah, for example, or Greek Easter. Marginal notes provide tips, kitchen tricks, information about ingredients, and other supplementary information. When a particular tradition calls for specialized ingredients, I've included a "pantry" list. At the back of the book you'll find resources for finding ingredients and cooking supplies: farmer's markets, specialty stores, and the like. If you visit them, take time to start conversations, ask questions, and embrace the affluence of knowledge at each stop.

Cook's Notes

All the recipes were tested by home cooks in home kitchens. Lacking the "batterie de cuisine" of the professional kitchen, I have not been overly meticulous about some things. Joy leaves the kitchen when you scurry for a ruler to measure a dish like some overwrought TV chef. There's not really much difference between a 10-inch or 12-inch skillet; most baking dishes come in small, medium, and large.

On oven temperatures and cooking times: I don't know your oven as well as you do. It may run hotter or cooler than mine, so the optimum cooking temperature may differ by 25 to 50 degrees. A higher or lower oven temperature alters the cooking time, so I have included a range of times in most recipes, along with some visual clues for doneness.

Feel free to tune the flavors to your taste buds; take liberties with the seasonings, using more or less if one agrees or disagrees with you. I have left amounts of salt and pepper to the cook's taste, but black pepper is always freshly ground.

I hope you find the next pages are delicious, informative, and fun. Your food memory may not coincide with that of the family next door, but the flavors and stories may return you to a kitchen table you cherish and enjoy.

Acknowledgments

My sincere thanks to all those who contributed data, direction, details, wisdom, and wit: Kelsey Atwood, Patricia Brown, Bob Cahill, Joe Carlin, Bill Cashman, Pete Chianca, Janet Christiansen, Lorralee Cooney, Frank Costello, Laurie Curtis, Linda Daley, Abner Darby, Mary Ann Esposito, Martin Foley, Joe Garland, Bob Garrity, Mary Gil, Gary Gill, Delphin Gomes, Tony Graffeo, Terry Golson, Bette Hunt, Paula Jackson, Nancy Jenkins, Tina Karalekas, Patricia Kelly, Dick Kent, Eleanor King, David Knisely, Barbara Kuck, Pharnal Longus, Brian Magrane, Jane Marshall, Jim McAllister, Peter McCarthy, Janet McKay-Smith, Marisol Navas, Sandra Oliver, Mary Palmer, Jerry Ryan, August Schumacher, Frank Pellino, David Shea, Nina Simonds, Bob Smith, David Solimine, Sr., Phil Sweeney, Michelle Topor, Ken Turino, Jim Webb, Fraffie Welch, and Barbara Wheaton.

Particular thanks to the North Shore cooks who are profiled here and gave me a few of their favorite recipes: Joe Carlin, Brendan Cronin, John W. Galanis, Lillie Jones, Denise Kiburis-Graffeo, Barbara Lazarides, Nikki Louk, Nancy Matheson-Burns, Ana Ortins, Barbara Schneider, and Anthony Verga.

The Beverly Historical Society, Cape Ann Historical Museum, Lynn Museum, Marblehead Historial Society, Massachusetts Department of Agriculture, Newburyport Historical Society, the Wenham Museum, and especially Les Dames Escoffier Boston set my compass. Mary Benjamin, Rebecca Brown, Marian Bull, and Martha Bull tested recipes through a hot summer. Julie and David Tseki rescued the manuscript from the jaws of an errant computer. For two years, Judy Shields, Nancy Petersen, Barbara Kay, Susan O'Neill, Elaine Segal, and Debbi Wrobleski were my lifelines.

My appreciation to publishers Webster and Katie Bull and the team at Commonwealth Editions. A bit of magic always surrounds these sorcerers who weave books from ideas and yank a title out of a hat. Editor Penny Stratton gave this soul, color, and form, always projecting serene confidence. Janet Knott and Ralph Turcotte brought the cooks to life in photographs. Designer Joyce Weston, copyeditors Susanna Brougham and Andrea Chesman, indexer Kevin Millham, proofreaders Lida Stinchfield and Laura Tawater, and production specialist Jill Atkinson put the goods in "apple pie order."

My grandparents, Rosina and Sebastiano Perlino, and my parents, Mary and Vin Mitchell, started my life with a wholesome larder. My daughter, Marisa, read chapters, translated, and edited across continents. My son, Timmy, provided the important daily technical support and some relief on the soccer field and baseball diamond. And, my husband, Tim, cheerfully pinch-hit for all of the above, on a moment's notice, lending palate and patience punctuated with a sense of humor.

Further Reading

I consulted the following works and have cited some of them in the cookbook. You might find it interesting to read some of them as well.

Arndt, Alice. *Seasoning Savvy.* Haworth Herbal Press, 1999.

Baggett, Nancy. *The All-American Cookie Book.* Houghton Mifflin, 2001.

Behr, Ed. *The Art of Eating* Newsletter.

Bulfinch's Boston Faire, Past and Present. Doric Dames, 1985.

Cahill, Robert. *Sugar & Spice and Everything.* Old Saltbox, 1991

Connolly, James B. *The Book of Gloucester Fishermen.* John Day, 1927.

Culinary Historians of Boston Newsletter.

Gamage, Virginia C., and Pricilla Sayer Lord. *The Spirit of '76 Lives Here.* Chilton, 1972.

Eldridge, Sherri. *Coastal New England Summertime Cooking.* Coastal New England Publications, 1995.

Emery, Sarah Anne. *Reminiscences of a Nonagenarian.* William H. Huse, 1879.

Esposito, Mary Ann. *Ciao Italia: Bringing Italy Home.* St. Martin's Press, 2001.

Farmer, Fannie Merritt. *The Boston Cooking-School Cook Book.* Little, Brown, 1896.

Gunst, Kathy, and John Randolph. *The Great New England Food Guide.* William Morrow, 1988.

Herbst, Sharon Tyler. *The New Food Lover's Companion.* Barron's, 1995.

Jones, Evan. *American Food: The Gastronomic Story.* Overlook Press, 1990.

Kurlansky, Mark. *Cod: A Biography of the Fish That Changed the World.* Walker & Co., 1997.

Larcom, Lucy. *A New England Girlhood.* Corinth Books, 1961.

Leonard, Jonathan Norton. *American Cooking: New England (Foods of the World)*. Time-Life Books, 1970.

Mariani, John. *The Dictionary of American Food and Drink*. Ticknor & Fields, 1983.

Murphy, Edward. *Yankee Priest*. Doubleday, 1952.

Neustadt, Kathy. *Clambakes: A History and Celebration of an American Tradition*. University of Massachusetts Press, 1992

Oliver, Sandra L. *Saltwater Foodways*. Mystic Seaport Museum, 1995.

Ortins, Ana. *Portuguese Home Style Cooking*. Interlink, 2000.

Palmer, Mary. *Cucina di Calabria*. Faber & Faber, 1997.

Root, Waverly. *Eating in America*. William Morrow, 1976.

Schneider, Elizabeth. *Uncommon Fruits and Vegetables*. Harper & Row, 1986.

Simmons, Amelia. *American Cookery*. Hudson & Godwin, 1796.

Stern, Jane, and Michael. *Real American Food*. Knopf, 1986.

Sternberg, Rabbi Robert. *The Sephardic Kitchen*. Harper-Collins, 1996.

The Taste of Gloucester: A Fisherman's Wife Cooks. The Fishermen's Wives of Gloucester, 1976.

Valldejuli, Carmey Aboy. *Puerto Rican Cookery*. Pelican. 1993.

White, Jasper, *Lobster at Home*. Scribner, 1998.

The Yankee Magazine Cookbook. Harper & Row, 1981.

FROM APPLE PIE
TO PAD THAI

EARLY COOKERY TRADITIONS
From Harbor to Hearth

The North Shore's early British settlers were hardscrabble fishermen and farmers. Cod was the gold of the Massachusetts Bay Colony. Mere fishermen made fortunes off the rich Grand Banks, elevating their families to a status of wealth and privilege, called the "codfish aristocracy." The dried and salted fish were sold in the Mediterranean and, less proudly, fed slaves in the West Indies' point of Triangular Trade—molasses, rum, slaves. Cod was also the main component of chowder, a one-pot meal that drifted onto land and was embraced by home cooks. Cod was also shaped into cakes and fried.

Early settlers adapted their own culinary traditions with Native American methods of cooking beans. According to local legend, the recipe we know as Boston baked beans once was called Beverly baked beans. The recipe in this chapter will tell you why. Corn, another staple of Native Americans, was ground into cornmeal and substituted for flour. It was baked into bread and boiled into Indian or hasty pudding. Lobsters were once so plentiful that they crawled up onto beaches of their own accord. Colonials used the precious commodity as bait or food for prisoners. Today a lobster dinner, with steamers, corn on the cob, coleslaw, cornbread, and the ubiquitous bib, is one of the "top ten things to do" when visiting the North Shore.

Like much of New England, this area no longer counts agriculture as its major contributor to the economic base, but small farms, some passed down from the founding families, others revived with new ownership, thrive under new agricultural preservation laws that keep them as open space in perpetuity. There is new interest in heirloom seeds, boutique crops, garden herbs, and homemade jams and vinegars. Annually, the Topsfield Fair, headed up by local farmer Forrester "Tim" Clarke of Hamilton, celebrates agriculture during early October, the area's most beautiful season.

A North Shore Cook: Joe Carlin

In another era, Joe Carlin might have been called a Renaissance man. A tightly spaced professional biography cites multiple advanced degrees, military service, public administration, research, and writing. His experiences have set him down in Southeast Asia, on a Hollywood sound stage, and on a New England university campus.

Starting out with a degree in food marketing, Carlin found himself in the U.S. Air Force from 1966 through 1970. A graduate degree in nutrition followed. With his knowledge of marketing, transportation, and nutrition wrapped into one neat package, he was a natural to train staff administering meals programs under the Older Americans Act. Carlin settled in Ipswich to bring up his family. Currently a specialist in gerontological nutrition at the U.S. Department of Health and Human Services, he has built up a parallel reputation as a food historian and founder of Food Heritage Press.

"I started to read and think about the history of food nearly forty years ago, my curiosity piqued by a book I'd read in college. There were no courses at the university level on the subject, so I explored secondhand bookstores and combed town histories for tidbits about eating habits and dining practices in the distant past. . . . In 1981, a group of scholars from the fields of anthropology, culinary arts, dietetics, women's studies, and history converged to create the Culinary Historians of Boston, the first professional food history group in the country," says Carlin.

Carlin regularly scours the output from university presses. His mail-order company distributes scholarly books on culinary topics, an outgrowth of his interest in history. "I thought I could provide a service, seeking out books on food history that were not generally known and bring them to the attention of chefs, food writers, and others who were serious about food."

The Internet was the company's biggest boon. Daily inquiries pour into his Web site from as far away as Australia. Recently, he turned his first modest profit, but Carlin says it's not enough to quit his day job.

"I get hundreds of e-mails from kids who have been assigned American history projects on food in the colonies. They find my Web site looking for authentic American recipes. I tell them that we were a British colony, so, naturally, we cooked from British cookbooks."

As Carlin speaks, the advanced degree in critical and creative thinking kicks in. "Before the Revolution, I can't imagine a ship entering a colonial port without a supply of British cookbooks for housewives. Remember, colonists were here long before 1776. There's a disconnect about that: people just hone in on that date. I like to think that, perhaps, when Paul Revere was out on his midnight ride, his wife was at home preparing a plum pudding or something, from the same British cookbook used in Washington's, Jefferson's, and Franklin's households."

"With the new nation, along came American Amelia Simmons, writing about Johny Cake, Indian Pudding, and Indian Slapjacks, and the first recipe for pumpkin pie. Colonial housewives had probably been making them for years, but the recipes had never been recorded. . . . Simmons's book was the first to use the words *squash* and *slaw.* She used the word *cookie* for what the British called *cake.* And she suggested cranberry sauce as a companion to roasted turkey. What could be more American!"

Carlin has taken his act on the road. Appointed a distinguished lecturer by the Institute of Food Technology, he travels the country speaking on "Eating and Drinking in the Early Republic." His erudition turned the Hollywood spotlight on him and he served as a technical consultant for FoodTV's production of *A Century of Food: 1900 to 2000.*"

Carlin thinks that historic exploration not only represents a nostalgic look backward but also affects the present and the future. As a regular contributor to *Nutrition Today,* his pieces spin history, linking past to present, as in a recent piece on how our colonial ancestors forged a new national identity through food.

"There are more than a few health-related tips we could take from the colonists. . . . Fruits and vegetables were consumed fresh, within days or even hours of being harvested. . . . The lengthiest trip was the short hop from the field to the kettle on the hearth. . . . Revolutionary produce was bred primarily for taste, a quality it delivered with robust strength."

Even simple family events are likely to jumpstart his thinking processes. "I recently visited my nephew at the bed-and-breakfast he runs. He invited friends in, and we collected around the kitchen counter to make pizzas. I started to think about how the process of cooking and eating has changed. In the very distant past, oh, a hundred thousand years ago or so, the men hunted and the women foraged. . . . Everyone brought something to the preparation of food. . . . Everyone was familiar with it.

Now the kitchen is center stage. Everyone meets there. The making of the pizza, playing with the food, as you will, is entertainment. Perhaps we're reverting to a nearly tribal experience."

Looking to the future, Carlin notes, "My young grandson might expect to see a hundred years of culinary change." He pauses. You can almost hear the creative processes shifting into gear.

THE RECIPES

Homestyle Fish Chowder

Lobster Bisque

Baked Scrod

Lobster Roll

Grilled Lobster with
Lemon Herb Butter

Cape Ann Casserole

Welsh Rarebit

Roasted Turkey

Quick Turkey Stock

Chestnut Stuffing

Maple-Glazed Root
Vegetables

Beverly Baked Beans

Beverly Brown Bread

Onion Pie

Election Cake

Apple Pie

Maple Cream

Pumpkin Pie

Any Berry Crisp

Sage Cream Cheese

Cranberry-Lavender
Lemonade

Homestyle Fish Chowder

Serves 6 to 8

Purists insist on cod in their chowder. However, a mixture of cod's white-fleshed neighbors, such as haddock, hake, pollock, and flounder, makes delicious chowder in these days of depleted fishing banks. Chowder improves if it is stored in the refrigerator overnight and reheated the next day.

¼ pound salt pork or smoked bacon, diced
2 tablespoons unsalted butter, plus more to garnish
1 large onion, diced
1 teaspoon dried thyme
6 large boiling potatoes, cut into 1-inch cubes
3 to 4 cups fish stock or water
3 pounds skinless, boneless fresh fillets of white fish
2 cups whole milk, cream, or half-and-half
Salt and freshly ground black pepper
Chopped fresh parsley
Chowder crackers

1. In a large heavy pot, sauté the pork or bacon for 3 to 5 minutes. It will render some drippings. Add the butter, onion, and thyme. Sauté for 5 minutes, until the onions are soft.

2. Add the potatoes and 3 cups of the stock. Simmer for 20 minutes, until the potatoes are tender when pierced with a fork.

3. Add the fish and milk. Add more stock if the mixture seems too dry. Bring to a low simmer and cook for 8 to 10 minutes, until the fish begins to flake. Season with salt, pepper, and parsley.

4. Ladle the chowder, reaching right to the bottom of the pot, into bowls. Sprinkle the top with parsley, a bit of unsalted butter, and crackers.

THE SAGA OF CHOWDER

New England claims chowder as its own fishermen's stew, cooked aboard ships for centuries. The word itself is often attributed to a soup pot found in coastal France called a *chaudière.*

On the North Shore especially, fish meant cod: It was the backbone of the early Massachusetts economy. Fishermen, loading their boats on the Grand Banks between here and Canada, needed hearty, easy-to-prepare meals to fuel the day's work. To make chowder, ship's staples—salt pork and hardtack—were layered one on top of another. As they cooked and dried out, water or wine (early printed texts specify claret or Madeira as a component) was poured in. The mixture needed very little tending.

On land, chowder was embraced and altered over time: fattened with potatoes, refined with milk, enhanced with

CONTINUED

other finfish or shellfish. Most changes brought improvement with two exceptions—the addition of flour and tomatoes.

Flour is grudgingly accepted as a thickener in restaurant-style chowder. The tomato has never been welcomed in North Shore chowder pots, underlining an ongoing rivalry between New York and New England. Local cooks have never allowed the "corrupting influence" of the Manhattan-style preparation. In 1939, chef Louis DeGouy reported that tomato-laced chowder was "regularly prepared on the North Shore in Gloucester, Swampscott, and Nahant," but it's likely he confused it with Portuguese or Italian fish stews. The North Shore stands firm: no tomatoes!

However, a creative chef can be applauded for a modern garnish such as kernels of corn stripped from the cob after a few minutes over a charcaol fire.

CULINARY POETRY

The earliest printed recipe for "chouder," written in rhyme, appeared in *The Boston Evening Post* in 1751:

> First lay some onions to keep the pork from burning;
> Because in chouder there can be no turning.
> They lay some pork in slices thin
> Thus you in chouder must begin.
> Next lay some fish out crossways
> Then season well with pepper . . . salt and spice
> Parsley, sweet marjoram, savory and thyme
> Then biscuit next which must be soaked some time.
> Thus your foundation laid, you will be able
> To raise a chouder high as the Tower of Babel;
> For by repeating o'er the same again
> You may make chouder for a thousand men . . .
> Last a bottle of Claret with water eno' to smoke 'em
> You'll have a mess, which some call Omnium gather 'em.

Lobster Bisque

Serves 6

To get a silky bisque, strain twice through a fine-mesh sieve or once through a colander lined with a layer of cheesecloth. This recipe, even though it has been streamlined, takes some time. The once-a-year dish is a Thanksgiving treat for many families.

4 to 6 small live lobsters
1 tablespoon Madeira
8 tablespoons (1 stick) butter
1 cup chopped carrots
1/3 cup chopped celery
1/4 cup chopped shallots
1/4 cup thinly sliced leeks, white part only
1 teaspoon dried tarragon
3 tablespoons chopped fresh flat-leaf parsley
5 tablespoons brandy
2/3 cup dry white wine
4 tablespoons all-purpose flour
3 cups milk
1 cup half-and-half
2 large plum tomatoes, peeled, seeded, and chopped
Pinch cayenne
Salt

1. Cook the lobsters (page 13) 15 to 17 minutes. Cool them just enough to handle. Take out the meat. Gently toss the lobster meat and the Madeira together in a bowl. Set aside. Save the shells. (You do not need the tomalley or roe.)

2. In a large soup pot, melt 4 tablespoons of the butter over medium heat. Add the carrots, celery, shallots, and leeks. Sprinkle with the tarragon and parsley. Sauté for 5 to 7 minutes. The shallots will be softened.

CHOWDER CRACKERS

In the late eighteenth century, Sarah Anne Emery, the wife of a Newburyport butcher, described "biscuit-pudding" as a "favorite of Newburyport's sea-faring men." Most likely she meant "pilot crackers" or "pilot bread," hand-molded at John Pearson's commercial bakery, built in 1794. The crackers were an evolution of "ship's biscuits," or hardtack, a brick of baked flour that softened in chowder's simmering broth. Over two centuries, the Newburyport bakery morphed into the multinational corporation, Nabisco. The company discontinued the Crown Pilot crackers in 1996, but brought them back by popular demand, in a media event that delivered the cargo by ship to their native Newburyport. Crown Pilot crackers are sold at fish markets on the New England sea-coast.

HOMARUS AMERICANUS

There are lobsters all over the world, but tender, sweet New England lobsters are the only ones with those large meaty claws. Nothing looks like them or compares in flavor. They are classified by weight.

- Chicken: 1 pound
- Select: 1 1/2 to 2 pounds
- Jumbo: 3 to 5 pounds
- Cull: missing claws, usually available at reduced price

3. Add the shells to the pot. Pour in the brandy. Warm for 10 seconds. Light the brandy. Let the flame burn out.

4. Add 3 cups of water and the white wine to the pot, and partially cover it. Simmer for 15 minutes.

5. Make a roux in a small saucepan. Melt the remaining 4 tablespoons of butter. Add the flour and cook, stirring, about 3 minutes, until the flour becomes lightly golden.

6. Combine the milk and half-and-half in a small saucepan and warm. Whisk the mixture into the roux, and add it all to the stock. Add the tomatoes, cayenne, and salt, and cover the pot. Bring barely to a boil. Reduce the heat and simmer gently for 45 minutes.

7. Strain the mixture twice through a fine-mesh sieve, or once through a fine-mesh sieve lined with cheesecloth. It will be fine-textured and smooth.

8. Rinse out the pot. Return the soup to the pot and heat through, stirring in the marinated lobster meat before ladling into heated bowls.

Baked Scrod

Serves 6

You don't need to go to the city for real Boston scrod. There's plenty on the North Shore, where we don't "eat," "order," or "buy" it: we "get" it. Scrod is not a type of fish; rather, it is a local recipe. Although uneducated or unscrupulous dealers may claim that *scrod* means "daily catch," an authentic recipe starts with small cod, under two pounds. The fillets are breaded, buttered, and broiled or baked. Over the past century, home cooks have added their own touches. Some coat their fish not with oil but with beaten eggs, milk, mayonnaise, or even olive oil.

> 2 tablespoons chopped fresh flat-leaf parsley
> 2 cups fresh white bread crumbs
> Salt and freshly ground black pepper
> 6 tablespoons (¾ stick) unsalted butter
> Juice of 1 lemon
> Oil, to film sheet pan and dip fillets
> 6 small cod fillets (6 to 8 ounces each)
> Half a fresh lemon

1. Preheat the oven to 400°F. Mix the parsley, bread crumbs, salt, and pepper in a shallow dish. Melt the butter in a saucepan. Cool it, and stir in the lemon juice.

2. Lightly film a sheet pan with oil. Pour a small amount of oil separately on a plate, and dip the fish pieces into the oil, shaking off any excess. Then dip them into the bread crumb mixture to coat. Lay the fish fillets on the sheet pan. Drizzle with the lemon butter.

3. Bake about 5 minutes. The bread crumb crust will start to turn golden. Flip the fillets over with a spatula. Bake about 4 minutes more. The crumb coating will be golden brown. Squeeze the fresh lemon half over the fish before serving.

THE "SACRED COD"

A carved gilded cod, circa 1784, hangs in the visitors gallery of the House of Representatives in the Massachusetts State House. The Doric Dames, a group dedicated to the building's historical preservation, refute the lore that the "Sacred Cod," as it is nicknamed, faces left when Democrats are the majority party and right for Republicans. However, elected mem-bers of that governing body like to keep the myth alive. To visitors seated in the gallery, the cod faces left; to members seated in the chamber, it faces right, so legislators show it off from the vantage point of their party affiliation.

MORE HISTORIC COD

Two copper codfish weather vanes cast by Paul Revere still remain. One is atop the State House roof; the other is at the top of Marblehead's Old North Church on Washington Street.

HOW TO COOK LOBSTER

Some cooks flavor the cooking water for lobster with white wine, fresh lemon juice, celery stalks, shallots, or seawater laced with seaweed.

- **Boiling:** Bring a large pot of water to a mad, rolling boil. Plunge the lobster in, headfirst, and bring the water back to a boil. Cook for about 10 to 12 minutes. Fully cooked lobsters will be bright red.

- **Parboiling:** Follow the directions for boiling, but cook the lobsters for only 3 minutes. They will keep most of their natural color. Finish the cooking process by baking or grilling shortly afterward.

- **Steaming:** Place a colander in a large pot filled with about two inches of water. Bring it to a boil. Put the lobsters in the colander above the water. Cover and steam for 10 to 15 minutes. Fully cooked lobsters will be bright red.

Lobster Roll

Serves 2

Fraffie Welch of the *Marblehead Reporter,* lives in Marblehead and spends part of each summer on an island off the coast of Maine. Her role as the paper's food writer is a labor of love, and her strongly held, no-nonsense views on lobster rolls describe the definitive recipe.

"Start with a plain Nissen's hot dog roll. It should be toasted. Mayonnaise, the good brand, should be just enough to moisten. A lettuce leaf on each side to line the roll is fine, but no using it as filler. The lobster must be freshly cooked, still warm, not left over—although I can't imagine leftover lobster—and cut into pieces large enough to know that you're eating claws and tails. Stuff it into the warm rolls. No salt or pepper. Serve on paper plates with paper napkins, potato chips, and pickle spears."

> 2-pound live lobster
> 2 hot dog rolls
> Mayonnaise
> 4 small lettuce leaves
> Potato chips, for serving
> Dill pickle spears, for serving

1. Cook the lobster according to directions for boiling described in the sidebar at left. When it is cool enough to handle, remove the shell and cut the claw and tail meat into large chunks.

2. Toast the rolls. Spread mayonnaise lightly on the insides of the rolls.

3. Line the rolls with lettuce leaves. Stuff the rolls full of lobster meat, using meat from a claw and half a tail for each one.

Grilled Lobster with Lemon Herb Butter

Serves 4

I first tasted this grilled lobster at my cousin Andrea Carey's annual family reunion. While we waited for the main event, we munched on crackers spread with the green lobster tomalley. It had been cooked over medium heat with butter, salt, and pepper, and then cooled and whisked with a little mayonnaise and lemon juice.

1/2 cup (1 stick) butter
1 tablespoon freshly squeezed lemon juice
1 tablespoon grated lemon zest (the yellow portion of the peel)
3 tablespoons minced fresh herbs, such as basil, tarragon, flat-leaf parsley, or chives
4 live lobsters, about 1 1/2 pounds each

1. Start the grill. Meanwhile, melt the butter. Stir in the lemon juice, lemon zest, and herbs. Set aside.

2. Parboil the lobsters (see sidebar, page 13) for 3 to 5 minutes. They will keep most of their natural color.

3. Put the lobsters on their backs. Cut them lengthwise up the center with a heavy, sharp knife. Scoop out the tomalley and/or roe, and save it for a separate use. Crack the claws over the sink so that any cooking water drains.

4. Put lobsters on the hot grill, cut side down. Grill 4 minutes. Turn and grill for 2 minutes on the other side. Turn again. Brush the cut side with some of the herbed butter. The meat will be white and juicy. Serve with the remaining butter for dipping.

EDIBLE PARTS OF A LOBSTER

"Meat" is the edible inside part of the lobster. New Englanders refer to the inedible shell as the "body."

- **Claws:** Crack claws, pull them apart, and take the meat out with a fork. Eat first.

- **Uropods:** Break off the fanlike portion of the end of the tail. There are small morsels of delicious meat there, which you can pull out with a tool called a lobster pick.

- **Tail:** Push the largest portion of lobster meat out through the tail end with a fork or knife. The interior also contains green tomalley. Red coral, also called roe, is in the female. Despite health warnings about tomalley and roe, most people do not eat enough lobster in a week, or even a year, to cause concern. Some consider these the best parts.

- **Walking legs:** There are eight legs, to eat last. Break off and slurp each one like a soda straw for the last few tastes.

THE CLAMBAKE OR SHORE DINNER

The clambake or shore dinner is a coastal feast meant for large outdoor gatherings, preferably on long summer weekends—Memorial Day, Fourth of July, Labor Day. The all-day process involves digging a pit in the sand, gathering wood and seaweed, and heating rocks in a pit. While clams, unshucked corn, and potatoes cook in the pit, there's time for swimming and games on the beach.

Culinary historians are still unearthing the origins of this "foodway." Food historian Sandra Oliver writes that the clambake is constantly evolving and that the shore dinner is a modern aspect of that evolution. Today, the menu may include any or all of the following: clam chowder, freshly dug clams, lobster, farm-fresh corn on the cob, cornbread, tangled heaps of coleslaw, fried chicken, strawberry or blueberry shortcake, watermelon—and plenty of paper napkins! However it evolves, it still tastes best in the rough— beach, porch, deck, or backyard. Woodman's of Essex specializes in delivering a "clambake" by truck to your door.

Cape Ann Casserole

Serves 8 to 10 as a luncheon dish

Old New England community cookbooks contain entries for shellfish baked into a refined pudding of bread, eggs, cheese, and milk. It was a popular ladies' luncheon dish from the Magnolia, Pride's Crossing, or Beverly Farms neighborhoods on Cape Ann, where there is easy access to fresh seafood.

    8 ounces cooked crabmeat
    9 slices white bread, crusts removed, cut into 1-inch
        cubes
    12 ounces mild cheddar cheese, grated
    8 ounces cooked lobster
    8 ounces cooked shrimp
    2 tablespoons butter, melted and cooled
    3 large eggs, beaten
    1/2 teaspoon Dijon-style mustard
    3 cups milk

1. Butter a large casserole.

2. Arrange the crabmeat on the bottom of the casserole. Top it with one-third of the bread. Sprinkle on one-third of the cheese. Layer in lobster, then half the remaining bread. Top it with half the remaining cheese. Next, arrange the shrimp and the last layer of bread. Top with the remaining cheese.

3. Beat together the butter, eggs, mustard, and milk. Evenly pour this mixture over the casserole. Cover and refrigerate for 2 to 4 hours.

4. Preheat the oven to 350°F. Bake, covered for 1½ hours. The top will be golden and crusty. Serve hot.

Welsh Rarebit

Serves 6

This earthy melting of a few bits of cheese and ale can probably be traced back to the medieval British sop of stale bread with something wet poured over it. But during the Great Depression, elegant hostesses seized on it as an economical way of home entertaining, especially when spooned from a silver chafing dish. It remains a stalwart at Sunday-night family supper. You can prep all the ingredients ahead and actually cook the rarebit in a chafing dish, silver or not, right at the table. Use a fine-textured white bread for the toast, such as Pepperidge Farm.

    12 ounces sharp cheddar cheese, diced
    3/4 cup milk, beer, or ale
    1/2 teaspoon dry mustard powder
    1 teaspoon Worcestershire sauce
    1 large egg, beaten
    12 slices white toast, crusts removed

1. In the top of a double boiler set over simmering water, gently whisk together cheese, milk, mustard, and Worcestershire sauce. Heat, stirring constantly, until the ingredients are blended.

2. Add the egg. Continue cooking and stirring until the sauce is smooth and well blended.

3. To serve, arrange the toast on individual plates and pour the sauce over the toast.

Roasted Turkey

Serves 10 to 20

Pat Rischer roasts the turkeys at Raymond's Turkey Farm in Methuen. She recommends "roasting turkey at 350° for 20 minutes a pound, or until it reaches 185°F. I've cooked thousands of turkeys, and I don't believe in pink juices: Rare is not an option! . . . The only way to know if it is done is to check the temperature. Six fresh 15-pound turkeys in the same oven will each be ready at a different time."

Mrs. Rischer feels that fresh turkey is so flavorful it doesn't need butter for basting. She recommends three essential pieces of equipment: a heavy-duty roasting pan, a meat (instant-read) thermometer, and a large bulb baster. This recipe is based on her directions.

    12- to 22-pound turkey
    Water
    Dried herbs (combination of rosemary, thyme, sage),
        optional

1. Preheat the oven to 350°F. Put a layer of foil on the bottom of a heavy roasting pan.

2. Remove the neck and giblets from the cavity of the turkey and reserve for making stock (see page 19). Place the turkey in the roasting pan. Pour about ¼ inch of water into the pan to keep the bird from sticking. Sprinkle the herbs into the cooking water and over the bird.

3. Roast for 20 minutes per pound, basting every 20 minutes or so with the juices that collect in the bottom of the pan. To test for doneness, insert a thermometer into the thickest part of the thigh. When the turkey is cooked, it should register between 175°F and 185°F. Wiggle the leg at the joint. The juices will run clear.

RAYMOND'S TURKEY FARM

More than 12,000 North Shore families buy their Thanksgiving bird from Raymond's Turkey Farm in Methuen, where phone orders begin pouring in on Labor Day weekend. Claire Rischer Ford and her son, James Rischer, are partners in a family business. James's wife, Pat, is the kitchen manager. Their kids work in all aspects of the business. Turkeys are sold ready to cook or roasted with 24 hours' notice, except on the third Thursday in November. Savvy customers also pick up prepared squash, turnip, cranberry-orange relish, and mashed potatoes. The farm is busy year-round, offering a variety of products including turkey cutlets, turkey steaks, turkey sausage, and ground turkey.

WILD TURKEYS ON THE NORTH SHORE

Wild turkeys proliferated on the North Shore in colonial times. They had all but disappeared until a few years ago. Today they are regularly sighted along wooded roads in Rowley, Ipswich, Danvers, Georgetown, Groveland, Topsfield, and North Andover.

4. Take the turkey out of the oven and tent the pan with aluminum foil. Let rest for 20 to 30 minutes to distribute the juices evenly. The turkey will continue to cook from residual heat. Put the turkey on a platter and set aside the pan with juices for making gravy.

Quick Turkey Stock

Makes 5 cups

This stock is for stuffing or gravy, not soup. Do not use the liver. If you can't decipher which of the innards is the liver, use only the neck, and the stock will turn out fine. Simmer for as little as 30 minutes, longer if you have time.

    Neck and giblets from 1 turkey
    1 large yellow onion, cut in quarters
    1 large carrot, trimmed and cut into 4-inch chunks
    Tops of 1 bunch celery
    Salt and freshly ground black pepper
    6 to 8 cups water
    2 tablespoons freshly squeezed lemon juice,
        optional

1. Combine the turkey neck, giblets, onion, carrot, celery, salt and pepper to taste, and water in a saucepan. Bring to a boil. Reduce the heat to a simmer and cook for 30 to 60 minutes.

2. Add lemon juice to brighten the flavor, if needed.

Chestnut Stuffing

Serves 12 to 20

This stuffing is for a 16- to 20-pound bird. Any stuffing that doesn't fit can be baked alongside in a separate casserole.

    ¹/₄ cup (¹/₂ stick) butter
    4 ribs celery, chopped
    2 medium onions, chopped
    1 pound chestnuts, peeled and chopped
    2 cups bread cubes
    1 tablespoon dried crumbled sage
    1 tablespoon salt
    1 teaspoon freshly ground black pepper
    2 tablespoons chopped fresh parsley
    3 large eggs, beaten
    1 cup Turkey Stock (see recipe, page 19)

1. Melt the butter in a medium skillet over medium-high heat. Add the celery and onions. Cook, stirring, for 5 to 7 minutes, until the vegetables are soft.

2. Toss the celery, onions, and chestnuts with the bread cubes in a large bowl. Add the sage, salt, pepper, and parsley. Toss again with eggs and stock until blended. Stuff loosely into the turkey cavity or bake in a casserole, covered, for 30 to 40 minutes, right alongside the turkey.

PREPARING CHESTNUTS FOR STUFFING

I've tried a lot of ways to peel fresh chestnuts, and short of buying them in a jar already done, this method works best. Cut a deep X into the flat side of the chestnuts. Put them in a saucepan with enough water to cover them by 1 inch. Bring them to a boil. Turn the heat to low. Work in small batches, fishing out a few chestnuts at a time. Use a sharp paring knife to peel off the inner and outer skins, starting at the X. If the skins won't pull off, put the chestnuts back in the hot water, wait one minute, and try again.

**MENU FOR A
NORTH SHORE
THANKSGIVING**

Lobster Bisque

Roasted Turkey with
Gravy and Chestnut
Stuffing

Maple-Glazed Root
Vegetables

Mashed Potatoes

Pumpkin Pie

Apple Pie with Maple
Cream

Maple-Glazed Root Vegetables

Serves 6 to 8

This recipe is an updated classic. Traditionally, the root vegetables are boiled, then tossed in the glazing mixture. However, caramelization makes oven-roasted vegetables much more flavorful, and they look beautiful around the holiday turkey.

3 pounds root vegetables (an assortment of parsnips,
    carrots, turnips, sweet potatoes, to taste), peeled
    and cut in 2-inch cubes
2 to 3 tablespoons vegetable oil
6 tablespoons unsalted butter
3 tablespoons real maple syrup
1 teaspoon freshly squeezed lemon juice
Salt and freshly ground black pepper

1. Preheat the oven to 425°F.

2. Spread the vegetables in one layer on baking sheets. Drizzle with the oil and toss lightly to coat the vegetables. Roast for about 20 to 25 minutes. The vegetables will be tender and golden brown.

3. While the vegetables roast, melt the butter. Whisk in the maple syrup, lemon juice, salt, and pepper. Add hot water, a few drops at a time, if the mixture seems too thick. Set it aside over very low heat to keep warm.

4. Turn the oven down to 325°F.

5. Remove the vegetables from the oven. Drizzle the maple syrup mixture over the vegetables and return them to the oven for about 10 minutes. They will be lightly singed on the edges. Serve hot with roasted meats.

Beverly Baked Beans

Serves 6 to 8

Edward Murphy, born in 1892, recalled the baked beans of his Salem boyhood delivered "just around sunset" on Saturday night by Mr. Morgan and his horse Minnie. He would "whoa her to a stop at each steady customer's gate. . . . There in the box stood three big-bellied earthen pots. . . . I'd lick my chops holding out Mom's yellow mixing bowl to receive as much . . . as two thin dimes could . . . ladle up for our evening meal." Murphy vividly describes his mother's baked beans: "Soaked for hours in water, seasoned with sliced onion, sweetened with molasses, and surmounted with a hunk of salt pork," and the neighborhood custom of taking "the pot by the knotted end of a fresh white towel" to the "Old Grist Mill nearby . . . for the baking of Sunday breakfast."

North Shore cooks have long flavored their bean pots with fresh-picked apples, newly pressed apple cider, or maple syrup. During World War II, homemade baked beans had a renaissance as the commercially canned ones were sent to the army.

1 pound dry white navy beans
1/2 cup unsulfured molasses
1/4 cup maple syrup or packed brown sugar
2 tablespoons dark rum, optional
2 teaspoons dry mustard powder
salt and freshly ground black pepper
2 cups boiling water
6 ounces salt pork, trimmed of rind and cut into 1-inch
     cubes
1 small yellow onion, peeled
1 small McIntosh apple, peeled, cut in half and cored

BEVERLY BAKED BEANS

In 1890, in *A New England Girlhood*, Beverly author Lucy Larcom related that towns once gave each other nicknames. "Ours was called 'Bean-Town,' she wrote, because it adhered to "the Puritanic custom of . . . baking beans on Saturday."

According to historian Robert Cahill, the brown-and-white earthenware bean pots were produced at Lawrence Pottery in Beverly. In *Sugar & Spice and Everything*, Cahill recounts a Civil War reunion in Boston: "Beverly veterans brought a gift to every old Union soldier—a famous Beverly bean-pot. . . . Asked where they had obtained the lovely bean-pots, . . . the answer was Boston."

By 1896, when Medford neighbor Fannie Farmer put the recipe in the *Boston Cooking-School Cook Book*, both beans and pots were connected forever to Boston.

1. Rinse and pick over the beans. Place in a pot with enough cold water to cover, and soak overnight. Drain well. Rinse under cold running water. Return the beans to the pot and refill the pot with cold water. Bring to a boil. Immediately drain and rinse the beans once more.

2. Preheat the oven to 300°F.

3. In a saucepan, combine the molasses, maple syrup (or brown sugar), rum (if using), mustard, salt, pepper, and water. Bring just to a boil. Remove from the heat, stir, and set aside.

4. Place the beans in an ovenproof casserole. Pour the molasses mixture evenly over them. There should be enough liquid to cover the beans. Add the salt pork cubes and stir. Bury the onion and apple pieces down into the beans.

5. Cover the beanpot, and bake for 4 to 5 hours. Check the beans each hour and, if necessary, add water to cover so that the beans do not dry out. The beans will be plump and deeply browned, and tender when pierced with a fork. Discard the onion. Serve hot, right from the casserole.

Beverly Brown Bread

Serves 6 to 8

At the turn of the twentieth century, young Edward Murphy's bean supper was supplemented "with a loaf of brown bread, thick cylinder-shaped, hot, full of plums, from a bakery on Essex Street," Murphy notes. "No friends of ours ever dined more satisfactorily on Saturday night, since all of them had exactly the same fare."

To get the cylinder shape, bake the bread in a well-greased coffee can. I use butter-flavored shortening.

Butter-flavored shortening
1 cup yellow cornmeal
1 cup whole wheat flour
1 cup rye flour
1 teaspoon baking soda
1 teaspoon salt
1 1/2 cups buttermilk
3/4 cup molasses
1 cup raisins, optional

1. Preheat the oven to 325°F. Grease the inside of a clean 1-pound coffee can with butter-flavored shortening. Bring a saucepan full of water to a boil.

2. In a large bowl, combine the cornmeal, wheat flour, rye flour, baking soda, and salt. Stir in the buttermilk, molasses, and raisins, if using.

3. Pour the batter into the coffee can, filling it two-thirds to three-quarters of the way. Cover the open end tightly with two sheets of aluminum foil.

4. Stand the coffee can in a deep cake pan. Pour boiling water into the cake pan, so that it reaches halfway up the sides of the coffee can.

5. Steam for 2½ hours. Check the pan every 30 minutes and pour in more boiling water to replace any that has evaporated. To test for doneness, take the aluminum foil off the can. Pierce the bread with a skewer; the skewer should come out clean.

6. Remove the can from its water bath but leave the bread in the coffee can to cool for about 1 hour. Remove the bottom end of the can with a can opener, and gently push the loaf through and out of the can.

FARM-FRESH CORN

As a kid, I husked and ate fresh corn right in the garden despite adult admonitions that eating uncooked corn would lead to untimely death.

To pick fresh corn, take a leisurely stroll out to the garden. Once the corn is picked, sprint! Husk the corn on the run to a pot of water already at a rolling boil. Native Americans built their fires right in the field, saving the trip. Here are different methods of preparing fresh corn:

- **Boiling:** Bring a large pot of water to a boil; you don't need salt, sugar, or milk. Add the husked corn. Return the water to a boil. Turn off the heat and cover the pot. Let stand for 5 minutes. Remove the corn with tongs.

CONTINUED

- **Steaming:** Fill a large pot about one-quarter full with water. Bring to a boil. Fit a colander or steaming basket into the pot and add the husked corn. Cover. Steam for 10 to 12 minutes.

- **Roasting:** Preheat the oven to 425°F. Push the corn husks back to remove the silk without removing the husks. Rewrap the ears in the husks. Tear off a strip of husk to tie the open end shut. Soak the corn in water for about 15 minutes. Remove the corn from the water and put the ears directly onto the oven racks, as if baking a potato. Roast for 17 to 20 minutes. The husks will blacken.

- **Grilling:** Fire up the grill. Prepare the corn as for roasting. Put the corn directly onto the grill. Grill for 20 minutes, turning often. The husks will char.

Onion Pie

Serves 6

Danvers was once called "Onion Town" because miles and miles of farmland were dedicated to that crop. Today malls sprawl between Route 128 and Route 114 where onions once grew. Onion pie is a spin-off of the satisfying broccoli and spinach casseroles often found in community cookbooks.

1 egg white
1 tablespoon canola oil
2 cups chopped yellow onions
3 large eggs, beaten
1 cup skim milk
1 teaspoon Worcestershire sauce
3/4 cup grated Parmesan cheese

1. Preheat oven to 375°F. Grease a 9-inch pie plate.

2. Lightly beat the egg white. Brush it over the bottom and sides of the pie plate.

3. Heat the oil in a large skillet over medium heat. Add the onions and cook gently for 8 to 10 minutes, until the onions wilt. Set aside to cool.

4. Beat together the eggs, milk, and Worcestershire sauce in a bowl. Add the grated cheese and onions. Pour into the prepared pie plate.

5. Bake for 30 minutes. The top of the pie will be golden brown. Let the pie set for about 20 minutes before serving.

Election Cake

Makes 2 loaves

When historian Virginia C. Gamage described "Election Week" in Marblehead during the early years of the republic, she wrote of bonfires, dancing in the streets, and "election cakes filled with both currants and raisins," washed down with ale and "foaming, homemade root beer." Recalling similar festivities in late 1820s Beverly, Lucy Larcom wrote, "My mother always made 'Lection' cake. . . . It was nothing but a kind of sweetened bread with a shine of egg-and-molasses on top; but we thought it delicious." The earliest published recipe for the cake, in Amelia Simmons's 1796 *American Cookery,* calls for 10 pounds of butter, 30 quarts of flour, and 14 pounds of sugar, with yeast as the leavening agent. Food historian Sandra Oliver, in her erudite tome *Saltwater Foodways,* reworked an 1845 recipe into modern language. My respect for her grew as I tested and retested the loaf, leaving it to rise for longer and longer periods—at one point, impatiently altering its makeup to try it as a quick bread. When I told her about this, she explained that cooks in those times weren't as hurried as modern-day cooks. I found that leaving Oliver's cake to proof overnight gave it a more satisfying, although not modern, height. The appearance of the finished loaf is not merely rustic but downright primitive, and the flavor is intense. A heavy metal baking pan gets the best results.

1 package (2^1/2 teaspoons) active dry yeast, dissolved
    in ^{3}/4 cup warm milk
^{1}/3 cup butter
1 cup sugar
2 large eggs
^{1}/2 cup brandy
4^1/2 cups sifted all-purpose flour
2 teaspoons ground cinnamon

$^1/_2$ teaspoon grated nutmeg
1 cup raisins
1 cup chopped walnuts

1. Dissolve the yeast in the milk. Set aside. Generously butter two 9- by 5-inch loaf pans. Flour a work surface.

2. Pulse the butter and sugar in the workbowl of a food processor. Add the eggs and brandy. Add the yeast mixture. Pulse only once. Gradually, add 4 cups of the flour, the cinnamon, and nutmeg. Pulse after each addition to blend. The dough will form a ball.

3. Place the dough on the floured surface. Flour your hands. Knead in the raisins and walnuts. Add the other ½ cup flour, gradually, only if needed.

4. Divide the dough into two halves. Place each one in a loaf pan. Set aside, covered with a towel, to rise overnight. Do not expect it to double in bulk.

5. Preheat the oven to 350°F. Bake for about 45 to 55 minutes. The loaves will be deeply browned. Tip the loaves out of the pans and cool on a rack, for at least 30 minutes, before cutting.

Apple Pie

Makes one 9-inch pie

In 1999, Kim Bolgonese won the Ward's Greenhouse Apple Pie contest that Dick Kent, an accomplished baker, organizes annually. This recipe is an adapted combination of both their recipes.

2 1/2 cups all-purpose flour
2 teaspoons sugar
1/2 teaspoon salt
2/3 cup chilled unsalted butter, cut in 1-inch pieces
3 tablespoons chilled vegetable shortening, cut in pieces
6 to 8 tablespoons ice water
Egg wash (1 egg beaten with 1 tablespoon water)
1 cup sugar
2 tablespoons quick-cooking tapioca
1/4 teaspoon salt
2 teaspoons ground cinnamon
Pinch grated nutmeg
6 large apples (2 pounds), peeled, cored, and sliced
4 teaspoons freshly grated lemon zest
4 teaspoons freshly squeezed lemon juice
2 tablespoons butter, cut in bits
Maple Cream (recipe follows)

DICK KENT'S APPLE PIE WISDOM

- The best crusts are made with a combination of both lard and butter.

- Handle pie dough as little as possible.

- Chill the dough for an hour before rolling it out.

- Mix different apples for best flavor. Try Baldwin, Granny Smith, Gravenstein, Jonathan, and Macoun.

- Season apple pie filling with combinations of cinnamon, nutmeg, allspice, cardamom, lemon zest, or orange zest.

- Decorate pies with lattice work or braided strips of pie dough, cut-out leaves or apples, or slash an "A" for apple into the top crusts.

1. To make the crust, whisk together the flour, sugar, and salt. Cut the butter and shortening into the dry ingredients with two knives. It will form small, coarse lumps. Sprinkle half the ice water over the mixture and continue mixing. Add more ice water, a tablespoon at a time, while continuing to mix. It will form a moist dough that sticks together. Form the dough into two balls. Flatten them. Wrap them in plastic and refrigerate for 1 hour.

2. To make the filling, whisk together the sugar, tapioca, salt, cinnamon, and nutmeg in a bowl. Add the apples, lemon zest, and lemon juice, tossing to coat. Set aside.

3. Preheat the oven to 425°F.

4. To assemble the pie, roll the dough into two circles, each 10 inches in diameter, on a floured board. Place one crust in the pie plate. Fill it with the apples. dot the 2 tablespoons of butter over the apple filling. Place the second crust on top. Crimp the crust around the edges. Trim the crust if it hangs more than ½ inch over the edge of the pie plate. Cut three slashes in the center of the top crust to vent it.

5. Place the pie on the lowest rack of the oven to cook the bottom crust. Bake for 10 minutes. Lower the heat to 350°F. Move the pie to the center rack, and continue to cook for 45 to 50 minutes. The crust will be golden and the apples will be bubbling around the edges.

Maple Cream

Makes about 1¼ cups

Harley-riding auto body shop owner Bob Bolgonese surprised everyone when he took second prize in the same apple pie contest his wife won. He topped it with this sinfully delicious and easy topping for this pie. It tastes just as good on pumpkin pie.

1 cup heavy cream
5 tablespoons pure maple syrup

Whip the cream until soft peaks form. Continue whipping while slowly incorporating maple syrup. For best flavor, serve this within an hour.

Pumpkin Pie

Makes one 9-inch pie

Some cooks peel, seed, cube, and boil their pumpkin, but I find it easier to cut it in half, remove the seeds and fibers, and put the pumpkin, cut side down, in a roasting pan. I pour 2 to 3 cups of hot water into the pan, and cover the whole thing tightly with aluminum foil, then bake it for about 1 hour at 400°F. It's then very easy to scoop out the soft pulp and process it in the blender or food processor.

Consider the spice measurements as a suggestion only. If you love ginger, then by all means up the amount! The same goes for cinnamon, nutmeg, and cloves.

2 large eggs
2 cups cooked and mashed pumpkin
1 cup sugar
$1/2$ teaspoon ground cinnamon
$1/4$ teaspoon grated nutmeg
$1/4$ teaspoon ground ginger
$1/4$ teaspoon ground cloves
$1/2$ teaspoon salt
3 tablespoons butter, at room temperature
$2/3$ cup evaporated milk
9-inch unbaked pastry shell

1. Preheat the oven to 425°F.

2. Beat the eggs in a mixing bowl. Stir in the pumpkin, sugar, cinnamon, nutmeg, ginger, cloves, salt, butter, and evaporated milk. Pour the filling into the pastry shell.

3. Bake for 15 minutes. Lower the oven temperature to 350°F. Continue baking for about 50 minutes, until a knife inserted into the center will come out clean.

COBBLERS, CRISPS, AND CRUMBLES

For centuries, recipes passed from mothers to daughters. Cook's notes discovered on tattered pages of household journals are like buried treasure, a window into kitchens of times past. These homespun desserts often noted in homemakers' manuscript journals, are found throughout the country made with the fruits that grow best.

- **Betty:** Mix buttered bread, cracker, cake, or cookie crumbs with a "pudding" of flour, sugar, and butter. Layer with fruit before baking.

- **Buckle:** Fold together berries and yellow cake batter, pour into a pan, and bake. Serve cut into squares.
- **Cobbler:** Drop biscuit crust, like "cobble-stones," onto fruit, and bake.
- **Crisp or crumble:** Bake fruit with a topping of nuts, oats, sugar, flour, butter, and crumbs.
- **Grunt or slump:** Blanket fruit with a cobbler crust; the fruit "grunts" or the crust "slumps" into it when cooking.
- **Pandowdy:** "Dowdy" cooked cobbler still in the pan, by stirring fruit and biscuit together.

Any Berry Crisp

Serves 6

This recipe works with summer berries such as blackberries, blueberries, or raspberries—alone or in any combination. Use the same topping to make a crisp of apples or peaches as well. Baking times will vary according to the fruit used; for example, apples will take longer than berries. Try Bob Bolgonese's Maple Cream (page 29) dolloped on top.

5 to 6 cups berries
1/3 cup sugar
Grated zest of 1 lemon
1 cup all-purpose flour
1/2 cup brown sugar
1/2 teaspoon ground cinnamon
1/2 cup (1 stick) unsalted butter, cut into pieces
1/2 cup rolled oats
1/3 cup chopped nuts (walnuts, hazelnuts, almonds)
Whipped cream or ice cream for serving, optional

1. Preheat the oven to 350°F. Butter a square baking dish.

2. Toss together berries, sugar, and lemon zest in a large bowl.

3. Toss together the flour, brown sugar, and cinnamon in another bowl. Cut in the butter with this flour mixture until large crumbs form. Mix in the oats and nuts.

4. Transfer the berry mixture into the baking dish. Cover with the flour mixture.

5. Bake for about 35 minutes until the top is golden and crisp and the juices are bubbling.

6. Cool for about 10 minutes before serving plain or topped with whipped cream or ice cream.

Sage Cream Cheese

Makes about 2 cups

Rita Wollmering and Brooke Finn, former Peace Corps volunteers, pooled resources to rescue a hundred-year-old farm on the Amesbury-Salisbury line. The HERB FARMacy, on a sweep of woodland and open fields bisected by a stream, yields fresh herbs and heirloom vegetables. The owners give classes and workshops in the greenhouse on subjects from cooking to the art of Victorian bouquets called "tussie-mussies." This cream cheese spread, adapted from their classes, is wonderful on crackers, vegetables, or thick slices of homemade bread.

    16 ounces cream cheese, softened
    3 tablespoons lemonade concentrate
    1/2 cup fresh sage leaves, loosely packed
    1 clove garlic, minced

Thoroughly blend the cream cheese, lemonade concentrate, sage leaves, and garlic. Refrigerate for at least 2 hours. If you make it 24 to 48 hours ahead, it will have stronger flavor.

TOPSFIELD FAIR

For ten days in early October, culminating on Columbus Day weekend when autumn foliage peaks, the epicenter of the North Shore is the Topsfield Fairgrounds on Old Route One.

Established in 1818, it is the oldest continuously held country fair in the United States. Visitors jam the fairgrounds for parades, fireworks, and competitions for every-thing from the fattest geese to the most sublime chili. Booths run down the midway like so many piano keys, offering tastes from corn on the cob to souvlaki to fried dough.

Forrester "Tim" Clark, president of the fair, says, "One of the most eagerly anticipated events is the annual Giant Pumpkin Weigh-Off. Growers from all over New England compete for cash prizes. We awarded a $10,000 bounty in 2000 to the first pumpkin to reach 1000 pounds!"

Cranberry-Lavender Lemonade

Serves 8

At summer farmers' markets, Rita and Brooke from The HERB FARMacy always offer this lemonade made with their homegrown lavender.

    4 cups cranberry juice
    4 cups lemonade
    1 handful (about 8 sprigs) lavender leaves, rinsed
    1 fresh lemon, sliced

1. Mix the cranberry juice and lemonade in a half-gallon container. Gently stir the lavender into the juice mixture. Cover, refrigerate, and let the mixture infuse for 3 to 8 hours.

2. Strain out the lavender leaves. Add the fresh lemon slices. Serve well chilled.

THE PORTUGUESE TRADITION

From Shipboard Stew to Sardine Barbecue

More than two hundred years ago, Portuguese seamen were seduced to the North Shore by the siren song of the whaling industry. Some scholars suggest that Portuguese explorers and fishermen had struck gold much earlier in the form of cod on the Grand Banks between New England and Canada. Whether legend or history, one thing is fact: Portuguese seamen were renowned for their oceangoing prowess, and that is how they found their place here. Whaling captains, at the industry's height in the late eighteenth century, recruited men from the Azores to New Bedford and Nantucket. Others were drawn to settle around the protected harbors of Cape Ann, north of Boston. From the top of Gloucester's "Portuguese Hill," the view of the present-day harbor, scattered with a colorful confetti of yellow, red, and turquoise fishing boats, speaks of a lively culture. The rugged men who captained and crewed these boats brought in huge hauls of cod—until just a few years ago. Today, with cod stocks in danger of depletion, fewer boats go out, returning with government-regulated smaller loads.

The early twentieth century saw a new immigration of men, women, and children from Portugal and the Azores Islands. They left a life of poverty to find ample work in Peabody's booming leather tanneries and formed a tight-knit community around the city's center. Markets and bakeries sprang up to provide the neighborhood with familiar old-country products made locally. Today markets like Tremont Market and Casa Portugal draw customers from all over the North Shore for imports from Portugal and local specialties—meats, sausage, breads, pottery, copper, and linens.

Clubs and churches in Gloucester and Peabody remain centers for Portuguese-American cultural life, fielding soccer teams and teaching the language and traditional crafts.

The Feast of the Holy Ghost

Our Lady of Fatima Church in Peabody was originally built as a Catholic mission for Portuguese immigrants. Each spring since 1916, the parish has celebrated Pentecost Sunday, the feast of the Holy Ghost, forty days after Easter, with a colorful procession. Children, dressed in white, carry red roses to the lovely church before a solemn high mass. When the service is over, everyone gathers on the grounds for a meal prepared by the best cooks in the parish, who have spent the previous few days peel-ing, slicing, marinating, and braising in a festive atmosphere. When the committee members take off their aprons for lunch, they set a table with hand-crocheted cloths and sparkling wine glasses. After courses of fried cod, vegetable salad, home-made bread, and cool wine, they re-turn to the kitchen, refreshed, to finish preparing the meal.

MENU FOR THE
FEAST OF THE HOLY GHOST

Holy Ghost Soup

Roast Beef

Spiced Potatoes

Raised Corn Bread

Sweet Rice Pudding

A North Shore Cook: Ana Ortins

Ana Patuleia Ortins grew up in Peabody's center, a bustling melting pot built around the leather-tanning industry, in the 1950s. Her family had emigrated from Portugal's Alentejo province.

"I was brought up very traditional," she says. "Girls stayed close to home and learned all the Portuguese folk arts, such as crocheting, from the older women in the family. My mother, aunt, and grandmother were good at the domestic arts, but it was my father who taught me to cook."

The elder Patuleia discovered little Ana's talent for cooking. When he wasn't working, he was in the kitchen with his daughter. Side by side, they would whip up huge pots of the flavorful, thick soups and stews of his native land.

Soon after high school, she married Philip Ortins. "His father owned Ortins Market. They sold Portuguese specialty foods, their own homemade sausage, and beer and wine. Everyone knew them."

The couple settled down and raised a family. Ana entertained often, treating guests to an ever-expanding repertoire of international recipes, but her culinary signature remained her father's *Açorda de Bacalhau,* a bread-thickened soup made with salt cod and fragrant with fresh coriander and garlic.

"I'd get the call from Dad early on Saturday mornings. He'd say, 'Did you get the smell?' and immediately I knew he was making the soup. You could smell it all over the neighborhood. I'd always tell him to set a plate and I hurried over."

With kids off to college, Ana enrolled in culinary school and managed a country club snack bar during summer breaks. Members, many from Boston professional sports teams, were known to slip away from a golf game to nab some of her chocolate biscotti.

After graduation, Ana put her newly minted education to work launching A Panela, a Web site specializing in authentic Portuguese fare, but she wanted to reach a larger community.

"All the while I was in school, I had this wish to combine my heritage with my training. I didn't know just how to go about it, so I began putting recipes in my computer, the ones I'd been cooking for years. Then, I started talking to people in the community about their family recipes. It took years of interviews and watching people demonstrate their different dishes. I made some wonderful friends along the way." Her affectionate documentation of heirloom recipes, *Portuguese Homestyle Cooking,* was published in 2001 and continues to sell briskly.

THE RECIPES

Fisherman's Stew
Caldeirada

Holy Ghost Soup
Sopa du Espirito Santo

Kale Soup
Caldo Verde

Tuna Steaks
Bifes de Atum

Orange Braised Rabbit
Coelho de Laranja

Roast Beef
Carne Assada

Joao Borge's
Portuguese-American Paella
Arroz Valenciana

Spicy Clams
Ameijoas

Summer Vegetable Salad
Salada do Verão

Potatoes with Cilantro
Batatas com Coentro

Roasted Spiced Potatoes
Battatas Assadas

Tomato Rice
Arroz a Tomate

Raised Cornmeal Bread
Broa de Milho

Ana's Sweet Rice Pudding
Arroz Doce

Fresh Fruit in Port
Fruta Fresca em Porto

FISHERMAN'S STEW

A true fisherman's stew changes daily because the main ingredient, the seafood, depends on the day's catch. With the current depletion of the cod stocks on the Grand Banks, innovative Portuguese-Americans home cooks add under-utilized species, such as cusk, to this stew. Every family has its own ver-sion of the stew, a special combination of white fish (cod, had-dock, or cusk) and shellfish (mussels or clams), which causes friendly family rivalries.

Fisherman's Stew

Caldeirada

Serves 4

Choose your own fish to use in this stew.

2 tablespoons olive oil
1 yellow onion, chopped
2 cloves garlic, chopped
2 pounds russet potatoes, peeled and sliced
    $1/2$ inch thick
1 pound fresh skinless, boneless firm white fish
    (cod, haddock, cusk, hake)
4 plum tomatoes, peeled, seeded, and sliced into rounds
1 teaspoon paprika
$1/2$ teaspoon crushed red pepper flakes
1 cup water
1 cup dry white wine
1 pound fresh mussels, rinsed and debearded
Salt and freshly ground black pepper
$1/4$ cup chopped fresh flat-leaf parsley

1. In a large, heavy soup pot, heat the oil over medium heat. Add the onion and garlic in one layer to the bottom of the pot. Cook gently for 2 to 3 minutes. They will just begin to wilt. Layer on all potato slices. Cover them with fish pieces. Layer with the tomatoes. Sprinkle the paprika and red pepper over the top. Pour in the water and wine. (The ingredi-ents will make their own stock.) Bring the heat up to high, until the liquids bubble. Immediately lower the heat to a sim-mer. Cook for 7 to 10 minutes. The potatoes will be tender.

2. Add the mussels. Add salt and pepper. Cover and simmer for 15 to 17 minutes more. The fish will be falling-apart ten-der and the mussels opened. Discard any mussels that have not opened. Sprinkle the parsley over the top before serving right out of the pot.

Holy Ghost Soup

Sopa du Espirito Santo

Serves 6 to 8

When the home cooks of Peabody gather to make soup for the annual Holy Ghost feast, this is the one they make. Ana Ortins regularly joins a group of men and women who work for more than a week to produce the celebratory meal, with the recipe, adapted here, as its centerpiece.

1 onion, chopped
5 cloves garlic, peeled and left whole
1 bay leaf
$^1/_2$ cup white wine
8 cups water
3 slices bacon, chopped
1 pound beef brisket
1 $^1/_2$ pounds chicken pieces (legs, thighs, wings, breast)
8 ounces linguiça sausage
1 pound kale, stems discarded, and leaves torn into
    small pieces
2 pounds potatoes, peeled and quartered
1 small head cabbage, cored and cut into quarters
1 teaspoon coarse salt, or to taste
$^1/_2$ loaf day-old Portuguese country bread or sourdough
    bread, sliced
Mint sprigs for garnish

1. In a large soup pot, combine the onion, garlic, bay leaf, wine, and water. Bring to a boil.

2. Add the bacon, brisket, chicken, and linguiça. Reduce to a simmer, and cook for about 20 minutes. The meats will be tender. Remove meats from the pot. Set aside and keep warm.

3. Strain the broth and return it to the pot. Discard the onion, bay leaf, and bacon. Add the kale and potatoes. Bring

SOUPS AND STEWS

Soups and stews, *migas*, are the stalwarts of the Portuguese family table. These sturdy dishes staved off the blistering cold of our North Shore winters using the garden's bounty to stretch meager stores of meat and fish.

Portuguese soups, both basic *sopas* and bread-thickened *acordas*, begin with water rather than stock. The meat—whether a whole chicken, a cut of beef, or a piece of smoked sausage—does double duty, releasing its flavors to make stock, then cut into bite-size pieces and returned to the pot as part of the stew. Larger cuts of meat are sliced and served as a separate course.

SKIMMING FAT

To lighten a dish, skim the fat off the top of soups that contain sausage.

to a boil. Reduce the heat to a simmer and cook for about 10 minutes.

4. Add the cabbage. Simmer for about 15 minutes longer. Add salt to taste.

5. Slice the beef and linguiça into serving-size pieces. Place on a serving platter with the chicken pieces.

6. To serve the soup, tear slices of the bread and place in a soup tureen. Ladle the soup to fill the tureen. Garnish with fresh sprigs of mint. Serve the meat platter as a separate course.

Kale Soup
Caldo Verde

Serves 6 to 8

This fragrant, slightly spicy soup, laced with linguiça and grassy filaments of kale or collards, is also called Green Soup. To cut the greens, stack the leaves one on top of another on a cutting board, and roll them tightly. Then cut them crosswise, very closely, with a paring knife. The resulting strips resemble ribbons.

Although some Portuguese-American home cooks have cautioned me against using any type of stock base, others swear by it as a flavor enhancement. A good homemade or low-salt commercial stock might be a good compromise, but generally store-bought stocks are simply too salty. In this recipe I've left the decision to the cook.

FATS AND OILS

The major cooking fats of Portuguese cooking are lard, bacon drippings, and olive oil. In daily home cooking, Portuguese-Americans use lard and bacon drippings sparingly. Olive oil imported from Portugal is available in specialty markets. Pure Italian olive oil, not extra-virgin, may be substituted. Modern cooks often use lighter oils, such as canola.

1 large yellow onion, very coarsely chopped
1 clove garlic, chopped
4 ounces linguiça, thinly sliced
4 russet potatoes, peeled and coarsely chopped
Salt and freshly ground black pepper
2 quarts cold water or chicken stock
1 pound kale, stems discarded and leaves cut
    into slivers

1. Combine the onion, garlic, linguiça, potatoes, salt and pepper to taste, and water in a large soup pot. Bring to a boil. Turn down the heat and simmer for 20 to 25 minutes. The potatoes will be tender when pierced with a fork. (The soup may be cooked a day ahead up to this point. When refrigerated overnight, the fat will harden and rise to the top and it can be scraped off with a spoon.)

REFOGADO

A gentle sauté of aromatic vegetables, called *refogado*, is the basis of soups, stews, and sauces. Sweet onion is cooked slowly in oil, either alone, with garlic, or with peeled, seeded, and chopped tomatoes, until tender and richly colored.

CORIANDER OR CILANTRO

Which is it? Technically, the terms are interchangeable. Cooks have come to call the leaves of the plant cilantro and the dried and ground seeds coriander. Toss the zingy lemon-lime-scented leaves, which resemble flat-leaf parsley, into stews—with abandon!

2. With a slotted spoon, skim any fat that rises to the top of the soup. Remove the sausage, slice it diagonally, and set it aside.

3. In a blender or a food processor, roughly puree the remaining ingredients, or mash them with a heavy potato masher. (The puree is meant to be thick and hearty.) Return to the pot.

4. Add the kale. Simmer for 10 minutes. The kale will turn bright green. Serve the sausage as a garnish on the side of each bowl.

Tuna Steaks

Bifes de Atum

Serves 6

Fish should be "just cooked through" for best results. It continues to cook from the pan's residual heat after it is taken out of the oven. Tuna is well loved in Gloucester home kitchens, where you can find many versions of this recipe.

3 tablespoons olive oil
1 large yellow onion, chopped
3 cloves garlic, minced
6 to 8 canned plum tomatoes, drained and chopped
1/2 cup Madeira
3/4 cup dry white wine
2 to 3 lemons, thickly sliced
6 tuna steaks, about 8 ounces each
Salt and freshly ground black pepper
1/2 cup chopped fresh cilantro

1. Heat 2 tablespoons of the oil in a saucepan over medium-high heat. Add the onion, garlic, and tomatoes. Cook, stirring, for 10 minutes. The vegetables will be softened and lightly golden. Stir in the Madeira and wine. Bring to a boil, then lower the heat to a simmer. Cover and cook for 15 minutes.

2. Heat the oven to 375°F. Coat a shallow baking pan with the remaining 1 tablespoon oil.

3. Cover the bottom of the pan with a layer of lemon slices. Layer on the fish. Sprinkle with salt and pepper. Pour the wine mixture over the fish steaks. Top with the cilantro. Cover.

4. Bake for 10 to 15 minutes. The fish will be just cooked through. Serve it hot with rice.

Orange Braised Rabbit

Coelho de Laranja

Serves 6

If you're not happy about eating rabbit, substitute skinless chicken thighs.

2 tablespoons olive oil
1 medium onion, chopped
1 green bell pepper, chopped
8-ounce piece chouriço
2 small (2-pound) rabbits, cut into serving pieces
Salt and freshly ground black pepper
1 1/2 teaspoons dried oregano
1 cup Madeira
1 cup canned or homemade chicken stock
1/2 teaspoon hot pepper sauce, or to taste
1/4 cup orange juice

PORK PRODUCTS

Pork products in the form of sausage or ham, are staples of Portuguese-American kitchens. These most familiar products are available in small specialty shops, but increasingly you can find them in larger markets.

- **Chouriço:** Spicy smoke-cured link sausage flavored with paprika.

- **Linguiça:** Mild smoke-cured sausage made of chopped pork shoulder, garlic, and paprika, traditionally seared in a clay pot, doused with a liquor called *agua dente*, (hard water), and set aflame. Portuguese-Americans use brandy.

- **Presunto:** Air-dried ham, comparable to a Smithfield ham or Italian prosciutto.

O FADO'S BAR

In Portugal, *fado* is folk music often heard in small eateries where the bill of fare is simple food and drink. Here on the North Shore, O Fado is a neighborhood place tucked behind Peabody Square, where regulars gather at the bar for the "real food." No one posts a menu. The cook passes earthy fried cod or rabbit with great lashings of sausage and garlic through the kitchen window. Loyal patrons wash the food down with beer.

1. Heat the oil in a Dutch oven over medium heat. Add the onion, green pepper, and chouriço. Cook for about 10 minutes. The sausage will be browned and the vegetables softened. Remove the sausage and vegetables with a slotted spoon. Leave the drippings in the pan.

2. Sprinkle the rabbit pieces with salt and pepper to taste, and oregano. Add to the pan. Sear the meat on all sides, for about 10 minutes, until the rabbit is slightly browned on the outside but not fully cooked inside.

3. Return the vegetables and sausage to the pan. Add the Madeira, stock, and hot pepper sauce. Bring to a boil. Reduce to a simmer. Cover. Cook for 35 minutes. The meat will be cooked through and tender.

4. Remove the meats from the pan with a slotted spoon. Remove the pan from the heat. Chop the sausage into bite-size pieces and place it on a serving plate with the rabbit.

5. Stir the orange juice into the sauce. Do not cook. This keeps the orange flavor fresh. Pour over the meats and serve.

Roast Beef

Carne Assada

Serves 6 to 8

This flavorful beef dish, which is the centerpiece of the Holy Ghost feast dinner, is treated to a marinade, a quick oven searing, and a slow roast to mingle all the flavors perfectly. Home cooks may choose either a dry rub (mostly dry ingredients massaged onto the beef) or a wet marinade (mostly wet ingredients poured over the beef)—whatever has worked for cooks in their own family.

      3 large cloves garlic, minced
      1 teaspoon each coarse salt and freshly ground black
          pepper, or to taste
      1 tablespoon paprika
      2 tablespoons tomato paste
      1 to 2 teaspoons hot pepper sauce, to taste
      4-pound rump roast
      2 medium onions, sliced into rounds
      3 slices bacon, diced
      2 cups water
      3 cups white or rose wine
      1 bay leaf
      1/4 teaspoon ground nutmeg

1. Make a paste by whisking together the garlic, salt, pepper, paprika, tomato paste, hot pepper sauce, and a few drops of the wine, if needed. Rub the paste over the roast. Wrap tightly with plastic wrap and refrigerate overnight.

2. Preheat the oven to 400°F.

3. Toss the onions and bacon together. Put them in the bottom of a roasting pan. Pour the water and wine over them.

Add the bay leaf and sprinkle in the nutmeg. Place the beef on top of the onion and bacon mixture in the roasting pan.

4. Roast in the oven for about 15 minutes. The meat will be browned on top. Remove and turn the roast over, and cook in the oven about 15 minutes. Take the roast out of the oven and spoon some of the onion and bacon mixture over the top.

5. Lower the oven temperature to 350°F. Return the roast to the oven. Cook, about 1¼ hours, basting with pan juices every 20 or 30 minutes. When measured with a thermometer, the temperature will read 140°F. Slice and serve on a platter with pan juices.

Joao Borge's Portuguese-American Paella

Arroz Valenciana

Serves 2

Portugal shares the Iberian Peninsula with Spain, including a Moorish occupation that brought rice, and eventually paella, to that part of the world. On the North Shore, Borge's Iberian-American paella, chockful of the local catch, is crowned with a whole lobster split in half! Don't expect expensive saffron as in Spanish versions of the dish: Borge boosts the stew with a secret ingredient, Sazon powder, a seasoning powder found in the international section of the supermarket or Caribbean specialty stores.

This recipe, although lengthy, is not difficult. I've broken it down into short sections. If you are making this for six, double the recipe and get three lobsters.

To marinate the pork, you need:

1/2 cup dry white wine
1 clove garlic, crushed
1 tablespoon wine vinegar
1 teaspoon hot pepper sauce
1 teaspoon coarse salt
1 bay leaf
1/2 pound pork, cut into 1-inch cubes

Whisk together the wine, garlic, wine vinegar, hot pepper sauce, and salt in a large bowl. Add the bay leaf and the pork cubes and toss to coat the pork with the marinade. Cover and refrigerate overnight.

To make the rice, you need:

2 tablespoons olive oil
1/2 cup finely chopped onion
1 teaspoon crushed garlic
1/2 packet (3/4 teaspoon) Sazon seasoning powder
2 bay leaves
1 tablespoon tomato paste
2 1/2 cups water
1 cup rice
1/2 teaspoon salt
1/2 cup frozen carrot and pea combination

Heat the olive oil in a large skillet over medium-high heat. Add the chopped onion. Cook for about 3 to 5 minutes. The onions will begin to soften. Add the garlic, seasoning powder, bay leaves, and tomato paste. Cook, stirring, for about 2 minutes more. Do not let the garlic brown. Add the water and bring the mixture to a boil. Add the rice and salt. Return the rice to a boil. Stir in the carrots and peas. Do not stir again. Reduce the heat to low. Continue cooking for about 20 minutes. The rice will be tender and liquid will be absorbed. Fluff the rice with a fork, and set aside.

BOULEVARD
OCEANVIEW
RESTAURANT

Although Gloucester's Boulevard Oceanview Restaurant, near the famous fisherman statue, serves up great local seafood, savvy customers ask for the Portuguese menu, which yields delicious surprises like charcoal-grilled salt cod or *mariscada*, a mélange of fresh lobster, shrimp, littleneck clams, and mussels in savory broth.

At the end of the day, owner and cook Joao Borge brings his own plate to the dining room and eats with customers. A former fisherman, Borge has been happily dishing up his Portuguese-American specialties to locals for nearly 20 years—but in the last few years, since Hollywood discovered Gloucester as a movie backdrop (*The Perfect Storm, The Love Letter*), you never know who might sit down at the next table. Unspoiled by all the attention, Joao just adds a new coat of paint to the building and keeps on cooking fabulous fried fish and perfect Portuguese-American paella.

To make the sauce, you need:

2 tablespoons olive oil
1/2 cup finely chopped onion
1 clove garlic, crushed
1 teaspoon hot pepper sauce, or more to taste
1/2 packet (3/4 teaspoon) Sazon seasoning powder
1/2 cup clam juice
2 tablespoons tomato paste
1/4 cup white wine
1/4 cup tawny port wine

Heat the oil in a medium saucepan over medium heat. Add the onions. Cook, stirring, for 3 to 5 minutes. The onions will be wilted. Add the garlic, hot pepper sauce, and seasoning powder. Cook, stirring constantly, for about 2 minutes more. The garlic will be aromatic. Do not let the garlic brown. Stir in the clam juice, tomato paste, white wine, and port. Bring the pot to a boil. Lower the heat to medium-low. Simmer gently for about 15 minutes.

To assemble the paella, you need:

1 live lobster, about 1 1/2 pounds
3 chicken tenders, cut into 2-inch pieces
2 tablespoons olive oil
6 littleneck clams
10 mussels
4 ounces medium shrimp, peeled and deveined
4 ounces bay scallops
4 ounces squid, cleaned and cut crosswise into rings
1/2 cup white wine
1/2 cup finely chopped cilantro

1. Preheat the oven to 350°F. Drain the pork and discard the marinade. Boil or steam the lobster according to the directions on page 13. Set the lobster aside.

2. Heat the oil in a large ovenproof pan. Add the pork. Cook for about 5 minutes, making sure to brown it evenly. Remove the pork from the pan with a slotted spoon and set it aside.

3. Add the chicken to the pan and cook for about 5 minutes, browning evenly.

4. Add the clams, mussels, shrimp, scallops, squid, and wine. Cover and cook for about 2 minutes. Turn off the heat. Add the cooked rice, about three-quarters of the sauce, and the pork to the pan.

5. Move the pan to the oven. Cover and cook for about 15 to 20 minutes. The clams and mussels will be opened. Discard any that are still closed. Gently toss the mixture with the cilantro and remaining sauce. Serve garnished with the whole lobster to be shared.

Spicy Clams

Ameijoas

Serves 6 to 8

Mario Clarimondo owns a tiny import shop where he sells the hinged oven-to-table casseroles called *cataplana,* used for cooking clams. Joao Borge owns a beat-up *cataplana,* which he often uses to cook this dish for himself and his kitchen helpers.

HOT STUFF

The hot red pepper sauce Tabasco flavors many Portuguese-American dishes since it closely approximates *molho de piri-piri,* an incendiary sauce made from peppers native to Angola, once a Portuguese colony. Mary Gil keeps track of a variety of authentic sauces and dried hot peppers on the shelves of Peabody's Tremont Market.

    To make hot pepper sauce at home, pulse $1/4$ cup stemmed, but not seeded, whole fresh hot red chili peppers, 2 cloves garlic, $1/2$ teaspoon coarse salt, $1/2$ cup olive oil, and, 2 tablespoons red wine vinegar in a blender or food processor. Refrigerate, tightly covered, in a glass jar for 24 hours. Shake well before using.

    Always make hot pepper sauce in small batches, refrigerate it, and use within 5 days to avoid bacteria growth.

4 dozen littleneck clams
$1/4$ cup olive oil
1 medium onion, chopped
1 small green bell pepper, chopped
1 small red bell pepper, chopped
2 cloves garlic, minced
$2 1/2$ cups peeled, seeded, and chopped tomatoes
2 heaping teaspoons tomato paste
1 packet Sazon seasoning
1 cup dry white wine
Salt and freshly ground black pepper
Hot pepper sauce
Generous handful of chopped fresh parsley

1. Scrub the clams. Soak in enough cold water to cover for 2 to 12 hours to release any grit. Rinse and drain. Set aside.

2. Heat the oil in a large heavy pot over medium heat. Add the onion, bell peppers, and garlic. Cook, stirring occasionally, for 10 minutes. The onion will be translucent.

3. Reduce the heat to low. Stir in the tomatoes and tomato paste. Cover and "sweat" the mixture for 10 to 20 minutes, until the vegetables are dark red and sweetly flavored.

4. Stir in the Sazon seasoning and wine and bring to a boil. Reduce the heat to a simmer. Cook, uncovered, for 3 to 4 minutes. Add the clams to the pot. Toss gently to mix. Cover. Cook over medium heat for 10 minutes. The clams will open. Discard any that do not open.

5. Season with salt and black pepper to taste, and hot pepper sauce. Sprinkle liberally with parsley. Toss gently just before serving.

Summer Vegetable Salad
Salad do Verão

Serves 6

A summer accompaniment to large, fresh sardines, blessed with oil and lemon and charcoal grilled, this salad is distinctive for its piquant dressing. A nearly one-to-one ratio of olive oil and cider vinegar is not whisked, but instead splashed separately onto the vegetables, tossing after each addition.

    1 red onion, sliced into rounds
    3 medium green bell peppers, seeded, cored, and
        sliced into rounds
    4 large ripe tomatoes, peeled, seeded, and sliced
        into rounds
    1 small clove garlic, minced
    Salt and freshly ground black pepper
    6 tablespoons extra virgin olive oil
    4 tablespoons cider vinegar
    Cilantro leaves
    Parsley leaves
    Brined small black olives, pitted and chopped

1. Combine the onion, bell peppers, and tomatoes in a large bowl.

2. Sprinkle with the garlic and salt and pepper to taste. Drizzle with the olive oil and toss. Add the vinegar and toss again. Add the cilantro and parsley and toss, once more, gently.

3. Cover and marinate for 30 minutes.

4. Toss lightly and serve sprinkled with the olives.

Potatoes with Cilantro

Batatas com Coentro

Serves 6

The bright lemon-lime flavor of cilantro gives the potatoes zip.

12 new potatoes
2 tablespoons olive oil
1 tablespoon unsalted butter
3 to 4 cloves garlic, minced
1/3 cup finely minced fresh cilantro leaves
Salt and freshly ground black pepper

1. Combine the potatoes and water to cover in a saucepan. Bring to a boil. Lower the heat and simmer for about 15 to 20 minutes. Potatoes will be tender when pierced with a fork. Drain and cool. Peel the potatoes.

2. Warm the oil and butter in a large skillet over low heat. Add the garlic. Cook for 1 to 2 minutes. Add the potatoes. Cook, gently turning, for 2 to 3 minutes, until the potatoes are lightly golden. Sprinkle with cilantro. Cook for 2 more minutes, turning. The potatoes will be lightly coated with cilantro. Season with salt and pepper. Serve hot.

Roasted Spiced Potatoes
Batatas Assadas

Serves 6 to 8

The accompaniment of the traditional Holy Ghost festival roast, these potatoes are perfect with any oven-roasted meats.

  2 cloves garlic, minced
  1 tablespoon sweet paprika
  1 teaspoon tomato paste
  1/4 cup olive oil
  Salt and freshly ground black pepper
  2 tablespoons finely chopped fresh flat-leaf parsley
  6 to 8 large potatoes, peeled and cut into 2-inch chunks

1. Lightly oil a heavy sheet pan. Preheat the oven to 350°F.

2. Whisk together the garlic, paprika, tomato paste, oil, salt, pepper, and parsley in a large bowl. Add the potatoes and toss until they are coated.

3. Spread the potatoes in a single layer on the sheet pan. Roast in the oven for about 1 hour, turning occasionally. The potatoes will be golden brown on the outside and tender when pierced with a fork.

Tomato Rice
Arroz a Tomate

Serves 6

Invented in Portugal by country cooks so that falling-off-the-vine-ripe tomatoes were not wasted, this dish was transported to the North Shore, where it is a standby in the late August and early September glut of garden tomatoes. At the Boulevard Oceanview Restaurant, the cooks add a shot of tomato paste for a more full-bodied flavor. Home cooks find the tomato paste useful when they want to make this dish in winter.

    1 tablespoon olive oil
    2 strips bacon, finely chopped
    1 medium yellow onion, peeled and chopped
    1 clove garlic, minced
    4 to 5 medium tomatoes, peeled, seeded, and chopped
    3 to 4 tablespoons tomato paste, to taste
    2 cups water
    2 cups long-grain rice
    Salt and freshly ground black pepper to taste
    2 tablespoons minced flat-leaf parsley or cilantro

1. Heat the olive oil in a heavy saucepan over medium heat. Add the bacon, onion, and garlic. Cook, stirring, about 5 minutes. The vegetables will be lightly golden. Swirl in the tomatoes and tomato paste. Cover and simmer for about 15 minutes. The vegetables will be cooked down and darkened, not scorched.

2. Add the water and bring the mixture to a rolling boil. Stir in the rice. Lower the heat to simmer. Cover and cook for about 20 minutes. The liquid will be absorbed, with grains tender and separate.

3. Season with salt, pepper, and parsley or cilantro. Fluff with a fork before serving.

Raised Cornmeal Bread

Broa de Milho

Makes 4 loaves

Portuguese-style yeast-raised corn bread is a dense, crusty loaf, nothing like hoe cake or quick bread. The baking technique has roots in the Azores, a group of islands off the coast of Portugal, and the finished loaves resemble rounds of sourdough, complete with flour-dusted tops. Corn bread is a natural partner for winter's hearty soups or for summer's charcoal-grilled sardines.

    2 packages (5 teaspoons) active dry yeast
    1 1/2 cups lukewarm water
    2 cups sifted white cornmeal
    1 cup milk, scalded and cooled
    2 tablespoons corn or vegetable oil
    1 1/2 tablespoons salt
    5 to 5 1/2 cups all-purpose flour

1. Stir together the yeast and ½ cup of the lukewarm water in a large bowl. Add ⅔ cup of the cornmeal, wisking to remove any lumps. Cover the bowl with a cloth and set aside in a warm place to rise for 30 to 40 minutes. It will be bubbly. Stir it down.

2. Whisk together 1 cup lukewarm water, milk, oil, and salt. Add this and the remaining cornmeal to the yeast mixture.

3. Blend in 5 cups of the flour, one cup at a time, to form a soft dough. Flour a work surface. Turn out the dough. Knead for 5 minutes. The dough will be smooth and elastic. Shape this dough into a ball. Oil the inside of a bowl. Place the dough in the oiled bowl. Cover with a cloth. Set in a warm place to rise for about 1 hour. It will double in bulk.

SARDINE BARBECUE

All summer long, backyard barbecues in the Portuguese neighborhoods of Gloucester and central Peabody sizzle with fresh sardines, which are eaten with *broa,* raised corn bread, and cool cucumber salad. Cleaned and boned sardines are purchased fresh or frozen, never canned, with tails and often heads still attached. They are left to marinate under a layer of coarse salt for an hour or two. When the salt is washed off, and a charcoal fire has burned down to a white ash covering, the fish are brushed with olive oil and placed over the fire for 2 to 3 minutes per side. A spritz of lemon is nice, although not required, at the end.

4. Punch down the dough. Turn it onto the floured board. Again, knead for 5 minutes. Shape it into a ball. Once more set it in the oiled bowl, covered with a cloth, in a warm place. Let it rise again for about 1 hour.

5. Turn the dough onto the floured board. For a third time, knead for 5 minutes. Divide it into two equal pieces. Shape them into rounds.

6. Preheat the oven to 500°F. Place a baking stone or two clean bricks on the bottom rack of the oven. Fill a spray bottle with cold tap water.

7. Grease two round cake pans. Place each round of dough into a cake pan. Sift some cornmeal over the tops. Then cover each with a cloth and set aside to rise, one last time, for 45 minutes.

8. Place the loaves on the center rack of the oven. Bake for 5 minutes. Open the oven and quickly spray water onto the baking stone to create steam. Repeat after 10 minutes, and 15 minutes. Then turn the oven temperature down to 400°F. Bake for an additional 30 to 35 minutes. The loaves will be deeply brown on top and firm to the touch.

9. Remove the loaves from the pans and cool them on a wire rack before cutting.

Ana's Sweet Rice Pudding

Arroz Doce

Serves 4 to 6

This is adapted from Ana Ortins's heirloom recipe for sweet rice pudding. Just before serving, she sprinkles the shape of a heart, a cross, or an honored guest's initials over the top with ground cinnamon. Make a paper template of the shape for best results. You can purchase stenciling templates at a craft shop for more ornate designs.

    1 cup short-grain rice
    2 cups water
    1/4 teaspoon salt
    Zest of 1 lemon, cut into strips
    1 cinnamon stick
    2 cups milk, scalded
    1 cup sugar
    Ground cinnamon

1. In a saucepan, combine the rice, water, and salt. Bring to a boil. Lower the heat, cover, and cook until the water is nearly absorbed, about 10 minutes.

2. Add milk, lemon zest, and cinnamon stick. Cook over low heat, stirring frequently, for about 20 to 25 minutes.

3. Add the sugar. Cook until the rice is tender and the sugar is dissolved, about 7 to 10 minutes. It will continue thickening as it cools. Ana says it should be as thick as oatmeal.

4. With a slotted spoon, remove the cinnamon stick and lemon zest. Pour the pudding into small serving bowls.

5. Make a design on top with ground cinnamon. Ana rubs the cinnamon between her thumb and index fingers, holding them closely over the surface of the rice so the cinnamon doesn't scatter all over. Chill until you are ready to serve.

Fresh Fruit in Port
Fruta Fresca em Porto

Serves 6

Port, a specialty wine from Portugal, makes this incredibly refreshing and easy dessert for summer very festive. A wonderful "adults-only" ice cream topping, it is nontraditional but a delicious counterpart to the rice pudding.

    1 quart whole fresh strawberries, hulled
    2 cups fresh pineapple, cut into 1-inch chunks
    5 tablespoons port
    Chopped fresh mint leaves, for garnish

1. Place strawberries in a glass bowl. Place pineapple in a separate bowl. Sprinkle each bowl of fruit with port. Toss gently to mix.

2. Chill 2 hours, covered. Toss the fruits together and sprinkle with mint before serving in dessert dishes or over ice cream.

THE AFRICAN-AMERICAN TRADITION

*From Molasses Cookies
to Momma's Kitchen*

Africans came to the North Shore by varied, and unusual, means of transportation. The first were brought here in colonial times as slaves or indentured servants. Some bought freedom with their labor; others were freed at the signing of the Declaration of Independence.

When Lucy Larcom wrote of her childhood in early nineteenth-century Beverly, she noted, "Families of black people were scattered about the place, relics of a time when . . . New England had not freed her slaves. . . . They lived among us on equal terms, respectable and respected." Sandra Oliver writes in *Saltwater Foodways* that blacks made their living as independent tradesmen or seamen. "Black sailors . . . enjoyed . . . comparative equality . . . as able seamen, but by the 1840s they were often shunted into more menial jobs as cooks or stewards."

A decade or so later, people of African heritage reached the North Shore under cover of night, passengers on the Underground Railroad, the trail to freedom for escaped slaves. Given shelter by the Society of Friends, also called Quakers, some chose to disembark here. The presence of a "Friend Street" in a neighborhood indicates the address of a Quaker meetinghouse.

After World War II, grandchildren of slaves migrated to northern cities to escape the rural poverty of the South. Unconscious memories of Africa merged with foodways of the American South in the food they prepared. Baked country ham, collard greens flavored with ham hocks, and corn bread to sop up pot liquor are vestiges of a country cooking that took few minor detours as its proponents became urbanized. Abner Darby of Lynn says, "Educated blacks are getting away from that kind of food; the younger generation eats healthier."

One celebrated culinary flicker remains from colonial times. A molasses-and-spice cookie was born in an America as shiny and new as the freedom of the man who made them famous.

Today authentic African foodstuffs find their way directly to the plate. A new consciousness emanates from local colleges where students of color explore African, Caribbean, and South American roots.

Karamu, the Kwanzaa Feast

Kwanzaa is a seven-day winter holiday observed in late December by people of African heritage. Each of the seven days is marked by a particular guiding principle; on each day, celebrants light a black, red, or green candle. On the North Shore, Dr. Pharnal Longus, professor emeritus of social work at Salem State College, has done a great deal to spread awareness of the holiday, bringing the message to elementary and high school students. Dressed in African garb, and speaking as a traditional African storyteller, he instills awareness of the seven principles, *nguzo sabo:* unity, self-determination, collective work and responsibility, cooperative economics, purpose, creativity, and faith.

> MENU FOR KARAMU,
> THE KWANZAA FEAST
>
> Peanut Soup
> Fried Chicken
> Baked Ham
> Fried Green Tomatoes
> Candied Sweet Potatoes
> Collard Greens
> Corn Bread
> Sweet Potato Pie

"We celebrate creativity during this season—the music, dance, and, yes, culinary arts. On the last night, when the last candle is lit and all seven candles burn at once, we teach our children to pass along faith—in themselves, their families, and their teachers—and we hold a feast, called *Karamu.*"

Family and friends celebrate, potluck style, with everyone tucking into heritage dishes such as fried catfish, collard greens, chitlins, corn bread, sweet potato pie, and rice pudding. Since the last day of the holiday is January 1, a dish of black-eyed peas for good luck is mandatory, as is African peanut soup. At Salem State College, the African-American Students Association holds a Kwanzaa Ball, blending these foods with African music.

A North Shore Cook: Lillie Jones

The secret to great fried chicken, according to Lillie Jones, is simply salt, pepper, and Lawry's Seasoned Salt. "Put it in the refrigerator overnight to flavor it. When you take it out, flour it, and deep-fry it in Crisco oil. Don't use any other kind of oil," says this mother of four, grandmother of six. "They're all too heavy."

If you're in search of authentic African-American cooking on the North Shore, all roads lead to "Momma Jones." Acknowledged by many as the "best cook in Lynn," she claims that her friends are good cooks, too. No matter. Jones is the one churches, schools, and others call on because she knows how to cook for a crowd. February, Black History Month, finds her directing groups of volunteers in the intricacies of preparing fried chicken, corn bread, black-eyed peas, and other specialties for up to two hundred. When word gets out that "Jones is in the house," it's standing room only! She's nearly as busy at Thanksgiving, when she'll bake seventy-five sweet potato pies for family and friends.

Born in South Carolina, Jones went to live in her grandmother's household as a young child. While her father was on active military duty, her mother became ill. Jones's only recollections of her mother are frequent, sad hospital visits until her death. Adopted by doting aunts and uncles, she often found herself in the kitchen with a favorite aunt.

"Aunt Ethel Brown was a great lady. She never married. She always provided for me. We lived on a cotton farm. We grew, and picked, and canned everything to get ready for the winter. Blackberries, tomatoes, corn, greens, all that stuff. When the land-lords slaughtered their animals, we got the feet, the tails, the necks, any parts they didn't want. We cooked those things up so they tasted good. Good for the soul. That's why we call it soul food.

"Oh, we had wonderful things. We flavored our collards with ham and pig's feet and neck bones. You know, the smoked ones are the best; they have more flavor. We had fried chicken on Sundays. Sometimes we had a roast chicken, but, well, we always liked fried best. And potato salad. Sweet potato pie and peach cobbler were our favorite desserts."

Jones married at eighteen and moved to Washington, D.C. She cooked when the family gathered.

"I was always good at math, so when we got together for a picnic, or Christmas, or Mother's Day, I figured out how much we needed. They'd say, 'Lillie knows how to do that,' and 'We'll let Lillie do it.' I'd figure out breakfast, lunch, and dinner. Then someone would drive me to get the groceries. I always did the cooking."

Mrs. Jones laughs as she recalls her move to the North Shore in 1962, where her first position was as a private cook.

"There was just one old lady in that big house, and she ate like a bird! She liked her bran muffin every morning . . . only one, but I had to make up a whole batch in these little, teeny muffin pans. . . . She'd eat about a teaspoon of anything I cooked.

"That first Friday night her family came for dinner, about ten or twelve of them. She wanted leg of lamb. Now, I'd seen lambs, but I didn't know people ate those things. Oooh, what a smell! I just don't like that smell! I put everything on it I could find in that kitchen to get rid of that smell! Then I just hoped. Well, they said they'd never tasted anything that good.

"They thought I could cook anything. Once, they wanted me to cook a deer. All I could say was 'Help me, Lord Jesus!' I marinated it in a lot of wine, or something, and let it roast for a long, long time, and they just thought it was delicious. I cooked a lot of things I never tried. Sponge cake. Pecan pie. They liked them all fine."

Eventually, Jones took her culinary talents to volunteer work with Girl Scouts, Girls' Club, and Operation Headstart. As a teacher's aide in the Lynn public schools, she devoted extra time to Black History Month projects. A few tastes of home cooking, brought to share with the staff one Martin Luther King's birthday, put her on the road to recognition. The little luncheon became an annual event, growing in size each year until she needed the whole cafeteria kitchen to prepare it. Word spread to neighboring communities, bringing TV camera crews who made sure to stick around to sample the collards.

"The secret to greens is pork fat. I use bacon or bacon drippings, white salt pork, ham hocks, or neck bones to flavor them. I like them smoked. They have a lot more flavor. When I first moved here, you couldn't find neck bones or chitlins [chitterlings]. Now, they're right beside the sausages.

"Chitlins, that's pork intestines. People don't like to talk about them, but that's what they fill when they make sausages. We boil them, batter, and fry 'em. My husband likes them that old-fashioned way. They're good boiled and cut fine, lighter that way. You put hot sauce and cider vinegar on them."

Lillie is rarely without a crowd around her, whether it is her children and grandchildren, fellow members of

Zion Baptist Church, or a gathering at the Bethel African Methodist Episcopal Church to toast her contributions to church and community. She's garnered awards from the Lynn Community Minority Cultural Center; Girls, Inc.; and Who's Who. Retired now, she still volunteers at a soup kitchen and lavishes attention on everyone around her. Her eyes flash with enthusiasm and interest in every conversation.

"Sometimes kids tell me they wish they had a mother like me. I tell them that their mothers are precious. I have no secret there. I just try to treat people the way they want to be treated."

She pauses a long moment. The voice lowers. "I guess I still wish for the mother I never had."

THE PANTRY

- **Black-eyed peas:** Creamy-colored dried beans with a black dot (eye), cooked and eaten for good luck on New Year's Day.

- **Chitlins (chitterlings):** Hog innards, literally intestines, rarely used owing to the intensive labor required to clean them.

- **Collards (collard greens):** Traditional greens of the American South, simmered slowly and flavored with a smoked pork product, such as ham hocks.

- **Fats and oils:** Bacon drippings, also called rendered bacon, and lard, rendered from the back of the pork loin available in bricks like butter. For health reasons, peanut, corn, and Crisco oils are substituted, sometimes with a bit of lard or bacon drippings added for flavoring.

- **Molasses:** Rich, dark by-product of sugar refining used as a sweetener.

- **Okra:** Green pod-shaped vegetable that creates its own thickener as it cooks. Okra is available fresh, frozen, or canned.

- **Peanut:** Legume of African origin often roasted and salted, a natural thickener in soups and stews. Peanut oil often replaces lard for frying in the modern kitchen.

- **Sweet potatoes:** Not to be confused with yams, which do not have the same yellow to orange interior. Available from autumn through winter.

THE RECIPES

Peanut Soup

Peach-Glazed Baked Ham

Lillie's Fried Chicken

Fried Fish

Collard Greens

Fried Green Tomatoes

Fried Okra

Picnic Potato Salad

Candied Sweet Potatoes

Black-Eyed Peas

Old-Fashioned Buttermilk
Biscuits

Corn Bread

Sweet Potato Pie

Peach Cobbler

Kwanzaa Rice Pudding

Joe Froggers

Roasted Pumpkin Seeds

Peanut Soup

Serves 6 to 8

Directly from Africa, this soup is popular on the Kwanzaa table. For a special touch, warm the peanuts in a skillet, stirring constantly, for about 2 minutes, watching carefully that they do not burn.

2 teaspoons cornstarch
2 cups whole milk
3 cups canned or homemade chicken stock
2 cups creamy peanut butter
2 thin slices yellow onion
1/4 cup chopped fresh parsley
Salt and freshly ground black pepper
1/4 teaspoon cayenne pepper
Chopped roasted peanuts for garnish

1. Whisk together the cornstarch and milk in a large heavy saucepan over low heat.

2. Add the stock, peanut butter, onion, half the parsley, salt and pepper to taste, and cayenne. Raise the heat to medium-high and bring just to a boil, stirring. Reduce the heat and simmer for 15 to 18 minutes. The mixture will thicken.

3. Cool the soup for about 10 minutes. Pour into a food processor or blender and pulse until smooth. Rinse the pot and return the soup to it. Bring the soup just to the boil to heat through.

4. Serve with a scatter of the remaining parsley and the peanuts over the top.

Peach-Glazed Baked Ham

Serves 10

A baked ham is an eagerly anticipated treat at Kwanzaa or a summer picnic. Ideally, the peach preserves would have been "put up" the previous summer.

5- to 7-pound smoked ham
1 cup freshly squeezed orange juice
3 tablespoons molasses
2 tablespoons peach preserves
2 teaspoons Dijon-style mustard

1. Preheat the oven to 350°F. Trim most of the fat from the ham, leaving a layer about ¼ inch to ½ inch all over.

2. Place the ham in a roasting pan. Bake for about 20 minutes.

3. Meanwhile, whisk together the orange juice, molasses, preserves, and mustard.

4. Remove the ham from the oven and baste with the orange juice mixture. Reduce the heat to 300°F and continue baking for 20 to 25 minutes per pound.

5. About 30 minutes before the cooking time is ended, remove the ham from the oven. Score a crisscross pattern into the fat with a sharp knife. Baste the ham again. Return it to the oven. Bake for about 30 minutes longer. The glaze will be golden brown. Serve hot.

FOOD SAFETY

When working with chicken, be careful that uncooked and cooked chicken do not come in contact with or touch the same surfaces.

Lillie's Fried Chicken

Serves 6

When Abner Darby of Lynn was growing up at the end of the Great Depression, chicken was reserved for weekends. "Mostly we'd eat beans and corn bread. On Sundays, the kids would help shuck corn and haul wood because we had no gas stoves. Sunday dinners tasted good, but there was nothin' good about the good old days."

Darby says that Lillie Jones's fried recipe, adapted here, is the best. Although he now bakes his chicken for healthier eating, he still uses the overnight seasoning technique.

> 3-pound frying chicken, cut into serving pieces
> Salt and freshly ground black pepper
> Lawry's Seasoned Salt
> 3/4 cup all-purpose flour
> Crisco oil for deep-frying

1. Wash and pat the chicken pieces dry. Season with salt (sparingly), pepper, and Lawry's salt. Place the chicken on baking sheets. Cover with plastic wrap and refrigerate, at least for a few hours, preferably overnight.

2. Put the flour into a large bowl. Toss the chicken in the flour, a few pieces at a time, to coat it lightly. Shake off any excess flour. Set aside.

3. Pour 4 inches of oil into a deep, heavy pot. Heat to 375°F. Slide the chicken into the hot fat, a few pieces at a time. Do not crowd the pot or the chicken will not be crispy. Cook for 20 to 25 minutes, turning once. The chicken will be golden brown on all sides.

4. Use a slotted spoon to remove the chicken from the pot. Drain on thick brown-paper bags. Keep warm on baking sheets in a 200°F oven until all the chicken is cooked. Serve hot.

Fried Fish

Serves 4 to 6

Originally this recipe was made with fresh river catfish, ide-ally caught on a summer afternoon. Today's catfish is farm-raised and caught at the supermarket. While the flabby texture of domesticated catfish is a matter of concern, this bacon-flavored cornmeal coating still tastes great on any freshwater or saltwater fish.

8 to 12 medium fish fillets
1/2 cup all-purpose flour
1/2 cup cornmeal
Salt and freshly ground black pepper
Drippings from 3 slices bacon
Hot pepper sauce

1. Rinse the fish. Pat dry with paper towels.

2. Mix the flour, cornmeal, salt, and pepper together in a bowl. Dredge the fish in the flour mixture, shaking off any excess. Set aside.

3. Heat the bacon drippings in a deep skillet to 375°F. Slide the fish, a few pieces at a time, into the pan. Work in batches, so the pan is not overcrowded. Cook for about 4 minutes. Turn and cook for about 3 minutes. The fish will be crispy and browned on both sides.

4. Remove the fish from the pan. Drain on thick brown-paper bags. Keep warm on a baking sheet in a 200°F oven until all the fish is cooked. Serve hot with a bottle of hot pep-per sauce on the side.

Collard Greens

Serves 4 to 6

I first met Lillie Jones one wintry afternoon when I volunteered to help stem, wash, and cook collards that filled four industrial-size pots. The aroma was intoxicating as they cooked. When we hauled the heavy pots off the stove, the savviest helpers already had bottles of hot sauce and vinegar in hand to sprinkle over the greens and corn bread to sop up the pot liquor. This recipe multiplies to serve 200 without losing flavor in the translation.

> 2 1/2 pounds collard greens
> Salt pork
> 2 to 4 smoked ham hocks or neck bones
> 4 cups water
> 1 teaspoon salt
> 1 teaspoon sugar
> Sliced hot chili peppers, hot sauces, vinegar, and/or
>   sliced onions for serving, optional

1. Wash and pick over the greens, removing any that are spotted or discolored. Stem the greens and discard the stems. Cut the leaves into halves.

2. Combine the salt pork and ham hocks in a large saucepan. Add the water, which should cover the meats by 1 inch. Stir in salt and sugar. Bring to a boil. Reduce to a simmer. Cook for 30 to 45 minutes, uncovered. Some liquid will evaporate. The meat should be thoroughly cooked.

3. Add the greens. Simmer for 20 to 30 minutes. The greens will be tender.

4. Remove the greens from the pot with a slotted spoon. Serve plain or with hot peppers, hot sauces, vinegar, or sliced onions.

WHY YOU WON'T FIND BARBECUED RIBS IN THIS COOKBOOK

Barbecue . . . it's the stuff of legend . . . of testosterone, of braggadocio . . . and of dreams. Try to find out about barbecue on the North Shore, and you'll find that you can eat barbecue, you can watch someone cook barbecue, but ain't nobody gonna give you a recipe for barbecue! Not for marinade. Not for barbecue sauce.

Abner Darby, veteran of the civil rights movement and former executive director of Lynn's Community Minority Cultural Center, is renowned for his barbecue. He cooks from "an old family recipe once or twice a year" at the Zion Baptist Church or the Community Brotherhood. Darby has one response when anyone asks for his recipe.

"I promised my grandmother I'd never tell the recipe," he repeats. "Grandma died when I was 16. She was 91 then . . . . born a slave. All us kids . . . had great respect for her.

"Everyone loves my barbecue. Closest I ever tasted was Kansas City. I worked in a place there for a short time. The owner chased me all over trying to see how I did it, but I never let on. Now one of my cousins is trying to market his barbecue sauce. I'm kind of thinking along those lines myself."

Then there's former Boston Red Sox great George "Boomer" Scott. For a few short, golden years, he coached professional baseball—and offered Boomer's Mississippi Barbecue—in Lynn. People lined up to watch the Massachusetts Mad Dogs and feast on whole racks of pork ribs, cooked Boomer-style, right beyond third base in a custom-built smoker, a sight never before seen this far north.

When I interviewed Scott for *North Shore Sunday*, he told me, "That gizmo cost me five thousand dollars. It's all in the marinade. . . . Mississippi-style barbecue, you use two. Dry and wet. I mix just a little of the wet with the dry one; I rub it into the meat and leave it overnight. If you put sauce on meat and put it right on the fire, it will burn. . . . The wet sauce goes on just before you put it in the smoker. Then it cooks for five, maybe six or eight hours . . . and the wet stuff just sinks into the meat."

Scott learned barbecue from Leonard Gates, who played ball with the Negro League. He says it took 15 years to perfect. He let me watch the process: marinate, sear, mop, and smoke, but I never saw the raw ingredients.

Says Scott, "I never tasted any sauce like mine. I'm one of the best in the world. Someday I'm gonna open a place near Fenway."

Fried Green Tomatoes

Serves 6

At summer's end, when you know the tomatoes still on the vine won't have enough sun to ripen, make this. Save the rendered bacon to sprinkle over a fried tomato sandwich slathered with mayonnaise.

5 to 6 large green tomatoes
$1/4$ cup all-purpose flour
2 tablespoons yellow cornmeal
1 teaspoon Lawry's Seasoned Salt
Drippings from 2 slices bacon
Freshly ground black pepper

1. Preheat the oven to 250°F. Slice the tomatoes thickly. Salt and set aside on paper towels. The extra juices will drain off.

2. Mix the flour, cornmeal, and Lawry's salt in a large bowl. Dredge the tomato slices in this mixture and set on a plate.

3. Heat the bacon drippings in a large skillet. Add the tomatoes and cook, turning once, for 2 to 3 minutes on each side, until the tomatoes are golden brown. Work in batches; do not overcrowd the pan.

4. Keep warm on a platter in the oven until all the tomatoes are cooked. Sprinkle with pepper before serving hot.

Fried Okra

Serves 6

To overcome the challenge of slimy okra, dry it on paper towels before coating it with cornmeal. Then barely film a nonstick skillet with just enough oil to keep the okra from sticking. Cook it at high heat. Never cut off the ends.

    3 slices bacon
    1 pound fresh (or frozen) okra, as small as possible
    ½ cup cornmeal

1. Cook the bacon in a large skillet over medium-high heat until it is golden brown and crisp. Crumble it and set it aside. Leave the drippings in the skillet.

2. Wash the okra and snap off the stems. Set aside. Place cornmeal in bowl. Toss the okra with cornmeal, making sure it is coated.

3. Raise the heat under the skillet to high. Add the okra. Cook, turning, for 3 to 5 minutes. Turn it over gently with a spatula or tongs. Do not pierce the okra while turning. Turn once more, if necessary. The coating will be golden brown and crisp. Serve hot, sprinkled with crumbled bacon.

RENDERING BACON

It's easy to get drippings from bacon. Simply put some bacon in a skillet over medium-high heat, and cook it until crisp, turning occasionally. Save the bacon for another use. Strain the drippings through a fine-mesh strainer and store in a jar in the refrigerator.

MUSIC

African-American food always seems to go hand in hand with music. In Chicago, it's the blues, but on the North Shore of Boston, it's a mixture of styles and the band of note is Mamadou Diop and the Jolole Band. Two of the members—Mamadou Diop, who writes the music, sings, and plays rhythm guitar and hand drums, and Ibrahima Camara on djembe, sabar, and tama hand drums—are originally from Senegal.

Picnic Potato Salad

Serves 10 to 12

When North Shore Community College holds its annual multicultural festival each spring, the culinary expo is the place to taste the best dishes from around the world. But you'd better get in line early to taste Lillie Jones's potato salad.

You will need these 10 to 12 servings for 6 people because everyone wants seconds. This recipe multiplies to feed up to 200 without losing its character.

5 pounds waxy potatoes, such as California whites
2 cups sweet pickles, diced
6 to 8 hard-cooked eggs, chopped
1 medium onion, diced
1/2 cup chopped celery
1/2 cup diced green peppers
1 cup mayonnaise
1/4 cup yellow mustard
Salt and freshly ground black pepper

1. Wash the potatoes. Combine them in a pot with enough water to cover by about 2 inches. Bring to a boil. Reduce the heat to a simmer. Cook for 20 to 25 minutes, until the potatoes are tender when pierced with a fork. Peel and cut into 1/2-inch cubes. Set aside to cool for about 10 minutes. The potatoes should still be warm when tossed with the dressing, so that they absorb the flavors.

2. Gently toss the pickles, eggs, onion, celery, green peppers, mayonnaise, and mustard together in a large bowl. Add salt and pepper to taste.

3. Add the potatoes and toss thoroughly, but gently. Refrigerate for at least 2 hours before serving.

Candied Sweet Potatoes

Serves 6

In 1929, Marshmallow Fluff, a wonderfully gooey marshmallow cream in a jar, went into production on Brookline Street in Lynn. Home cooks found the local product more convenient and the topping much creamier than chopped marshmallows.

MARSHMALLOW FLUFF

Marshmallow Fluff is the ingredient that elevated the mere peanut butter-and-jelly sandwich to a lunchbox classic, the Fluffernutter, and blends with crispy rice cereal to make heavenly bar cookies, called Marshmallow Fluff Treats. Marshmallow cream was born in Swampscott, the brainchild of confectioners H. Allen Durkee and Fred L. Mower. They later moved to a larger plant in Lynn.

    3 to 4 sweet potatoes (about 3 pounds), scrubbed, not peeled
    3/4 cup brown sugar
    1/2 teaspoon grated nutmeg
    1/2 teaspoon ground cinnamon
    1/2 teaspoon grated orange zest
    8 tablespoons (1 stick) butter
    1/3 cup orange juice
    7-ounce jar Marshmallow Fluff

1. Bring the sweet potatoes and enough water to cover them to a boil in a large pot. Reduce the heat to a lively simmer. Cook for 20 to 30 minutes. They will be fork-tender. Peel. Slice into ½-inch-thick rounds.

2. Preheat the oven to 400°F.

3. Layer the sweet potatoes, sugar, nutmeg, cinnamon, and orange zest in a 2-quart casserole in two layers. Pour in the orange juice. Cut 4 tablespoons of the butter into small bits and strew over the top.

4. Bake for 20 to 30 minutes, basting once or twice with the casserole juices. The potatoes will look glazed on top.

5. Melt the remaining 4 tablespoons butter in a small saucepan. Whisk in the marshmallow cream.

6. Remove the casserole from the oven. Lower the oven heat to 325°F. Drizzle the marshmallow mixture over the sweet potatoes. Bake for 5 to 10 minutes. The marshmallow mixture will be bubbly and brown. Serve hot from the oven.

Black-Eyed Peas

Serves 6

1 pound dried black-eyed peas
1 smoked ham hock or neck bone
4 to 5 strips bacon
1 onion, peeled but left whole

1. Pick over the peas and discard any damaged ones. Put the peas in a bowl with enough water to cover. Soak overnight or for at least 8 hours. Drain the soaking water. Rinse well under cold running water.

2. Combine the peas, ham hock, bacon, and onion with fresh water to cover in a large pot. Bring to a boil.

3. Reduce the heat. Cover the pot and simmer for 40 to 45 minutes. The peas will be tender. Discard the ham hock, bacon strips, and onion before serving hot.

Old-Fashioned Buttermilk Biscuits

Serves 10 to 12

Many home cooks swear by lard, which is sold in pound blocks, like butter, in the supermarket. Vegetable shortening, however, does produce a decent biscuit.

    3 cups all-purpose flour
    1 teaspoon baking soda
    1 teaspoon cream of tartar
    1 teaspoon salt
    1/3 cup vegetable shortening
    3/4 cup buttermilk

1. Preheat the oven to 400°F. Flour a work surface. Grease a baking sheet.

2. Combine the flour, baking soda, cream of tartar, and salt in a bowl. Cut in the shortening with two forks or knives. The mixture will look like coarse cornmeal.

3. Gradually pour in the buttermilk, stirring.

4. Transfer the dough to the work surface and work with your fingertips to blend.

5. Roll out the dough to a thickness of about ½ inch. Cut into 10 to 12 circles with a biscuit cutter. Arrange on the baking sheet.

6. Bake for 12 to 15 minutes. The biscuits will be pale golden in color. Serve warm.

Corn Bread

Makes 1 loaf; serves 4 to 6

The negligible amount of sugar is the clue that the recipe migrated from Southern kitchens, where the corn bread is tender and savory. It may be baked in a cast-iron pan or a dark loaf pan for a more authentic finish.

Serve it hot from the oven with butter. Toast leftovers for breakfast. Use it to mop up the pot liquor from collard greens.

3/4 cup all-purpose flour
3/4 cup yellow cornmeal
2 tablespoons sugar
1 tablespoon baking powder
1/2 teaspoon salt
3/4 cup whole milk
1 large egg
3 tablespoons peanut or corn oil

1. Preheat the oven to 425°F. Grease a 5 by 9-inch loaf pan.

2. Toss together the flour, cornmeal, sugar, baking powder, and salt in a bowl. Gradually beat in the milk, egg, and oil. The batter will be smooth. Pour the batter into the loaf pan.

3. Bake for about 20 minutes. The corn bread will be golden and slightly puffed on top. Cool 20 to 30 minutes on a rack before cutting.

Sweet Potato Pie

Makes one 9-inch pie

Lillie Jones's son, Marcus, entered her recipe in a contest, and I've adapted it here. Although in the past, cooks used lard for the "perfect" crust, vegetable shortening works just fine. Lillie prefers to pour the filling in an unbaked crust; I partially bake the crust first. You can decide which you prefer.

1/2 teaspoon salt
1 cup plus 1 tablespoon sifted all-purpose flour
1/3 cup vegetable shortening
3 tablespoons ice water (or more, as needed)
3/4 cup sugar
2 large eggs, beaten
1/4 cup evaporated milk
6 tablespoons (3/4 stick) butter, at room temperature
1 teaspoon nutmeg
1 teaspoon lemon extract
4 to 6 cooked sweet potatoes, cooled and mashed
    (about 1 1/2 cups)

1. To make the crust, preheat the oven to 400°F. Flour a work surface.

2. Combine the salt and 1 cup of the flour in the workbowl of a food processor, pulsing once or twice to blend. Gradually add the shortening through the feed tube, pulsing to mix. The mixture will have a coarse texture.

3. With the motor running, add the ice water, a few drops at a time. The dough will start to form a ball. Remove it from the food processor. Shape the dough into a ball, then flatten it slightly into a circle. Wrap tightly in plastic wrap. Refrigerate for about 30 minutes.

4. Roll the dough lightly outward from the center with a rolling pin so that it forms a circle large enough to fit the pie plate. Crimp the edges, squeezing with your fingers. Pierce the bottom of the pie crust many times with tines of a fork.

5. Bake the crust for 15 to 18 minutes. It will be very lightly golden. Set aside to cool. Turn the oven heat down to 350°F.

6. To make the filling, beat together the sugar, eggs, milk, butter, 1 tablespoon flour, nutmeg, and lemon extract. If the mixture sticks, rinse the beater, then continue beating. The mixture will be smooth and creamy. Add the sweet potatoes, mixing until well blended.

7. Pour the filling into the piecrust. Bake for 45 to 60 minutes. Check once or twice after 45 minutes to be sure that the crust does not burn. The center will be tender, not wobbly, and the crust golden brown. If the crust browns before the filling is cooked, shield it with a strip of aluminum foil. Serve the pie warm or chilled, plain or with whipped cream.

Peach Cobbler

Serves 6

New England, native peaches are available at farm stands and farmer's markets for only a few fleeting weeks in late August.

2 1/2 to 3 pounds fresh peaches, skinned, halved, and
   pitted
1/2 cup plus 1/4 cup sugar
1 1/3 cups plus 2 tablespoons all-purpose flour
1/2 teaspoon ground allspice
1 tablespoon freshly squeezed lemon juice
2 teaspoons baking powder
1/4 teaspoon salt
1/4 teaspoon baking soda
4 tablespoons melted butter, cooled
1/3 cup buttermilk
1/4 teaspoon lemon extract

HOW TO SKIN A PEACH

To remove skin from fresh peaches, bring a large pot of water to a rolling boil. Have a bowl of ice water handy. Cut a small X just through the skin on the bottom of the peach. Gently drop two or three peaches at a time into the boiling water for 30 to 40 seconds. Remove them with a slotted spoon and immediately plunge them into the ice water. The skins should pull off easily.

1. To make the filling, preheat the oven to 425°F. Butter a 2-quart baking dish. Flour a work surface.

2. Toss together the peaches, 1/2 cup sugar, 2 tablespoons flour, allspice, and lemon juice. Spoon the mixture into the baking dish. Place the baking dish in the oven for 20 to 25 minutes. The peaches will be bubbling.

3. While the peach mixture is in the oven, make the topping. Combine the 1 1/3 cups flour, 1/4 cup sugar, the baking powder, salt, and baking soda in a bowl. Whisk together the butter, buttermilk, and lemon extract. Stir the wet ingredients into the dry ingredients. The mixture will form a soft dough.

4. Take the peach mixture out of the oven. Reduce the heat to 375°F. Drop tablespoons of the dough onto the peach mixture, spacing them so they do not touch. Bake for 15 to 20 minutes. The top will be golden and the fruit bubbling. Cool on a rack for 15 to 20 minutes before serving.

Kwanzaa Rice Pudding

Serves 6 to 8

Dr. Pharnal Longus, of Salem State College's African-American Studies Department, notes that rice pudding is a favorite Kwanzaa dessert. Serve it warm from the oven or prepare it a day in advance, refrigerate, and bring to room temperature. Dollop with vanilla-and-nutmeg-scented whipped cream to heighten the flavor.

4 cups milk
1/4 cup long-grain rice
1/4 cup sugar
1/4 teaspoon salt
1/2 cup sweetened shredded coconut
1 teaspoon vanilla extract
1/4 teaspoon freshly grated nutmeg
1/8 teaspoon ground cloves

1. Preheat the oven to 300°F. Butter a large casserole dish.

2. Mix together the milk, rice, sugar, salt, and coconut. Pour into the casserole dish.

3. Bake, uncovered, for about 2 hours, stirring every 20 to 30 minutes.

4. Remove from the oven. Stir in the vanilla, nutmeg, and cloves. Bake for about 30 minutes longer. The pudding will be tender and creamy, with a golden crust on the top. Serve warm or chilled.

Joe Froggers

Makes about 4 dozen 3-inch cookies

Recorded descriptions of the original cookies differ. Some say the dough was thinly rolled and cut in circles eight inches in diameter to resemble lily pads in Black Joe's pond. Others claim the dough was thick, so that the cookies plumped out like fat frogs. Either way, the measurements of ingredients seldom vary, although recipes have been printed and reprinted in newspapers, magazines, and community cookbooks over the last hundred years.

> 7 cups all-purpose flour
> 1 teaspoon salt
> 1 tablespoon ground ginger
> 2 teaspoons baking soda
> 1 teaspoon ground cloves
> 1 teaspoon grated nutmeg
> 1/2 teaspoon ground allspice
> 1/4 cup dark rum
> 2 cups molasses
> 1 cup vegetable shortening
> 2 cups light brown sugar

1. Toss together the flour, salt, ginger, baking soda, cloves, nutmeg, and allspice in a bowl.

2. Beat together the rum, molasses, shortening, and brown sugar in another bowl with an electric hand mixer at medium speed.

3. Alternately add the dry ingredients to liquid ingredients until a dough forms. It will be stiff but not dry. If dry, add a tablespoon or two of water as needed. Roll the dough between pieces of waxed or parchment paper until it is about 1/4 inch thick. You may need to roll out two to four sheets of it. Stack the sheets of dough between clean sheets of paper. Refrigerate for 2 to 4 hours.

JOE FROGGERS, THE MARBLEHEAD COOKIE

On holiday weekends, and throughout the summer months, shops all over Marblehead sprout signs reading "Joe Froggers are here!" That means a limited supply of the town's signature molasses cookies is on hand. They sell out quickly.

According to local legend recorded by historian Virginia C. Gamage, the cookies hark back to George Washington's administration, when Lucretia Creesey and Joseph Brown settled beside a pond on a hill overlooking Marblehead harbor. The couple, whose parents were freed slaves, forged a living out of their home near the raucous waterfront. Sailors and fishermen caroused at "Black Joe's" Tavern while "Auntie Creesey" produced genteel

CONTINUED

confections such as wedding cakes and gingerbread in the kitchen. The area was dubbed Gingerbread Hill and the pond called Black Joe's Pond, but the couple's collaboration sowed the seeds of the legend. When Lucretia baked molasses-and-spice cookies, Joe sold them on the docks to seafarers.

In Marblehead, where they still spin yarns about how the cookies got the name Joe Froggers, it's traditional to pack the treats when sailing out of the harbor or wrap them as parting gifts for guests. Folklorist Lynn Nadeau gave them as favors at her son's wedding with a note: "Save this for your leave-taking; your passage will be sweeter!"

The building that housed "Black Joe's" Tavern still stands on Gingerbread Hill.

4. Preheat the oven to 375°F. Grease two or three baking sheets.

5. Cut the dough into 3-inch cookies with a round cookie cutter, using all the dough. Transfer them to the baking sheets. Bake for 10 to 12 minutes. The cookies will be dark around the edges and firm at the centers. Set the baking sheets on a rack to rest for 2 to 3 minutes. Transfer the cookies to a rack to cool and firm before serving.

Roasted Pumpkin Seeds

Makes 2 cups

This is one more recipe directly from Africa. It's a great snack if you happen to be making pumpkin pie or carving a jack-o'-lantern. I like pumpkin seeds when they're still warm, out of a paper-towel-lined basket. They won't last long.

2 tablespoons vegetable, canola, or peanut oil
2 cups, or more, fresh pumpkin seeds
Coarse salt

1. Preheat the oven to 350°F. Film a baking sheet with the oil.

2. Rinse the seeds and put them on the baking sheet. Toss to coat them with the oil. Then spread the seeds out in one even layer on the baking sheet.

3. Bake for about 8 minutes. Stir the seeds lightly and continue baking for 2 to 3 minutes more. They will be lightly toasted on both sides. Sprinkle with some salt while they are still on the baking sheet. Place on paper towels to drain, and salt again before serving.

THE IRISH TRADITION
From Empty Pots to Cornucopia

The Irish swept over the North Shore in the nineteenth century following crop failures and widespread famine. They shared a collective wish to forget the painful past and simply become Americans. Unlike immigrants who came in later decades, the Irish at least were not hampered with learning a new language. Men found work in the mills and a living in the building trades; women found work as cooks, some in private residences, others in family-style restaurants, perhaps answering newspaper ads for "a plain Irish cook." Rising to economic security, Irish-Americans created a parallel universe to a society not yet ready to accept them, putting their own stamp on it in the process. Spires on their brick churches, built with volunteer labor, pierced the sky, as did the austere white wooden structures already occupying the landscape; their alternative school system emphasized religion as well as letters. They formed social organizations like the Ancient Order of Hibernians, and, with prosperity, some of the North Shore's grander country clubs grew up around a roster of Celtic names. Most notably, Irish-Americans organized politically, gaining a foothold into the governmental structure and a firm control of their futures.

At the table, Irish cooking had roots in British foodways, so there was a continuation of sustaining, hearty foods. Corned beef and cabbage is next of kin to the New England boiled dinner. Finnan haddie, a breakfast dish in Ireland, was converted to a Sunday-night chafing-dish supper, served over toast. The term "sacred cod" took on a whole new meaning as the North Shore's plentiful, inexpensive supply of fish became nearly sacramental on meatless Fridays—fried, smoked, and creamed.

Today, Americans with Irish ancestry want to trace their familial lines. Magrane Travel in Lynn is known for personalized trips to Ireland. Owner Brian Magrane says, "Irish-Americans have a need to unearth the past. It's a romance there that harks back to the Druids, the Celts, Saints Patrick, Brendan, and Colmcille . . . poetry and music . . . and, yes, food."

According to Magrane, "Grandchildren and great-grandchildren of immi-grants return from travel with more than snapshots, having discovered dishes that never made it here with their forebears. . . . Myriad preparations for pota-toes, mixed grill of newly butchered lamb and freshly made sausages. There are no giant food corporations. It's local farmers and purveyors . . . garden veg-etables, fresh herbs, farmstead cheeses, homemade jams and jellies. But, if there's one food that speaks of Ireland most, it's salmon, smoked at breakfast and poached at sunset."

An Irish-American Breakfast

A hearty breakfast is a tradition in Ireland. The groaning board includes meats and fish, plain cooking that seems exotic to the American palate before noon. The Irish-American breakfast has taken a lot of detours in more than a century.

Edward Murphy, born in 1892 to Irish immigrants in Salem, wrote of fam-ily breakfast on Derby Street: "It seemed a ban-quet. . . . It consisted of what Mom called 'turns,' pieces of dough . . . kneaded the night before and left in a round tin pan in the pantry to rise . . . fried in lard to a crispiness . . . not only tasted but smelled good, especially . . . with melted butter and cups of tea or milk." His meager breakfast was a far cry from the "fry" described by Chef Cronin. Phil Sweeney of Marblehead, founder of the Black Rose Restaurant and Pub in Boston, points out that the breakfast black-and-white blood pudding, made with oatmeal and bacon, is only recently available in the United States. He fea-tures them in a "Dublin coddle" on his lunch menu at his newest pub, Sweeney's Retreat. On this side of the Atlantic, we can choose our favorites for an Irish-American breakfast.

MENU FOR AN
IRISH-AMERICAN BREAKFAST

Pork Sausage

Finnan Haddie

Fried Tomatoes

Potatoes O'Brien (page 219)

Eggs, any style

Buttermilk Scones

Soda Bread

Tea

A North Shore Cook: Brendan Cronin

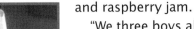

When Brendan Cronin speaks of food, his thoughts interconnect in a poetic, Joycean monologue. In his kitchen at the Tupper Mansion on the Endicott College campus, where he heads the culinary portion of the Hospitality and Tourism Administration Program, Cronin talks about a childhood far different from earlier Irish immigrants. Growing up in the twentieth century on a dairy farm in Belmullet in the west of Ireland, he never knew hunger.

"Our family life centered a lot around food and all aspects of farm work. My parents had little, but they had great spirit. We had a farmhouse with a lot of empty rooms, so my mother took in lodgers, a bed-and-breakfast. . . . The house was divided down the center. The dining room was in the front portion, off limits to us. The guests ate there. We usually had six."

"Each morning my mother made six full Irish breakfasts, what we called a fry, for the guests . . . two fried eggs, two bacon rashers, two slices of black pudding and two slices of white pudding, one or two breakfast sausages, fruit, cornflakes, jugs of milk, tea, and homemade blackberry and raspberry jam.

"We three boys all slept in one big bed and got up early to feed and milk the cows.

"Then my mother made breakfast for the family, but not a fry. We had porridge, bread, jam, and butter . . . in the kitchen. Before we left for school, we bottled, capped, and loaded the milk for Dad to deliver. And we couldn't escape a teaspoon of cod liver oil.

"My mother made her own butter. She would separate the cream from the milk, and save it at room temperature. The cream would sour slightly, giving the butter a wonderful, refreshing tang. It's now the rage around Europe. Homemade butter was the thing. There was homemade and then there was 'shop' butter . . . a definite faux pas. It indicated that you were not an adequate provider. You always made your own cakes, and jam, and butter."

When Cronin was 15, his mother encouraged him to interview for hotel school since he had shown an aptitude for making "fancy" cakes. He was accepted and set off for a five-year training program in Galway, hours away from home.

One of Chef Cronin's annual assignments is a traditional Irish St. Patrick's Day dinner. Students must research every aspect, including ingredients, recipes, music, and table settings, presenting the final product in Endicott's Tupper Hall dining room overlooking the sea. They are often surprised to discover the difference an ocean can make in the menu.

"St. Patrick's Day in Ireland is a religious day. There was mass and we were allowed to go into town for the procession. Easter at the end of Lent was a big holiday. On Friday there was major fasting. We went to confession on Saturday. We didn't eat before mass on Sunday. . . . There was a roasted leg of lamb for dinner, kind of an upgrade from lamb chops.

"At Christmas dinner, we had turkey with bread sauce. My mother would take a pint of milk and set it on the side of the fire. We had a turf fire going for heat all the time. She added a whole onion stuck with cloves, and a bay leaf, then left it for one hour, seasoned it with salt and pepper, and added white bread crumbs. She cut all the crusts off the bread, then rubbed it on the grater into crumbs and put them into the milk to thicken it.

"We started the Christmas cakes in late October. My parents would buy an enormous box of spices, flour, lemon peel, almonds, and dried fruits. . . . We soaked them in so much porter and whiskey that there was no spoilage. Once cooked, they stayed at room temperature. At the country fair, the cakes would be the subject of much discussion, as in, 'Have you started your Christmas cakes and puddings yet?'

"A cake was baked; a pudding, steamed. It needed weeks to mellow, for the flavors to infuse. My mother would make five puddings to be eaten on Christmas Day, New Year's Day, Epiphany, St. Patrick's Day, and Easter Sunday."

After his apprenticeship, Cronin worked in a series of five-star hotel kitchens in Ireland and Switzerland, then "set out to conquer the world." In his travels, he acquired a family and fluency in two more languages. His two children were born in Singapore and Switzerland.

Chef Cronin and his family enjoy American culinary traditions, especially Thanksgiving. His mother's bread sauce appears on the table as a nod to his heritage, although he finds cooking the meal daunting.

"I find it a strain cooking for fewer than forty or fifty people. Fortunately, Christine, my wife, is an excellent cook."

THE RECIPES

Ham and Peas Soup

Serves 6

8 ounces dried green split peas
1 tablespoon butter
1 tablespoon vegetable oil
1 medium onion, chopped
2 medium carrots, chopped
4 to 5 slices bacon, chopped
1 ham bone
5 cups water
Salt and freshly ground black pepper

1. Soak the peas for 6 hours in cold water. Drain. Rinse. Set aside.

2. Warm the butter and oil in a soup pot over medium-high heat. Add the onion, carrots, and bacon. Cook gently, stirring, for about 15 minutes. The vegetables will soften and the bacon will start to crisp.

3. Add the peas and ham bone to the pot. Add enough water to cover. Bring to a boil. Reduce the heat to a simmer. Cook for about 1 hour. The peas will be tender.

4. Discard the ham bone. Ladle out 1 cup of the soup mixture and puree it in a food processor or blender. Stir the pureed mixture back into the soup pot. Season with salt and pepper. Reheat just to the boiling point before serving.

IRISH CHOWDER

David Shea recalls corn chowder as a hallmark of the hearty cooking of his grandmother, Carrie Mahoney. "In a family of eight children, this was the kind of good wholesome food my mother could stretch to feed the family."

Shea uses leftovers from a baked ham or "ends" he buys at the deli counter and liberal amounts of ground black pepper. "My mother used salt pork. I'm sure that had more to do with economics than flavor. I tried salt pork, and later bacon, but I prefer the ham."

Corn Chowder

Serves 10 to 12

David Shea's corn chowder is the much-anticipated center-piece of his family's Fourth-of-July celebration. The amount of canned creamed corn, he notes, can be adjusted to make the chowder thicker or thinner. The recipe is easily modified for smaller or larger quantities. He allows "at least a half-hour after I add the corn" for flavors to develop before serving.

8 tablespoons (1 stick) butter
2 large onions, chopped
2 pounds diced ham
Freshly ground black pepper
3 or 4 medium potatoes, peeled and diced
Water
8 cups whole milk
5 to 8 (14-ounce) cans creamed corn
Salt

1. Melt the butter in a large heavy pot over medium-high heat. Add the onions and ham. Cook for about 10 minutes. The onions will be softened. Add pepper to taste, the more the better. Add the potatoes. Add water immediately to cover the ingredients. Bring to a boil. Reduce the heat and simmer for 7 to 8 minutes. The potatoes will be just tender when pierced. Be careful not to overcook the potatoes.

2. Turn the heat down to a simmer. Slowly stir in the milk. Simmer, do not boil, stirring often, so ingredients do not stick to the bottom and burn.

3. When the mixture is evenly heated, stir in the creamed corn. Add salt, if needed, and more pepper to taste. Keep over very low heat for about 30 minutes before serving.

Finnan Haddie

Serves 6

Smoked haddock was a supper staple in Irish-American households during the Lenten season, on meatless Fridays, and Christmas Eve. In Ireland, it is served over buttered toast at breakfast.

Two 2-pound pieces smoked haddock
3/4 cup milk
2 tablespoons unsalted butter
1/2 small onion, very thinly sliced
Freshly ground black pepper, to taste
Mashed potatoes for serving

1. Rinse the fish in cold water to remove excess salt.

2. Place the fish in a large skillet with water to cover. Add the milk, butter, onion, and pepper. Heat until the water bubbles around the edges of the pan. Reduce the heat and simmer gently for about 2 minutes. Remove the fish from pan. Set aside.

3. Cook the liquid in the skillet 2 to 3 minutes more. Return the fish to the skillet and immediately remove the skillet from the heat. Serve hot over mashed potatoes.

THE DRAMA OF FLAMING

When you flame food, you ignite the alcohol. Alcohol begins to evaporate as soon as it is poured. When lit, the flames follow the alcohol's path.

Warm the pan for only a few seconds after pouring in the liquor. If you are working at the stove, tip the pan slightly to catch flames from the burner. If you are flaming tableside, hold a lighted match just off to the side.

Safety tips:

- Don't flame food directly on the dining table. Use a separate small table.
- After pouring, set the liquor bottle away from the pan.
- Keep your face away from the pan.
- Keep table linens away from the pan.
- Have a lid handy. If the flame burns too high, clamp on the lid to deprive it of oxygen. Do not douse with water; this only spreads the flames.

Dublin Lawyer

Serves 1 or 2

No one seems to know the exact origins of this dish, but Irish chefs agree that only a lawyer from Dublin could afford the costly ingredients. A big-city dish in Ireland, it translated easily to New England lobster. Some cooks flame this elegant dish at the table. If you do this, use a chafing dish and be sure to have the lid within reach.

2- to 3-pound lobster
1/4 cup (1/2 stick) butter
1/4 cup Irish whiskey
1/2 cup heavy cream
Salt and freshly ground black pepper

1. Boil the lobster. (See the directions on page 13.) Cool. Remove the meat, keeping the body (shell) as much in one piece as possible. Cut the meat into bite-size chunks.

2. Warm the butter in a skillet (or chafing dish) over medium-low heat, just until foamy. Add the lobster meat to the pan.

3. Pour in the whiskey. Warm for 2 to 3 seconds, and ignite with a match. (Or, if you feel confident, tip the side of the pan, just slightly, to catch the flame from the burner.) When the flames subside, add the cream. Keep the pan over low heat until the cream thickens. Stuff the mixture back into the lobster shell to serve.

Corned Beef and Cabbage

Serves 6 to 8

Phil Sweeney of Marblehead is the founder of the landmark pub the Black Rose, and by the nature of his business as well as his heritage, an authority on traditional Irish-American fare. At the pub, he literally cooks this up by the gallon. Once, challenged in a TV interview about the authenticity of corned beef and cabbage, he eloquently defended its place on the Irish-American table. According to Sweeney, butchers in Ireland sold a cheap cut of beef called silverside. Home cooks tenderized it in a barrel of brining solution before simmering with potatoes, carrots, and cabbage. In the United States, they substituted brisket. The resulting dish resembled the New England boiled dinner, a meal in a pot that included turnips, parsnips, and beets. Jewish immigrants brined their brisket in a solution that turned the meat red. The more inviting red brisket caught on.

David Shea's grandmother, Carrie Mahoney, worked as a cook at Moutsakis' Restaurant in downtown Salem in the days when newspaper ads read "Wanted: Plain Irish Cook." Her version of this dish, learned from her mother in Ireland, was built around a smoked pork shoulder. Each year Shea and his brothers cook up a pot not on St. Patrick's Day, but on a day nearly as important to them—the annual fundraiser for the Salem State College women's basketball team that brother Tim has coached to many championships.

I've made provisions in this recipe to accommodate either Mrs. Sweeney's or Mrs. Mahoney's ingredients.

6-pound corned beef brisket (or smoked shoulder)
3 pounds thin-skinned potatoes, peeled and cut into
    4-inch chunks
10 to 12 large carrots, peeled and cut into 4-inch chunks
10 to 12 parsnips, peeled and cut into large chunks

BRAISING MEAT

When braising a large cut of meat, cover it with water, and bring it just to the brink of a boil. Reduce the heat to a very low simmer immediately or the muscle will contract and the meat will become tough and stringy—and no amount of cooking will remedy it.

1 large head green cabbage
1/4 cup (1/2 stick) unsalted butter

1. Place the meat in a large pot. Cover with cold water. Bring just to a boil. Drain immediately.

2. Refill the pot with water. Bring just to a boil. Reduce to a simmer. Do not let the meat boil. Simmer the meat very gently for about 2½ hours. The meat will be tender when pierced with a fork.

3. Skim any fat from the surface of the cooking water. Ladle 6 to 8 cups of water out of the pot and reserve. Add the potatoes, carrots, and parsnips to the pot. Add more water if the vegetables are not submerged. Simmer, covered, for 20 to 30 minutes. The vegetables will be tender.

4. Meanwhile, cut the cabbage into 4 to 6 wedges, leaving part of the core on each wedge so the wedges don't break apart. Pour the reserved cooking water from the beef into a medium pot with the cabbage. Add more fresh water to cover the cabbage. Bring just to a boil. Reduce the heat and simmer for about 10 minutes. It will be very tender when pierced with a fork.

5. Reserve a cup of the cooking water. Carve the meat and arrange it on a serving platter. Surround it with the cabbage and vegetables and dollop with butter. If the vegetables seem dry, sprinkle a little cooking water over them before serving.

Classic Baked Ham

Serves 8

A whole ham often needs soaking to remove excess salt. Your purveyor is the best guide for the ham you select. Parsley butter sauce is the traditional accompaniment to an Irish baked ham. This recipe is adapted from Brendan Cronin's method.

12-pound smoked ham
10 cups water
1 teaspoon ground mace
1 tablespoon freshly ground black pepper
Whole cloves
2 tablespoons brown sugar

1. Preheat the oven to 300°F.

2. Put the ham, water, mace, and pepper in a large roasting pan. Cover the pan with aluminum foil. Cook for 20 minutes per pound. The juices will run clear.

3. Remove the ham from the oven. Increase the oven temperature to 425°F. Score the ham with a crisscross pattern. Pierce cloves into the ham where the lines of the pattern intersect. Drain the water from the pan.

4. Return the ham to the roasting pan. Sprinkle the ham with brown sugar and return it to the oven for about 15 minutes. The top will be glazed golden brown.

Parsley Sauce

Makes about 2 cups

Johanna Theresa Cotter Sanderson, born in County Cork, Ireland, in 1889, emigrated to the North Shore as a young woman. To make ends meet, she sold homemade jams and jellies from her horse and wagon. Later she hired out as a cook in the "summer cottages" on Gloucester's Eastern Point, before moving into the tower at Hammond Castle. Her granddaughter, Lorralee Cooney, has kept John Hammond's signed handwritten notes of dinner instructions. Cooney remembers her grandmother shaking her head and saying, "This won't be any good," as she read some of the notes. Mrs. Sanderson often napped slices of baked ham or haddock poached in water, parsley, lemon, and butter with this sauce. Cooney vividly recalls her grandmother's directions to "always buy haddock with the skin on."

1/4 cup (1/2 stick) unsalted butter
2 tablespoons all-purpose flour
1 1/2 cups warm milk
1/4 cup finely chopped fresh parsley
Salt and freshly ground black pepper

1. Melt the butter in a saucepan over medium-low heat. Whisk in the flour. Slowly whisk in the milk. Heat until bubbles form around the edges, continually whisking for about 3 minutes. The sauce will thicken to coat a spoon.

2. Sprinkle in the parsley. Stir and cook for about 1 minute more. Add salt and pepper to taste. Serve hot.

Lamb Stew

Serves 6

Both Brian Magrane and Bill Cashman remember this stew, a staple on their mothers' tables. Usually water took the place of the stout, sometimes called dark beer.

3 pounds stewing lamb, cut into 2-inch chunks
All-purpose flour
2 tablespoons vegetable oil
2 medium onions, sliced
6 large carrots, sliced into rounds
3 pounds russet potatoes, sliced
1/4 cup finely chopped fresh parsley
Salt and freshly ground black pepper
2 cups water
1 cup stout

1. Preheat the oven to 350°F.

2. Dredge the lamb in the flour, shaking off any excess. Heat the oil in a deep ovenproof casserole over medium-high heat. Add the meat and sear on all sides for 5 to 7 minutes. Remove and set aside. Drain off most of the fat, leaving barely enough to film the bottom of the pan.

3. Layer the ingredients, meat on the bottom, followed by the onions, then carrots, and potatoes on top, sprinkling each layer with parsley, salt, and pepper. Reserve some parsley for later.

4. Pour the water and stout into the casserole. Cover and bring just to a boil. Remove from the stovetop and put into the oven. Bake for 1½ to 2 hours. The meat will be very tender.

5. If the gravy needs thickening, remove one or two slices of potato and some cooking juices. Puree together in a blender. Stir the puree into the casserole. Scatter the remaining parsley over the top before serving right out of the casserole.

Shepherd's Pie

Serves 6

Irish-American families passed down this stick-to-the-ribs supper, often substituting ground beef when children objected to the flavor of lamb. Some cooks substitute carrots or peas for the layer of corn kernels between the meat and potatoes. The optional addition of sour cream or grated cheddar cheese to the mashed potatoes gives added richness. Patricia Kelly, professor of food history at North Shore Community College, adds elegance, without discarding the dish's earthiness, with a layer of nutmeg-scented white sauce between the meat and potatoes. Use the recipe for Champ (page 104) for truly delicious mashed potatoes.

1 tablespoon vegetable oil
1 small yellow onion, chopped
1 teaspoon dried thyme
1 1/2 pounds lean ground lamb or lean ground beef
1 tablespoon all-purpose flour
1 cup hot beef stock
3 tablespoons chopped fresh parsley
1 tablespoon snipped fresh chives
Salt and freshly ground black pepper
1 cup corn kernels (frozen or canned)
About 3 cups mashed potatoes
2 tablespoons butter, melted
Snipped fresh chives or chopped parsley, for garnish

1. Preheat the oven to 375°F.

2. Heat the oil in a large skillet over medium-high heat. Add the onion and thyme. Cook for about 2 minutes until the onion is softened. Add the lamb or beef and cook, stirring, for about 10 minutes. It will still be pink. Drain off any excess fat.

3. Sprinkle the flour over the meat, and cook, stirring, for about 2 more minutes. Pour in the stock. Reduce the heat to low, and simmer for about 5 minutes. The sauce will thicken. Add the parsley, chives, and salt and pepper to taste.

4. Layer the lamb mixture, corn, then mashed potatoes in a 9 by 13-inch baking dish. Drizzle the top layer with melted butter.

5. Bake for about 25 minutes. Turn the oven up to broil for the last 5 minutes. The top layer will be golden brown and the casserole will bubble around the edges.

Colcannon

Serves 6 to 8

Generations of Irish-Americans called this recipe and the following one simply "mashed potatoes." In recent years, the old names have been rediscovered. If you subtract the cabbage and leeks, you get a dish of glorious plain mashed potatoes to use in other recipes in this book.

> 8 medium russet potatoes, peeled and cubed
> 2½ cups chopped cabbage
> ¾ cup heavy cream
> 2 small leeks, white part only, chopped
> 3 tablespoons plus 2 tablespoons butter
> Pinch grated nutmeg
> Salt and freshly ground black pepper

1. Place the potatoes in a large pot with water to cover. Bring to a boil. Reduce the heat to a healthy simmer. Cook for 10 to 12 minutes. The potatoes will be tender when pierced with a fork. Drain and return to the pot. Set aside. Cover to keep warm.

2. At the same time, bring another pot of water to a boil. Add the cabbage. Reduce the heat to a simmer. Cook for 10 to 12 minutes. The cabbage will be very tender. Drain well.

3. Bring the cream and leeks to a simmer in a small pan and allow to bubble very gently for 7 to 8 minutes. The leeks will be tender.

4. Mash the potatoes right in the pot with 3 tablespoons of butter. Mash in the cabbage, the leek mixture, nutmeg, and salt and pepper to taste. The mixture will not be smooth, but lumpy from the cabbage.

5. Heap the hot potatoes in a bowl and press the extra dollop of butter into the top before serving.

Champ

Serves 6 to 8

Irish-Americans always marveled that their mothers' mashed potatoes were the best.

8 medium russet potatoes, peeled and cubed
1 cup milk
2 scallions, trimmed and finely chopped
2 tablespoons plus 2 tablespoons butter
4 tablespoons minced fresh flat-leaf parsley
2 tablespoons minced fresh chives
Salt and freshly ground black pepper

1. Place the potatoes in a large pot with water to cover. Bring to a boil. Reduce the heat to a healthy simmer. Cook for 10 to 12 minutes. The potatoes will be tender when pierced with a fork. Drain and return to the pot. Cover to keep warm.

2. Heat the milk in a saucepan over medium-high heat. When it starts to bubble around the edges, add the scallions and take the pan off the heat. Set aside to cool slightly.

3. Mash the potatoes right in the pot with the scallion mixture and 2 tablespoons butter. Stir in the parsley, chives, and salt and pepper to taste.

4. Heap the hot potatoes in a bowl and press the extra dollop of butter into the top before serving.

Broiled Tomatoes

Serves 6 to 8

Broiled tomatoes are a ubiquitous side dish that brighten the Irish breakfast plate. It is easy to triple this recipe.

> 4 large ripe red tomatoes, cut in half crosswise
> Salt
> 1/2 cup dried bread crumbs
> Freshly ground black pepper
> 2 to 3 slices bacon

1. Slice the tomatoes in half crosswise. Salt, and turn cut side down on paper towels to drain for about 10 minutes.

2. Turn the tomatoes cut side up and sprinkle with bread crumbs, salt, and pepper, and gently push some of the crumbs into the hollows of the tomatoes. Place in a baking pan. Set aside.

3. Preheat the broiler.

4. Fry the bacon in a skillet until almost crisp. Pat dry with paper towels.

5. Crumble the bacon over the tomatoes. Place the tomatoes under the broiler for 2 to 3 minutes. The tops will be golden brown and the bacon brown and crisp. Serve hot.

Sliced Tomatoes in Herb Dressing

Serves 6 to 8

Lorralee Cooney is descended from a long line of "good plain Irish cooks." Her great-grandmother, Fannie Bray Cotter, born in County Cork in 1850, was known for her homemade jams and jellies. Lorralee's grandmother, Johanna Sanderson, worked as a cook at the Hammond Castle in the Magnolia section of Gloucester.

Mrs. Sanderson didn't keep a formal notebook, just a Fannie Farmer cookbook stuffed with newspaper clippings, notes from her employer, John Hammond, and recipes written out in longhand on assorted scraps of paper. Lorralee kept the book. The binding is long gone, and the brittle-edged pages are held together with a well-worn garter. She has given up looking through the book for her grandmother's seasoned salt mixture, but recalls her drying the herbs that Hammond had specially shipped for the concoction. This is adapted from a recipe found tucked between the pages and could be the key to the seasoned salt.

1 teaspoon salt
$1/4$ teaspoon freshly ground black pepper
1 teaspoon dried basil
1 teaspoon sweet paprika
2 teaspoons chopped fresh chives
1 cup vegetable oil
$1/2$ teaspoon dry mustard powder
$1 1/2$ teaspoons water
1 tablespoon sugar
3 tablespoons freshly squeezed lemon juice
2 tablespoons red wine vinegar
6 large ripe tomatoes

1. Stir the salt, pepper, basil, paprika, and chives into the oil. Set aside for about 1 hour.

2. Whisk together the mustard and water. Whisk into the oil mixture. Add the sugar, lemon juice, and vinegar. Continue whisking until the dressing is slightly thickened.

3. Slice the tomatoes crosswise into ½-inch slices. Arrange on a platter, drizzle on some of the dressing, and serve immediately with the remaining dressing on the side.

Buttermilk Scones

Makes about 20

Salem chef Brian Kilroy grew up on his mother's good Irish-American cooking. Wisely, he kept all her recipes, now neatly cataloged in his computer. Her buttermilk scones, slathered with butter or jam, are his favorite.

    2 teaspoons baking powder
    1 teaspoon salt
    2½ cups all-purpose flour
    1 cup buttermilk

1. Preheat the oven to 400°F.

2. Mix together the baking powder, salt, and flour in a bowl. Stir in the buttermilk. Gather into a ball of dough. Knead gently on a floured surface, four or five times.

3. Roll out the dough. Cut into 2-inch circles. Place on a baking sheet. Do not butter the baking sheet.

4. Bake for about 15 minutes, until the scones are deeply golden on top. Cool for 5 minutes on a rack before serving warm.

Soda Bread

Makes 6 miniature loaves

Dr. Martha Brine recalls the individual raisin-studded breads that her mother baked for friends each St. Patrick's Day. Sour cream is the secret to the lusciously moist quick bread. Brine makes a huge batch of that bread each year for North Shore Community College's intercultural festival. "Students, faculty, and staff share cultures and arts at this event, but the food does more to connect people than any other campus event," says Dr. Brine. "Everyone takes part, including a maintenance man who is a Bosnian native."

Loralee Cooney adds chopped orange and lemon zest to her soda bread, a trick learned from her grandmother Johanna Sanderson.

To make individual treats, grease six miniature bread tins, follow the recipe for the larger bread below, baking for only 15 minutes.

2 1/2 cups sifted all-purpose flour
1/4 cup sugar
1/2 teaspoon baking soda
2 teaspoons baking powder
1/2 teaspoon salt
1/4 cup butter
1 large egg
1 cup sour cream
1/2 cup milk
1 1/2 cups golden raisins, tossed in 1 teaspoon
    all-purpose flour
1 teaspoon caraway seeds

REAL TEA

You need some basic ingredients and equipment to make a good tea.

- Loose tea
- Fresh water
- Saucepan or kettle in which to boil the water
- Real teapot
- Favorite teacups
- Garnishes: lemon, cream or milk, sugar, brown sugar, honey

The best tea doesn't come from a bag, but as loose, whole tea leaves. Start with fresh cold water. Bottled or tap water is fine as long as it's cold. Bring the water

CONTINUED

to a mad, rolling boil. Let it bubble away for 5 minutes.

Meanwhile, swirl hot tap water in the teapot and the cups to warm them and pour it out. Add the tea leaves to the pot. The usual amount is 1 teaspoon per cup and "one for the pot." The boiling water should be ready now. Don't let it sit around; real tea lovers claim it goes flat.

Let the tea steep for about 5 minutes, a bit longer if you like your tea dark and strong; shorter if you like it more delicately flavored. Tea is best right after it is made; don't let it cool. Pour into cups immediately.

1. Preheat the oven to 375°F. Grease an 8-inch round cake pan.

2. Sift the flour, sugar, baking soda, baking powder, and salt into a large mixing bowl. Blend in the butter, crumbling with your fingertips.

3. Beat together the egg, sour cream, and milk in another bowl. Stir in the raisins and caraway seeds. Blend the wet and dry ingredients together to make a slightly lumpy dough. Turn it into the pan.

4. Bake for 35 to 40 minutes. The tines of a fork pierced into the center will come out clean.

5. Cool for about 15 to 20 minutes on a rack before cutting. The bread is delicious warm, at room temperature, or toasted.

Tomato Soup Cake

Makes one 2-layer cake

Faced with the Great Depression of the 1930s, Irish-Americans were undaunted. Nothing was as bad as what their families had left behind fifty years before. This innovative spice cake is a product of that time, and although the recipe is likely the invention of the company that canned the soup, Irish-Americans embraced it. Katie Bull recalls her mother still baking it in the late 1950s. Don't let the tomato soup scare you off.

    2 cups all-purpose flour
    1 1/3 cups sugar
    4 teaspoons baking powder
    1 teaspoon baking soda
    1 1/2 teaspoons ground allspice
    1 teaspoon ground cinnamon
    1/2 teaspoon ground cloves
    1 (10 3/4-ounce) can tomato soup
    1/2 cup shortening
    2 large eggs
    1/4 cup water
    Cream cheese frosting

1. Preheat the oven to 350°F. Grease and flour two 8-inch round cake pans, shaking out the excess flour.

2. In a large mixing bowl, combine the flour, sugar, baking powder, baking soda, allspice, cinnamon, and cloves. Add the soup, shortening, eggs, and water. Beat together into a smooth batter. Pour into the cake pans.

3. Bake for 35 to 40 minutes. The tines of a fork pierced into center will come out clean.

4. Cool in the pans for 10 minutes. Remove the cakes from the pans and finish cooling on wire racks. Cool completely, about 2 hours, before frosting.

5. Layer and frost the top and sides with your favorite cream cheese frosting.

Whiskey Cake

Makes one 2-layer cake

Madelyn Cashman owned an Irish import shop for many years. Her husband, Bill, said that mere flour became the food of angels in her hands. He kept her kitchen notebooks, where he found this recipe.

    5 large eggs
    1 1/4 cups superfine sugar
    1/4 cup (1/2 stick) butter, melted and cooled
    1 teaspoon vanilla extract
    1/2 cups plus 3 tablespoons water
    4 1/2 cups cake flour
    1 teaspoon baking powder
    1/4 cup granulated sugar
    3 tablespoons Irish whiskey
    Vanilla frosting
    Toasted flaked almonds

1. Preheat the oven to 375°F. Grease two 9-inch cake pans, lining the bottoms with waxed or parchment paper.

2. Beat eggs and sugar together in a large mixing bowl until pale and foamy, about 5 minutes. Stir in the melted butter, vanilla, and 3 tablespoons water.

3. Mix together the flour and baking powder. Sift gradually into the egg mixture, folding gently until combined. Pour the batter into the two cake pans.

4. Bake in the center of the oven for 20 to 25 minutes. The top of the cake will spring back when pressed. Cool for 10 minutes on wire racks.

5. To make the sugar syrup, bring the sugar and ½ cup water to a boil in a small saucepan over medium-high heat. Reduce the heat to a simmer. Cook, stirring, for about 2 minutes. Remove the pan from the heat. Add the whiskey. Drizzle the syrup over the cakes.

6. Layer and frost the top and sides with vanilla frosting. Sprinkle the top with toasted almond flakes.

Bailey's Irish Cream Cheesecake

Makes one 10-inch cake

Brian Kilroy is the executive chef at the Salem eatery Finz "oh-so-hip" Seafood. He uses "an old Irish trick to keep the cheesecake from cracking" as it bakes. He adds a tablespoon of flour to the cheesecake batter. He also likes the creamier texture he gets by mixing the filling in a food processor. At the restaurant, Kilroy drizzles this with caramel sauce, something he doesn't recommend making at home. Instead, he suggests heavy cream whipped with a little more of the liqueur.

    3 to 4 tablespoons butter, melted
    2 cups graham cracker crumbs
    1½ pounds cream cheese
    4 large eggs

1 cup Bailey's Irish Cream liqueur
1/2 cup sugar
1 tablespoon all-purpose flour

1. Preheat the oven to 350°F. Butter a 10-inch springform pan.

2. Work the butter and cracker crumbs with your fingers until they hold together. Press the crumb mixture into the bottom of the pan and about one-quarter of the way up the sides.

3. Blend the cream cheese, eggs, liqueur, sugar, and flour in a food processor until smooth, stopping to scrape down the sides with a spatula. Pour the filling into the crust.

4. Bake for 45 to 50 minutes. The top will be pale gold and slightly puffed up.

5. Remove the sides of the springform pan. Set the cake to cool on a rack for at least 1 hour. Refrigerate at least 3 hours before cutting.

SUNDAY BRUNCH AT THE CLUB
Home Cooking Refined

Home cooking is enduring and comforting, but it doesn't always stay at home. We still crave the familiar when we eat out. Each in its own way, the private club and the diner bring satisfying neighborhood foods to the table. Their styles may be different, but the basis is still Grandma's table.

Men of means once cloistered themselves in private clubs built up around golf or sailing. The linen-draped dining rooms preserved the foodways that evolved from early American times. Perfectly roasted beef and gravy; lemon-crumbed broiled haddock fillets; and Indian pudding with real whipped cream are still plated up here, but more likely for families gathering at a festive Sunday brunch buffet to celebrate a holiday or other special occasion. Grandmother's favorite chicken fricassee, fragrant roasted chicken, or creamy fish chowder are served up alongside scrambled eggs and pancakes under silver domes. And someone is always on hand to carve Grandpa's favorite roast beef or whole salmon. The coffee is poured from silver carafes.

In recent years, the stuffy chefs who once presided over those kitchens have given way to a new breed, who maintain excellence while enlivening the table with a new array of specialties that reflect

SUNDAY BRUNCH

Bloody Marys and Mimosas

Tenderloin of Beef with
Provençal Crumbs

Eggs Florentine

Potatoes O'Brien (page 219)

Seafood Newburg

Gorgonzola-Walnut Tart

Grapenut Pudding

today's polyglot culture. Professionals like Denise Kiburis-Graffeo, Joe Occhipinti, and Phil Devlin balance tradtional with cutting-edge offerings and recruit new young talent to their kitchens.

A North Shore Cook: Denise Kiburis-Graffeo

Denise Kiburis-Graffeo buzzes around town in a snappy red convertible, license plate CHEF DEE. If that doesn't say she's proud of her profession, note the angle of her toque and her impeccably starched white jacket with the words *Executive Chef* embroidered on the pocket.

It's mid-morning, and she's curled over paperwork in a tiny office tucked behind the kitchen at Eastern Yacht Club. There's a comforting clatter outside the door as the cooks prep lunch. As the produce or linen or ice deliveries arrive, the drivers call out, "Chef Dee!" as they enter.

"When I got married, the delivery guys didn't know what they were going to call me. They weren't sure if I'd change my name or what. So it was Chef Dee."

As a college student, Kiburis-Graffeo started cooking to pay tuition. She was the first woman to work in the kitchen of a posh Boston hotel, where the volatile French chef had difficulty accepting her. He assigned her to making salads and refused to let her work at any other station, but when-ever something went wrong, she got the blame. His rages served only to gain her the respect and acceptance of the kitchen staff.

"They liked that I took it like a man, but that didn't stop the guys from a little good-natured hazing. One day, I tried to move a soup pot that wouldn't budge. I couldn't figure it out because I lifted that pot just fine every day. When I stirred it, my spoon hit something! The guys had put cinder blocks in my soup! When the chef found out, he threw a 20-minute tantrum. No French I'd ever heard, but I got the gist. I started a new pot, but he kept on screaming, 'Strain eet and serve eet!' I hate to think of the people in the dining room that day.

"I learned a lot in that kitchen. I learned how to barter. A lot of the guys liked to drink beer on their breaks, so if I kept a few extra cans around, life was a lot easier. See, once you picked up your list of stuff from the storerooms or refrigerators for the day, they got locked. And stayed locked. That was the rule, even if Jackie Onassis ordered caviar! And, wouldn't you know, that's exactly what happened to me. The chef threw one of his famous fits, but I managed to trade a beer for the caviar. He, of course, took all the credit with Mrs. Onassis."

Kiburis-Graffeo got her degree, but she never left cooking. Working her way through some of Boston's finest kitchens, she eventually became the first woman executive chef in a private club in the Northeast, a position she has held for more than twenty years.

The climb inspired her to nurture young talent through organizations such as Les Dames Escoffier and the Epicurean Club, two prestigious professional organizations where she is a key person on scholarship committees and a tireless fund-raiser. She provides hundreds of culinary students with financial support, networking opportunities, and job placement within the industry. In recognition, she's been named chef of the year many times over, both locally and nationally. A wall in her office is lined with framed honors and gold medals.

The Epicurean Club provided more than a medal. Tony Graffeo, a Boston executive chef, introduced himself on his way to a meeting with the group one snowy night.

"I had broken my leg, and it was in a huge cast, and there I was balancing on one good leg and one crutch, using the other crutch to open the door. Tony came along and opened it, and we've been together ever since."

The fifty-something couple determined to marry in chefs' whites, going from the kitchen, where they would prepare the meal for 250 guests, to the church. But the many cooks whose careers they'd promoted got there early to chop vegetables, roast meats, ladle soup, and pop the champagne. A mix of cooks, purveyors, TV personalities, and club members danced the night away at the gala.

Chef Dee sees the club membership as family. Her menu is a dazzling merger of classic and cutting edge kept fresh with frequent culinary workshops and world travel. China and Italy are favorite destinations.

"When I want to try a new dish, I introduce it at the Sunday brunch buffet. It's more fun than taking a poll. We did an 'Alice Through the Looking Glass' theme to try out Asian and Caribbean dishes. The guests entered the buffet line through a 'mirror' and chose the Asian or Caribbean path. We updated the menu with their favorites."

Eggs Florentine

Serves 2 to 4

Phil Devlin was a culinary student when he took a summer job at Essex County Club in Manchester-by-the-Sea. By year's end, and at the top of his class, he was asked to step up to sous chef, second-in-command of the kitchen. It was a perfect fit. A year later the executive chef retired, and Devlin neatly stepped into the top job.

"We do Sunday brunch on holidays and special occasions," says Devlin. "Mother's Day brings out our largest attendance of the year, so we do two seatings to make it comfortable. Eggs Benedict is always our most popular dish. I like to play with the recipe, so it doesn't get boring; sometimes we do the classic one with Hollandaise, other times we vary the sauce or the base, maybe Florentine-style on a bed of tender sautéed spinach."

Chef Devlin uses a classic béarnaise sauce with tomato puree added, which is called a Choron sauce. I've adapted his recipe to make it easy to do at home.

1/4 cup tarragon vinegar
2 tablespoons minced shallot
2 tablespoons minced fresh tarragon leaves, or
    2 teaspoons dried
Salt and freshly ground black pepper
7 large eggs
1 cup (2 sticks) unsalted butter, melted and cooled to
    room temperature
1 tablespoon fresh tomato puree
1 to 2 tablespoons olive oil
1 medium shallot, chopped
12 ounces fresh spinach, tough stems discarded
1/3 cup white wine
1 tablespoon white vinegar
2 English muffins

1. To make the sauce, combine the vinegar, shallot, tarragon, and salt and pepper to taste in a saucepan and bring just to a boil. Reduce the heat to medium-high and simmer. It will reduce to 1 tablespoon.

2. Combine the reduced vinegar and the eggs in a food processor or blender. Pulse on, then off quickly. With the motor running, add the melted butter a drop at a time at first, then in a slow, steady stream. The sauce will thicken to mayonnaise-like consistency. Whisk in the tomato puree. Cover. Set aside and keep warm.

3. To cook the spinach, warm the olive oil in a skillet. Add shallot and cook for 2 to 3 minutes on medium heat. It will be wilted.

4. Lower the heat to medium and add the spinach. Cook, stirring for about 2 minutes. Season with salt and pepper. Add the white wine. Cover the pan and steam for 3 to 4 minutes. The spinach will be wilted down to one-third of its volume. Keep warm.

5. To cook the eggs, crack each egg into a separate small cup or bowl.

6. Fill a skillet with about 2 inches of water and bring to a boil. Add the vinegar and salt.

7. Gently lower two eggs into the water. Cover and cook for about 3 minutes. Take eggs out of the skillet with a slotted spoon. Drain on paper towels. Repeat with two more eggs.

8. Split and toast the English muffins.

9. To assemble the dish, place two toasted English muffin halves on each plate. Top each equally with the sautéed spinach, then a poached egg on top. Nap the eggs with the sauce. Serve immediately.

Popovers

Makes 6

These light puffs of dough happily accept butter, jam, or honey. The modern innovation of cholesterol-free eggs seems to improve the results. You can easily double or triple this recipe to feed a crowd.

    2 eggs
    1 cup all-purpose flour
    1 cup milk
    Pinch of salt

1. Preheat the oven to 425°F. Grease 6 nonstick popover or muffin cups generously.

2. To make the batter, blend the eggs, flour, and milk in a food processor or blender, or with a whisk, until smooth.

3. Pour an equal amount of the batter into the muffin tins. Fill them about three-quarters full.

4. Transfer the pan to the oven. Reduce the heat to 400°F. Bake for 20 to 25 minutes. The popovers will be tall and golden brown on top. Gently pierce the top of each one with the point of a knife to allow steam to escape. Remove them from the baking pan and serve hot.

Tenderloin of Beef
with Provençal Crumbs

Serves a crowd

Chef Dee's brunch is usually built around a carving station, and this beef often appears there. She's been getting requests for this very simple recipe for years. Use it as the centerpiece for a special bash.

> 5 to 7 pounds whole tenderloin of beef
> 2 tablespoons vegetable oil
> 1/3 cup Dijon-style mustard
> 2 cups fresh white bread crumbs
> 1/4 cup dry bread crumbs
> 1/4 teaspoon white pepper
> 1 teaspoon minced garlic
> 1/2 cup olive oil
> 1/4 cup chopped fresh parsley

1. Trim all the outer fat from the tenderloin. Tie it along its length using butcher's twine so it's the same thickness all over.

2. Heat a sauté pan over high heat. Add the tenderloin and brown, quickly and evenly, on all sides. Cool on a platter for about 20 minutes. Meanwhile, preheat the oven to 375°F.

3. Remove the string. Coat the entire outside of the roast with mustard.

4. Mix the fresh and dried bread crumbs, pepper, garlic, oil, and parsley together to make Provençal crumbs. Cover the tenderloin with the crumbs. Place it in a roasting pan. Roast for about 45 minutes. A meat thermometer inserted into its thickest part will read 140°F to 145°F.

5. Let the meat stand for about 15 minutes before slicing.

Seafood Newburg

Serves 6 to 8

The Corinthian Yacht Club is perched on the rocks overlooking Marblehead Harbor. David Titus, for eight years the executive chef, recently became clubhouse manager, a job with "long hours, but time to think," he says. "A chef needs to make every decision on the spot. As manager, I have time to follow up on staff, see what's happening in the dining room."

After college, Titus worked his way from dishwasher to executive chef of the Lyceum, a historic Salem restaurant. He went on to a number of Boston kitchens before landing on "the Neck," the section of Marblehead where the club is located.

At the Corinthian, he oversees brunch every Sunday from May through October.

"We change it up weekly. Sometimes we'll do cold shrimp with a dill mayonnaise or a smoked salmon salad tray. Cobb and Caesar salads are popular. We always have a supply of fresh croissants and muffins, and savory hot dishes. Seafood Newburg is a favorite. As soon as we lift the dome, there's a line!" I have adapted his recipe for the home kitchen.

$1/4$ cup ($1/2$ stick) unsalted butter
$1/4$ cup all-purpose flour
2 teaspoons sweet paprika
4 cups milk
Salt and freshly ground black pepper
1 cup sherry
1 pound fresh haddock, poached
8 ounces fresh sea scallops, poached
8 ounces medium shrimp, peeled, deveined, and
    cooked
4 to 8 ounces fresh cooked lobster meat, cut into
    1-inch pieces
Fresh bread crumbs
Chopped fresh flat-leaf parsley

1. To make the sauce, melt the butter in a skillet over medium heat. Stir the flour and paprika into the butter with a wooden spoon. Turn the heat to low. Continue to cook and stir for about 5 minutes. The mixture will be pale gold.

2. In a large saucepan over medium-high heat, heat the milk to the boiling point. Immediately, turn the heat to low. Continue to simmer. Whisk in the flour mixture, until all of it is incorporated into the milk. Keep stirring for 1 to 2 minutes. The mixture will be thick and smooth. Season with salt and pepper.

3. Heat the sherry in a small saucepan. Tip the pan into the flame, or light with a match to burn off alcohol. Whisk the sherry into the sauce. Set aside, but keep warm.

4. For the seafood mixture, preheat the oven to 350°F.

5. Place a layer of haddock in the bottom of a large casserole or baking dish. This fish is very delicate when cooked and will break apart easily. Gently toss together the scallops, shrimp, and lobster. Layer over the haddock.

6. Ladle the sauce over the seafood until it is covered. Scatter the bread crumbs over the top.

7. Bake for 20 to 30 minutes. The crumbs will be golden brown and the sauce will bubble lightly. Sprinkle with parsley before serving.

Gorgonzola-Walnut Tart

Serves 6 to 8

After 25 years spent cooking around the world, Joe Occhipinti settled down as executive chef at Ipswich Country Club. A hotel and restaurant management degree launched him into specialty catering. He has cooked for heads of state Nelson Mandela, Mikhail Gorbachev, and Prince Charles; celebrities Arnold Schwarzenegger, Julia Child, and Rose Kennedy; and musicians from Yo-Yo Ma to Aerosmith.

"Cooking has always come naturally to me," he says. "I come from an Italian family and food was a considerable part of our lives. My mom and dad were excellent cooks, and I started baking with them."

Now, throughout autumn and winter, Chef Occhipinti uses the club dining room's breathtaking vistas of tall, ancient pines as a backdrop for Sunday brunch.

This savory cheesecake is adapted from Occhipinti's recipe.

1 cup all-purpose flour
2/3 cup chopped walnuts
1 tablespoon plus 1 tablespoon sugar
1/2 teaspoon plus 1/4 teaspoon salt
1/2 teaspoon dry mustard powder
1/8 teaspoon cayenne pepper
6 tablespoons (3/4 stick) cold unsalted butter,
    cut into cubes
1 to 2 tablespoons milk
2 tablespoons olive oil
1 large onion, diced
1 cup cranberries, fresh or frozen
1 tablespoon sugar
1 1/3 cups walnuts, corsely chopped
1 teaspoon minced fresh thyme
2 large eggs
1 cup heavy cream
2 to 3 ounces Gorgonzola cheese

1. To make the crust, combine the flour, walnuts, sugar, salt, mustard, cayenne, and butter in a food processor. Pulse until the mixture resembles fine bread crumbs.

2. Add the milk and pulse until the mixture forms a dough. Press the dough into a ball and transfer into a 9-inch tart pan. Working from the center out, press down on the dough in all directions until it covers the bottom and sides of the pan in an even layer. Freeze for 30 minutes.

3. Preheat the oven to 375°F.

4. Bake for 15 to 20 minutes. The crust will be lightly golden. Remove the crust from the oven and set aside to cool. Turn the oven temperature down to 350°F.

5. To make the filling, heat the oil in a heavy saucepan over medium heat. Add the onion, sprinkle with salt, and cook for 10 to 15 minutes, stirring frequently, until the onion is tender and caramelized. Add the cranberries and sugar. Cook until the cranberries pop. Stir in the walnuts and thyme. Set aside.

6. Whisk together the eggs and cream until smooth.

7. Spoon the walnut-cranberry mixture into the baked tart shell. Crumble the Gorgonzola over the top. Pour in the egg mixture.

8. Bake for 15 to 20 minutes. The top will be golden and the custard set.

9. Cool for 15 minutes before serving.

Grapenut Pudding

Serves 6 to 8

Homely grapenut pudding is a regular on most country club menus. The spelling—"grapenut," not "grape-nuts" as it appears on cereal boxes—is a New England idiosyncrasy. The origins have been lost, but that's been the spelling in kitchen diaries and community cookbooks here for as long as anyone can recall.

    4 cups milk, warmed
    1 cup Grape-Nuts cereal
    4 egg yolks, beaten
    ½ cup sugar
    Bare pinch of salt
    4 egg whites, beaten to soft peaks
    1 tablespoon vanilla extract
    Grated nutmeg

1. Preheat the oven to 350°F. Butter a 2-quart ovenproof baking dish.

2. Pour the milk over the Grape-Nuts. Allow to soak for about 5 minutes.

3. Stir together the egg yolks, sugar, and salt. Add to the Grape-Nuts mixture. Fold in the egg whites and vanilla.

4. Pour into the baking dish. Sprinkle the top with nutmeg.

5. Place the baking dish into a larger one. Pour hot water into the larger baking dish until the water comes about halfway up the smaller one. Bake for 40 to 45 minutes. A knife inserted near the center will come out clean. Serve warm dolloped with whipped cream.

THE NORTH SHORE'S PRIVATE CLUBS

- Beverly Golf and Tennis, Beverly
- Boston Yacht Club, Marblehead
- Corinthian Yacht Club, Marblehead
- Eastern Yacht Club, Marblehead
- Essex County Club, Manchester-by-the-Sea
- Georgetown Country Club, Georgetown
- Haverhill Country Club, Bradford
- Indian Ridge Country Club, North Andover
- Ipswich Country Club, Peabody
- Kernwood Country Club, Salem
- Myopia Hunt Club, Hamilton
- Salem Country Club, Peabody
- Singing Beach Club, Beverly Farms
- Tedesco Country Club, Swampscott

THE ITALIAN TRADITION

From Tomato Sauce to Checkered Tablecloths

When Italians emigrated to the United States in the late nineteenth and early twentieth centuries, they brought foodways formed by a topography that, until 1870, had fragmented their native land into many separate countries. Each separate region developed its own customs, crops, cooking techniques, and dialects.

On the North Shore, immigrants from Sicilian coastal towns easily slipped into the fabric of Gloucester's fishing industry. Those from the Campania, Calabria, and Abruzzo regions settled into the thriving shoe industry capitals of Lynn and Haverhill or worked as masons or gardeners on country estates in Hamilton, Ipswich, and Beverly Farms. In the cities, they opened vegetable markets, bakeries, and eateries where fragrant pots of simmering tomato sauce enticed customers. Italian cooking gradually became Italian-American cooking as cooks whipped up "Sunday-best" dishes, such as lasagna and *melanzane parmigiana,* to impress non-Italian patrons. Food historian Michelle Topor says that restaurant cooks, responding to the demand for meat, piled meatballs onto the plates of pasta, inventing the "side of spaghetti," and substituted veal for the eggplant in another dish, creating "veal parmigiana."

At home, fare was still pasta and vegetables with small amounts of meat, except on Sunday, when extended family gathered for a multicourse meal highlighted by a long-simmered meat-and-tomato sauce.

Education and affluence prompted new generations to flee the cities for the leafier communities of Lynnfield, Saugus, and Methuen. The dream to own land for vegetables and flowers, a headquarters where Grandpa could gather the family, was realized.

Sunday Dinner

Sunday was a *festa*, the day of the week when the extended Italian-American family gathered for a dinner that began after church and stretched into early evening. The event called for the best china, linens, and silver.

Savory bites of cured meats or marinated vegetables whetted the appetite while the pasta water bubbled on the stove. The pasta, or "macaroni," was enveloped in rich, meaty tomato sauce, the meats served on a separate platter. Roasted meats followed—beef or poultry or both. Then came vegetables and a green salad to aid digestion.

After the women cleared the table and spread a new cloth, there was cheese and fresh fruit and pastry, then cups of thick black coffee with liqueurs, some directly spicing the coffee. The afternoon was paced slowly with plenty of time for digestion, lively conversation, or a game of bocce.

> **MENU FOR SUNDAY DINNER**
>
> Fried Eggplant
>
> Macaroni with Meat Sauce
>
> Rolled Beef
>
> Meatballs
>
> Roasted Chicken with Potatoes
>
> Stuffed Peppers
>
> Baked Artichoke Hearts
>
> Mixed Green Salad
>
> Fresh Fruit, Pastry, Espresso

Sunday dinner was the template for all family celebrations. At weddings, the pasta was ziti (literally, "bride-grooms"). On Easter, it was lasagna. A Thanksgiving turkey slipped nicely into the roast course, while pumpkin and mincemeat pies shared the table with *cannoli*. On Christmas Eve, *La vigilia di Natale,* there was fish in place of meat, and, for dessert, tangerine wedges dipped in red wine, their skins a perfume roasting with the chestnuts.

A North Shore Cook: Anthony Verga

Anthony Verga stops to say hello to friends and neighbors nearly every morning. The soft-spoken man with salt-and-pepper hair sits at a table for four in a breakfast spot near the Route 128 exit to Boston, where he represents Essex, Rockport, and Gloucester in the Massachusetts Legislature. He found his way to public service gradually after a life in and around the fishing industry. Since Verga is the grandson of a Sicilian-born Gloucester fisherman, his conversations inevitably turn to family and food.

"I grew up with good food. My dad was the cook on a fishing boat. Summers in high school, I went out with him. He cooked pasta every night, sometimes with greens, sometimes mackerel, and sometimes shrimp. Always different. Always good. It was hard work. I weighed a lot less then, even eating pasta every day.

"There was a coal stove on that boat. My father could do anything on that thing. In the morning, he soft-boiled eggs. To this day I like two soft-boiled eggs for breakfast. The first one, I knock off the top, dip in the toast. I drink the second. A lot of Italians drink their eggs, some with a shot of vermouth.

"Other times, my father pulled the top off the stove and char-cooked steaks on it. He made a two-sided grate to hold fish, grilled them over the coals, too.

"My father went to sea when he was five years old. His family was so poor that he was sent to sea so he could eat on the boat. He was adopted, never knew his real parents. I always thought he had a sadness about him, like something was on his mind. Maybe he wondered about them."

Verga grew up in a large, lively household. His parents had eight children. His mother did the cooking at home.

"My mother baked her own bread," he remembers. "She would pull it out of the oven with her bare hands—she had hands like asbestos gloves!—then she sliced it open, poured on green olive oil, some salted mackerel or anchovies, and cheese, and while it was still hot, she broke off pieces to pass around the table.

"When she fried mushrooms, she threw a coin into the pan. If it turned black, she said the mushrooms were no good. We kids were more interested getting that quarter!

"She bought chickens live, brought them home in burlap sacks. She left them by the kitchen door, and I remember tripping over them and hearing them clucking in the bag. She wrung the necks herself, then dipped them in a pot of hot water to take out the feathers. The little yellow eggs would be still inside. She put those in the chicken soup.

"We always had fish. It was a staple. Free. Fresh. In summer, we had mackerel. In winter, haddock, sole, scup. Occasionally we got lobster, mussels, or quahogs. Anything we call underutilized species today, my mother cooked it. She made miracles with skate. She turned it into a soup with lemon and garlic in the broth. The fish was so tender, you could eat the cartilage!"

Tony met his wife, Adrienne, in high school. She was from the Portuguese parish, Our Lady of Good Voyage, and he from St. Ann's, the Sicilian parish: the ideal Gloucester union. They have eight children and fifteen grandchildren. All live in Gloucester, "five within yelling distance," near Fisherman's Memorial Park. Holidays are filled with noise and laughter and at least twenty-four around the table.

Never far from the sea, Verga's experience included a stint in the Navy and fishing off the San Diego coast. With a growing family, he worked in real estate for a while, but found his way back to the edge of the sea as a manager of the Main Deck, a restaurant that had been badly damaged by fire, and then opened the Schooner Race across the street. Both establishments were heavily patronized by the fishing community.

"We always had something good cooking—staples, you know: chicken, lasagna. Eggplant parmigiana—I crumbed and fried it back then. Now I do it in the oven, not so many calories. I would start my [tomato] sauce the day before. I'd add so much wine, the sauce was purple 'til the alcohol burned off. It would go all day. Sometimes, I just did it to get people hungry."

Verga smiles and takes a breath as if inhaling the cooking aromas. "You know, the smell of frying onions and peppers gets the senses going. I can do the sauce in an hour on Sunday morning, but it's better cooked a day before. I use good green olive oil, onions, loads of garlic, sugar or wine to cut the acid of the tomatoes. For meat, I use sausage and meatballs. I make them with bread crumbs, lots of garlic, and grated cheese. Once, someone brought a tuna to the restaurant. I cooked it in the sauce, just like a roast. We still talk about it."

His next venture was the White Star Fish Market, where he recalls giving cooking tips over the counter, usually family recipes. For Verga, family is always intertwined with food.

"Adrienne cooks my mother's food with her own touch. She makes delicious tripe with potatoes and adds mushrooms. Now my kids cook, too. One daughter-in-law is from China. She cooks Italian food, but she does it with a Chinese accent. It's delicious!"

More people stop by Representative Verga's table, one with an invitation to a

Girl Scout event the following weekend. Across the room, he spots Vito Calomo, the executive director of Gloucester Fisheries. They wave affectionately. Representative Verga takes a last sip of his tea—hasn't touched coffee in years—before heading for the State House.

"It's not a bad place to be at my age."

THE PANTRY

- **Anchovies:** Italian-Americans buy their anchovies in tins, the anchovies inside bathed in olive oil. Drain before using.
- **Basil:** This fragrant fresh herb, also called sweet basil, has bright green rounded leaves. Available year-round, it is more expensive in winter. Don't substitute dried basil.
- **Cheeses:** Real Parmigiano-Reggiano, is imported from that region of Italy, the words stamped onto the rind. Look for wheels or wedges so you can read the stamp. It is expensive, but worth it.

    You don't need to seek out imported mozzarella. Domestic brands are authentic to Italian-American cooking. Small balls of mozzarella, called *bocconcini*, are easy antipasti or wonderful in a salad. Another cheese frequently used is provolone. A full-flavored, densely textured cheese, provolone is sliced into sandwiches or rolled for antipasto platters.

- **Cold cuts:** Salami, pepperoni, and mortadella are cooked sausages that have found their way into sandwiches or antipasti platters. Italian-Americans used domestic prosciutto since it was not imported until recent years.
- **Fats and oils:** Use 100 percent olive oil for cooking. Its clean taste doesn't alter when heated. Save full-bodied extra virgin olive oil for drizzling over salads and vegetables. Salt pork, the once-discarded fatty end, available at the meat counter or butcher, is often rendered to flavor tomato sauce.
- **Flat-leaf parsley:** Also called Italian parsley, this is darker green, more flavorful, and easier to chop than the frilly variety. It is available fresh year-round.
- **Oregano:** The "pizza herb" is equally at home with meats, fresh fish, or strewn into salads. Use fresh abundantly; use dried sparingly as it can taste burnt.
- **Pasta:** Good-quality dried pasta is widely available and preferable to most store-bought fresh pasta.

THE RECIPES

Fried Eggplant
Melanzane Fritti

Fried Dough with Anchovies
Zeppole con Alici

"Little Rags" Soup
Stracciatella

Chicken Stock
Brodo

Pasta and Beans
Pasta e Fagioli

Quick Tomato Sauce
Marinara

Smooth Tomato Sauce
Il Sugo di Pomodoro

Sunday Sauce
Il Sugo, Ragú

Meatballs
Polpetti

Rolled Stuffed Beef
Braciole

"Little Ears" Pasta with
Broccoli Rabe
Orecchiette con Broccoli Rapi

Chicken with Red Peppers
and Potatoes
Pollo con Peperoni e Patate

Sausage and Peppers
Salcisse e Peperoni

Vegetable Omelet
Frittata di Verdure

Baked Artichoke Hearts
Carciofi Cotto

Braised Mushrooms
Funghi

Oven-Roasted Potatoes
Patate Arrosti

Ricotta Pie
Pastiera

Italian Ice
Granita di Limone

STANDARD BREADING PROCEDURE

At the words "standard breading procedure," a food professional instinctively lines up three plates. The food to be coated is dipped consecutively into the plates of flour, egg wash, and bread crumbs. Then it is placed on a baking sheet at the end of the line and refrigerated for at least 30 minutes before cooking.

Fried Eggplant
Melanzane Fritti

Serves 6 to 8

Serve these hot or at room temperature. Cut them into strips for a mixed antipasto platter, or tuck into crusty rolls lined with tomato slices, provolone cheese, and fresh peppery greens like arugula, then drizzle with olive oil.

These are the fried eggplant slices that become "parmigiana" by layering in a baking dish with tomato sauce and thin mozzarella slices, starting and ending with sauce. Top with grated Parmesan cheese, and bake at 350°F for 20 to 25 minutes. The cheese will melt and the sauce will bubble.

> 2 medium eggplants, about 1 pound each
> Salt
> ¹/₂ cup all-purpose flour, or more as needed
> Freshly ground black pepper
> 1 cup dried bread crumbs
> 3 tablespoons minced fresh herbs (basil, oregano, flat-leaf parsley, or mint)
> 2 large eggs, beaten well with 2 tablespoons water
> Olive oil for frying

1. Wash and dry the eggplants. Do not peel. Slice crosswise into ¼-inch-thick rounds.

2. Salt each slice heavily and place in a colander. Set aside for 20 to 30 minutes, to "sweat" out bitter juices. Rinse each slice under cold running water. Pat them dry with paper towels.

3. Season the flour with salt and pepper. Toss the bread crumbs with the herbs.

4. Coat the eggplant slices in flour, then in the egg wash, then in the bread crumbs, shaking off any excess. Set aside on a tray. Refrigerate for about 30 minutes.

5. Pour the olive oil about 1-inch deep into a large skillet over medium-high heat. Add the eggplant in batches; do not crowd the pan. Cook for 2 to 3 minutes on each side. The slices will be deeply golden. Drain on paper towels. Keep the finished eggplant in a warm oven until the entire batch is done.

Fried Dough with Anchovies
Zeppole con Alici

Makes 20 to 25

North Shore native Mary Palmer recalls these savory, salty puffs of dough, adapted here, in her book *Cucina di Calabria*. I was thrilled to find the recipe that my family had long forgotten. For the sweet version, skip the anchovies and drizzle the puffs with warmed honey. These antipasti are finger food—and deliciously addictive.

    1 package (2 1/2 teaspoons) active dry yeast
    1 1/4 cups lukewarm water
    3 cups all-purpose flour
    1/4 teaspoon salt
    2-ounce can flat anchovies, drained and coarsely
        chopped
    1 cup mixed vegetable and olive oil, for frying

1. Stir the yeast into the lukewarm water until it dissolves. Flour a work surface.

ROASTED PEPPERS

My grandmother, Rosina Perlino, roasted peppers directly in the flames of the big stove that heated her kitchen, turning them with a long kitchen fork until their skins charred all over. After steaming them in a tightly closed paper bag for about 20 minutes, she gently rubbed off the charred skins and pulled out stems and seeds, often burning her fingers in the process. She served the peppers as an antipasto on a platter, blessed with salt and a drizzle of good olive oil.

My grandaunt Zia Antonetta often roasted a single pepper, picked from her garden, in the toaster oven after removing seeds and stem. It was her closest brush with fast food!

You can roast peppers on the backyard grill or on a rack under the oven broiler, heated to 500°F. Turn often, so that they char evenly. Steam them in a paper bag or wrapped loosely in foil. Rub the skin off under cold running water.

2. Sift the flour and salt into a bowl. Make a well in the center. Pour the yeast and water mixture into the well, mixing until it forms a dough.

3. Transfer the dough to the work surface. Knead for 3 to 5 minutes. The dough will be smooth and elastic. Set it aside in an oiled bowl. Cover it with a towel. Let it rise in a warm place for about 2 hours. It will double in bulk.

4. Preheat the oven to 200°F. Pinch off about 20 pieces of dough about the size of a golf ball. Stretch each piece into a rectangle, press a few anchovy pieces into the center, and fold the dough over, twisting it on the ends to close. Set aside on waxed or parchment paper.

5. Pour the oil into a deep, heavy skillet until it is about 2 inches deep, and heat over medium-high heat. Add the dough pieces a few at a time to the pan. Do not crowd the pan or they will not brown. Turn with a spatula or tongs to cook all sides, about 3 to 4 minutes. They will be golden and crisp. Remove them with a slotted spoon to drain on paper towels. Then place them on baking sheets in the warm oven until the whole batch is done. Pile them on a serving platter while they are hot.

"Little Rags" Soup
Stracciatella

Serves 6

Immigrants brought the custom of keeping "backyard chick-ens," even in the city. As children, my brother and I adopted my grandfather's newborn chicks as pets. My dad had a few words with him before we were old enough to equate their gradual disappearance with the chicken dishes on his table. Most Italian-American neighborhoods had a "chicken man," a shop where customers selected live chickens to be prepared for cooking. All parts, including feet, were packaged to go.

8 cups Chicken Stock (recipe follows)
1 large head escarole, trimmed, washed, drained, and
    coarsely chopped
4 large eggs
1/4 cup grated Parmigiano-Reggiano cheese
Salt and freshly ground black pepper

1. Bring the chicken stock to a boil in a large pot over medium-high heat.

2. Add the escarole to the chicken stock. Lower the heat to medium. Simmer for 10 minutes.

3. While the escarole cooks, beat the eggs and cheese together in a bowl. Pour the egg mixture into the bubbling stock in a thin, steady stream. Whisk gently. The mixture will form strands, or "little rags," in the soup.

3. Add the escarole to the simmering broth. Bring just to a boil. Reduce the heat to a simmer. Cook for 2 to 3 minutes. While the soup is still bubbling, pour in the egg mixture in a steady stream while whisking gently. It will form strands in the soup.

4. Remove the soup from the heat. Season with salt and pepper and serve immediately.

Chicken Stock

Brodo

Makes 4 quarts

Freeze any extra stock. It keeps up to a month.

2¹⁄₂ to 3 pounds chicken, cut into pieces,
    including neck
6 quarts water
2 large carrots, trimmed and coarsely chopped
2 medium onions, quartered
4 celery ribs, including leaves, coarsely chopped
2 plum tomatoes, cut in half, *or* 1 tablespoon
    tomato paste
1 bay leaf
Few sprigs fresh flat-leaf parsley

1. Rinse the chicken. Combine the chicken and water to cover in a soup pot. Bring to a boil. Reduce the heat and simmer for 2 to 3 minutes. Drain the chicken. Discard the water.

2. Return the chicken to the soup pot. Add 6 quarts fresh water, the carrots, onions, celery, tomatoes, bay leaf, and parsley. Bring to a boil. Reduce to a simmer. Cook for 2 to 2½ hours. The stock will be golden.

3. Strain through fine-mesh sieve. Discard the solids. Cool. Refrigerate the broth for about 2 hours or overnight. Any fat will congeal on top and can be lifted away.

4. Bring the stock to a boil. Reduce the heat and simmer for about 15 minutes. For clearer stock, strain once more, through cheesecloth or a paper coffee filter.

Pasta and Beans

Pasta e Fagioli

Serves 6

Somewhere between a soup and a pasta, the name of this nutritious dish, standard Friday night and meatless Lenten fare, was mispronounced "pasta fa-zool."

2 tablespoons olive oil
Crushed red pepper flakes (start with 1/8 teaspoon),
    to taste
1 to 2 cloves garlic, peeled and cut in half
1 1/2 pounds peeled, seeded, chopped fresh plum
    tomatoes, *or* 1 (32-ounce) can plum tomatoes, drained
Salt
2 (15-ounce) cans red kidney beans, drained and rinsed
4 cups water
12 ounces short tubular macaroni (such as elbows,
    ditalini), cooked
Grated Parmigiano-Reggiano cheese for sprinkling
Chopped fresh parsley for sprinkling

1. Heat the oil over medium heat in a deep pot. Add the pepper flakes and garlic. Cook gently for 3 to 5 minutes. The garlic will be lightly golden and fragrant. Do not let the pepper flakes burn.

2. Add the tomatoes and salt to taste. Bring to a boil. Reduce heat. Cook for about 3 minutes. Add the water. Simmer about 15 minutes more. The liquid will reduce and the stock thicken.

3. Add the pasta. Cover and heat, about 2 minutes. The pasta will be hot. Remove the garlic. Sprinkle with grated cheese and parsley before serving.

PRINCE MACARONI COMPANY

The city of Lowell, neighboring the North Shore, was once the home of the Prince Macaroni Company. After World War II, its marketing to home cooks included a catchy TV slogan, "Wednesday is Prince Spaghetti Day," free recipe booklets, and special offers for inexpensive kitchen gadgets like box graters.

TOMATO SAUCE

Three basic tomato sauces complement Italian-American dishes
- a quick-cooking marinara, or sailor's sauce, for quick pasta dishes
- a smooth-textured sauce, for dolloping between layered baked dishes such as lasagna and eggplant parmigiana
- a hearty long-cooking meat sauce, for Sunday and holiday pasta

Quick Tomato Sauce
Marinara

Makes about 4 cups

This quickly made, textured sauce was named for sailors who wanted their pasta right away! This was weekday sauce especially useful for meatless Lenten meals. To make it spicier, add plenty of red pepper flakes.

2 tablespoons extra virgin olive oil
2 cloves garlic, peeled and split
Crushed red pepper flakes, optional
1/4 cup dry white table wine
3 pounds fresh (or canned) plum tomatoes, seeded and coarsely chopped (peeling is optional)
Salt and freshly ground black pepper
Chopped fresh basil

1. Heat the oil in a large saucepan over medium heat. Add the garlic and red pepper flakes, if using. Cook gently for 2 to 3 minutes. The garlic will be lightly golden, not browned. Discard the garlic.

2. Add the wine. Cook for 2 to 3 minutes, stirring.

3. Add the tomatoes, salt, and pepper. Simmer, uncovered for 10 to 15 minutes. Stir in the basil to warm and release its oils, 2 to 3 minutes. The oil and tomatoes will not completely blend. Serve hot.

Smooth Tomato Sauce
Il Sugo di Pomodoro

Makes 6 cups

Originally made from fresh-picked or home-canned tomatoes, resourceful immigrants adapted to the North Shore's unforgiving climate by using commercially canned tomatoes. A pinch of sugar or a splash of wine cuts any acidity. Home cooks had a trick of swirling water in the empty tomato can to enrich the pot with any stray tomato clinging to the insides. This sauce goes between layers of eggplant for parmigiana or between sheets of noodles and cheeses for lasagna.

2 (32-ounce) cans peeled plum tomatoes
2 tablespoons olive oil
1 small onion, cut in half
1 whole clove garlic, crushed
2 tablespoons tomato paste
3/4 cup dry red or white wine *or* 1 to 2 teaspoons
    granulated sugar
Salt
12 fresh basil leaves, cut into fine shreds
1/8 to 1/4 teaspoon crushed red pepper flakes, optional

1. Force the plum tomatoes through a fine-mesh sieve or food mill to remove seeds.

2. Warm the oil in a heavy pot over medium-high heat. Add the onion and garlic and cook for 2 to 3 minutes. The onion and garlic will soften and be pale gold. Discard the onion and garlic.

3. Stir in the tomatoes and tomato paste. Add the wine or sugar. Bring to a boil. Simmer for 20 to 30 minutes, depending on the juiciness of the tomatoes. The mixture will thicken.

RAGÚ OR GRAVY?

RAGÚ OR GRAVY?

Eighteenth-century Neapolitan nobles sent their household cooks to train in France. There they learned French culinary techniques and language. On their return, they put their new skills to work—with an Italian accent. The newly acquired title *monsieur* (sir) became *monzu; gateau* (cake) became *gatto*, and *ragout* (stew) became *ragù*. That *ragù* underwent further transformation when the men—all professional cooks were men—substituted tomatoes for stock, creating a meaty tomato sauce.

Two centuries later, Italian immigrants to Boston renamed the sauce "gravy," just like any other sauce cooked with meat. Home cooks also know it as "big sauce," a nod to the amounts of time and meat that go into preparation, or simply "The Sauce" (*il sugo*), because there is no equal! I call it Sunday Sauce because it's the one my grandfather started at dawn on Sunday and simmered for hours.

4. Stir in salt to taste, basil, and red pepper flakes, if using. Heat through for 3 to 5 minutes more. The sauce will be smooth and thick and the basil fragrant.

Sunday Sauce

Il Sugo, Ragú

Makes 3 quarts

Here it is: The Sauce, *il sugo, ragú*, or "gravy" for Sunday dinner and celebrations. The meats cooked in the sauce are served on a separate platter. Each family recipe is influenced by regional roots and personal tastes and flavored with combinations of beef, lamb, pork, chicken, meatballs, sausages, or stuffed rolls of steak called *braciole*. Groveland businessman Dan Roland's sauce, based on his mother's recipe, is spiked with mint, a gift of her Sicilian heritage. Tony Verga recalls pigs' feet and pork rind in his mother's sauce.

4-ounce piece salt pork
Braciole (see recipe, page 146)
Olive oil to film the bottom of the pot
Meatballs (see recipe, page 145)
1 onion, cut in half
2 cloves garlic, peeled
2 carrots
2 ribs celery, with leaves
3 tablespoons tomato paste
1/2 to 3/4 cup dry red wine, to taste
4 large (32-ounce) cans Italian plum tomatoes, pureed in food processor
Salt and freshly ground black pepper
2 good-size sprigs fresh basil (or mint), if available

1. Pat the outside of the braciole dry.

2. Warm the oil over medium-high heat in a large heavy pot. Sear the salt pork, meatballs and braciole for 3 to 5 minutes on each side, until they are browned on the outside. Cook each separately and do not crowd the pot. Remove the meatballs and braciole from the pot and set aside.

3. Pour off any excess fat from the pan. Add the salt pork, onion, garlic, carrots, and celery to the pot, and cook for 2 to 3 minutes, removing each vegetable as it turns lightly golden and begins to soften. The carrots will take the longest. Do not allow them to brown. Discard the onion, garlic, carrots, and celery. Return the salt pork to the pot.

4. Stir in the tomato paste and wine. Cook, stirring, for 1 to 2 minutes. Add the pureed tomatoes. Fill the four empty tomato cans about three-quarters full with water, swirling to remove any tomato clinging to the inside. Pour the water into the pot. Bring the pot to a boil. Reduce to a simmer, and cook, partially covered, for about 2 hours.

5. Return the meatballs and braciole to the pot. Add the salt and pepper and the basil or mint. Simmer very gently for 1 to 1½ hours. If the sauce thickens too much, add ½ cup warm water, as needed. To serve, remove and discard the salt port and garlic, and arrange the meats on a serving platter. Toss the sauce with your favorite pasta on a separate platter.

SPAGHETTI AND MEATBALLS

Restaurants opened by Italian immigrants got rave reviews from non-Italian diners who couldn't get enough of checked tablecloths and candlelight glowing from straw-covered wine bottles. These eateries gave birth to the dish spaghetti and meatballs. At home, meatballs were stuffed with raisins, cubes of mozzarella, pine nuts, or capers and served on a separate platter.

Meatballs
Polpetti

Serves 6

For her meatballs, my grandmother always added fresh bread crumbs soaked in milk.

1 cup fresh bread crumbs
1/3 cup milk
1 pound lean ground beef
2 large eggs, beaten
1/2 cup grated Parmigiano-Reggiano cheese
1/3 cup minced fresh flat-leaf parsley
Salt and freshly ground black pepper
Olive oil
Sunday Sauce (see page 143)

1. Combine the bread crumbs and milk in a bowl. Set aside to soak for about 20 minutes.

2. Mix the bread crumb mixture, beef, eggs, cheese, parsley, and salt and pepper to taste. With wet hands, shape the meat mixture into balls of whatever size you like.

3. Go to step 2 in the Sunday Sauce recipe, or heat a large skillet over medium-high heat. Swirl in enough olive oil to film the bottom. Add the meatballs, being careful not to crowd the pan. You may have to work in batches. Cook, turning often, until lightly browned on the outside.

4. Drain on paper towels. Gently—to prevent splashing—lower the meatballs into a simmering pot of Sunday Sauce to cook until the sauce is finished.

Rolled Stuffed Beef
Braciole

Serves 6

Frank Pellino of Danvers grew up on this type of family fare. Today, as chef/owner of Pellino's Fine Dining in Marblehead, he presents elegant Tuscan fare, updated seasonally, to a loyal clientele.

$\frac{1}{3}$ cup minced fresh flat-leaf parsley
$\frac{1}{2}$ cup grated Parmigiano-Reggiano cheese
1 clove garlic, peeled and cut in half
Salt and freshly ground black pepper
1$\frac{1}{2}$ pounds beef round
Olive oil

1. Toss the parsley, cheese, and garlic together. Season with salt and pepper.

2. Slice the beef into pieces about 3 by 5 inches each. Place the beef slices on a work surface. Pound with a meat mallet or the bottom of a heavy skillet to flatten. The slices should be ¼ inch thick.

3. Spread the parsley mixture over one side of each slice. Roll the beef. Tie on each end and across the center with kitchen string.

4. Go to step 2 in the Sunday Sauce recipe, or heat a large skillet over medium-high heat. Swirl in enough olive oil to film the bottom. Reduce the heat to medium and add the rolls of beef. Cook, turning, until the rolls are lightly browned on all sides.

5. Add the rolls to the simmering Sunday Sauce to cook for about 1½ hours, until the meat is very tender. Remove the strings before serving.

"Little Ears" Pasta with Broccoli Rabe

Orecchiette con Broccoli Rapi

Serves 6

Broccoli rabe is a bitter green that looks like tiny, leafy broccoli. In Italy, the bulbous roots were thrown to farm animals while the family feasted on the prized greens. My grandmother Rosina Perlino maintained that a woman who cooked root vegetables for her husband would ruin her marriage.

> 1 pound broccoli rabe
> Salt
> 1 pound orecchiette pasta
> 1/4 cup olive oil
> 2 cloves garlic, peeled and cut in half
> 3 to 5 anchovy fillets, drained and rinsed
> Crushed red pepper flakes
> 1/2 cup grated Parmigiano-Reggiano cheese

1. Set aside a large bowl of ice water.

2. Wash the broccoli rabe. Coarsely chop the tops into pieces about 1-inch long and discard the stems. Bring a large pot of salted water to a boil. Add the broccoli rabe. Cook for 1 to 2 minutes, until it is bright green and tender. Remove the broccoli rabe with a slotted spoon or tongs, leaving the cooking water in the pot. Immediately plunge the vegetable into ice water. Drain. Set aside.

2. Bring the cooking water back to a boil. Add the pasta and cook until al dente.

3. While the pasta cooks, heat a large skillet over medium-high heat. Swirl in the olive oil. Add the garlic and anchovies and cook for 2 to 3 minutes, until the garlic is pale gold, not

browned. Discard the garlic. The anchovies will soften. Mash them with a fork so that they dissolve into the olive oil. Add red pepper flakes to taste. Remove the skillet from the heat.

4. Drain the pasta, reserving 1 cup of the cooking water. Toss the pasta and the broccoli rabe directly into the hot skillet with the olive oil mixture. Sprinkle with the cheese and toss again. If the mixture is too thick, add a tablespoon or more of the reserved cooking water, until you like the consistency. Serve hot.

Chicken with Red Peppers and Potatoes

Pollo con Peperoni e Patate

Serves 2

In the past 50 years, second- and third-generation Italian-Americans exited the North Shore for the suburbs. With *Nonna* no longer in the same house, on the same block, or standing at the stove, there's a nostalgia for her cooking. Enter classically trained chef Gaetano "Danny" DeSimone, who re-creates *la cucina di famiglia* at his tiny Saugus eatery. Huge platters and congenial atmosphere are part of the charm at La Vita Mia. Loyal clientele line up every night of the week, even in below-zero temperatures. I've adapted DeSimone's recipe.

You can find vinegar peppers in Italian specialty shops or on the international shelves of the supermarket.

1 chicken breast, skin on, cut in half and flattened
All-purpose flour for dredging
Olive oil

PACE'S MARKET

Joe Pace (pronounced pah-chay) moved his successful Italian specialty market, Joe Pace & Sons, north to Saugus from Boston's North End when the Big Dig (a massive road construction project) kept his customers away. The new location boasts its own bakery and fresh meat case, as well as cured meats and cheeses. There are shelves of pasta and cases of cookies and other sweets. Joe, or one of his knowledgeable staff, will sell you a wedge of authentic Parmigiano-Reggiano cheese or grate it for you while you watch. He always asks if you want the rind to simmer in your chicken stock or tomato sauces.

¼ Spanish onion, sliced
2 large vinegar peppers, cut into strips
1 large potato, scrubbed and sliced into ¼-inch slices,
    skin optional
1½ cups Chicken Stock (see recipe, page 139)
Salt and freshly ground black pepper
1 tablespoon butter
1½ teaspoons chopped fresh flat-leaf parsley

1. Preheat the oven to 450°F.

2. Dredge the chicken in the flour, shaking off any excess.

3. Heat a large ovenproof skillet over medium-high heat and swirl in enough olive oil to film the bottom. Add the chicken. Cook for 3 to 5 minutes on one side, until golden. Turn the chicken. Add the onion and vinegar peppers to the pan. Cook for 7 to 9 minutes. The chicken will be golden on both sides.

4. Meanwhile, heat another large skillet and swirl in enough olive oil to film the bottom. Add the potato slices and cook on both sides until they are lightly browned. Remove the potatoes with a slotted spoon, so there is no extra oil, and add them to the skillet with the chicken mixture. Place the pan in the oven and bake for 15 to 25 minutes. The potato will be tender and the chicken cooked through. Place in a colander to drain any excess oil.

5. Add the stock to the skillet. Add the salt, pepper, butter, and half the parsley. Bring to a boil. Reduce the heat and cook for 5 to 7 minutes to blend the flavors and reduce the sauce slightly.

6. Transfer the chicken mixture to a platter. Pour the sauce over it and scatter the remaining parsley on top. Serve hot.

Sausage and Peppers

Salcisse e Peperoni

Serves 10 to 12

Every summer, my dad arranged a country picnic for our extended family, some forty to fifty grandparents, uncles, aunts, and cousins. Assorted *nonnas* never flinched at feeding this multitude, cooking for days to fill coolers and baskets with every treat. Considering it barbaric to dine on wooden picnic tables, they induced the men to lug hampers filled with linens, china, and silver to the picnic site, where they warmed huge pans of sausage and peppers over the fire. Dad happily pushed aside hot dogs and burgers to make room. Feel free to reheat a pan of these over a charcoal fire.

18 to 20 Italian sausages, sweet and hot mixed
8 red bell peppers
8 green bell peppers
2 large sweet onions, optional
1 cup red wine or water

1. Preheat the oven to 400°F.

2. Pierce the sausages several times with a fork. Place on baking sheets; use two baking sheets so that the sausages are not crowded and can brown evenly. Bake for 20 minutes, turning once, until the exteriors are lightly browned. Remove the sausages from the oven. Drain on paper towels. Pour the excess fat from the baking sheets, leaving just a light coating.

3. While the sausages cook, cut the stems, seeds, and ribs out of the peppers. Cut each in half lengthwise and each into 4 lengthwise slices. Cut the onions into rings.

4. Slice the sausages diagonally into thirds. Place the sausages, peppers, and onions on the baking sheets. Drizzle

SAUSAGE AND PEPPERS

Sausage and peppers was the food of street festivals held in honor of patron saints Rocco, Francis, Anthony, and Mother Cabrini. Colorful ribbons pinned with paper money offerings streamed from the statues that "strong men of good character" carried through the streets. Later, there were games, music, dancing—and food. Sausages and peppers cooked over coals was the signature aroma in the air. The most popular dish, it spread to all outdoor festivals. Today that same aroma greets revelers at October's Topsfield Fair. It is coincidental that the fair is held over Columbus Day weekend.

with the wine. Bake for about 30 minutes. The sausages and onions will be deeply brown and the peppers will be lightly singed and fragrant. Serve hot.

Vegetable Omelet
Frittata di Verdure

Serves 6

Hot from the oven, the frittata, a cross between an omelet and a pizza, is a great one-dish supper with a green salad and crusty bread. Stuff the wedges, cold or at room temperature, into rolls with sliced tomatoes and provolone, or cut into strips for an antipasto. The frittata is a great way to use zucchini (or any vegetables) from an overabundant summer garden.

    2 medium zucchini
    2 tablespoons olive oil
    1 small onion, sliced in rings
    2 roasted red peppers, cut into strips
    7 large eggs
    2 tablespoons chopped fresh flat-leaf parsley
    Salt and freshly ground black pepper
    2 tablespoons grated Parmigiano-Reggiano cheese

1. Wash, but do not peel, the zucchini. Cut off the stems and cut the zucchini in half lengthwise. Remove the seeds with a melon scoop or a teaspoon. Slice crosswise thinly.

2. Heat the olive oil in a large ovenproof nonstick skillet over medium heat. Add the onion, and cook, stirring, about 4 to 5 minutes. It will be wilted and pale yellow. Add the zucchini and cook for about 5 minutes, then add the roasted red peppers. Cook for about 2 minutes. The zucchini will be lightly golden and soft.

3. Preheat the oven broiler to 500°F.

4. Beat the eggs, parsley, salt, and pepper together until frothy. Pour this mixture into the skillet, and cook until the eggs begin to set. Do not stir. Lift the edges of the egg with a spatula, and let the uncooked egg from the top run to the bottom of the pan.

5. Sprinkle the top of the eggs with the cheese, and place under the broiler for 2 to 3 minutes. The top will puff up slightly and the cheese will melt and turn golden. Cut in wedges like a pizza and serve hot, right from the pan.

Baked Artichoke Hearts
Carciofi Cotto

Serves 4 to 6

Fresh artichokes are plentiful and inexpensive in the spring. Then they are trimmed, stuffed, and braised. Home cooks used canned artichoke hearts when the vegetable is out of season.

   3 (14-ounce) cans artichoke hearts
   1 extra-large egg, well beaten with 1 tablespoon water
   1/2 cup dried bread crumbs
   1 to 2 tablespoons olive oil
   1/4 cup grated mozzarella
   2 tablespoons grated Parmigiano-Reggiano cheese

1. Rinse the artichoke hearts under cold running water. Cut each one in half. Drain on paper towels.

2. Dip the artichoke hearts into the egg wash, and then into the bread crumbs, in that order, shaking off any excess coating.

3. Over medium-high heat, heat enough olive oil to film a large skillet. Add the artichoke hearts and cook on all sides for 1 to 2 minutes. They will be lightly golden. Drain on paper towels.

4. Place the artichoke hearts in a baking dish in a single layer. Sprinkle with the cheeses. Bake in a 375°F oven for 7 to 10 minutes. The cheese will melt and bubble. Serve hot.

Braised Mushrooms

Funghi

Serves 6

My mother always put this on a holiday table.

2 tablespoons olive oil
1 clove garlic, peeled and split
1 1/2 pounds large white mushrooms, thickly sliced
1/4 cup Quick Tomato Sauce (see recipe, page 141)
1/3 cup red wine
Salt and freshly ground black pepper

1. Heat a large skillet over medium-high heat. Swirl in the olive oil to film the bottom. Add the garlic. Cook for about 3 minutes, until the garlic is lightly golden, not browned. Discard the garlic.

2. Add mushrooms to the pan. Cook for 3 to 5 minutes. Lower the heat. Add the tomato sauce and wine. Cook, covered, for about 15 minutes.

3. Remove the cover. Cook, uncovered for 5 to 10 minutes more, until the mushrooms are melded with the sauce. Serve hot.

Oven-Roasted Potatoes

Patate Arrosti

Serves 6

My cousins dubbed these "Auntie's Potatoes" because my mother makes them for every family gathering. They are perfect with roasted chicken, beef, or lamb basted with olive oil, garlic, and herbs.

    3 pounds russet potatoes
    1/4 cup olive oil
    Salt and freshly ground black pepper
    2 or 3 sprigs fresh rosemary or fresh thyme

1. Preheat the oven to 425°F.

2. Cut the potatoes into 4 to 6 wedges lengthwise, depending on their size.

3. Toss the potatoes, olive oil, salt, pepper, and herb sprigs in a bowl so that the potatoes are coated. Turn them onto a sheet pan in a single layer.

4. Transfer them to the oven. Turn the heat down to 400°F and cook for 20 to 25 minutes. Turn them to brown evenly on all sides. Roast for about 30 minutes longer. They will be golden brown. Serve them hot surrounding roasted meat.

USING DRIED ROSEMARY

If you cannot find fresh rosemary, finely chop 2 teaspoons dried rosemary with a little coarse salt. The salt keeps the brittle herbs from jumping around on the cutting board. You probably won't need to add salt with the pepper in that case.

Ricotta Pie

Pastiera

Makes one 10-inch pie

When my grandaunt, Zia Antonetta Petrilo, passed away, no one knew how to make her Easter pie. Then, one day as I flipped through the pages of Mary Ann Esposito's *Ciao Italia: Bringing Italy Home*, there it was, neatly written down. And the results were just like Zia's! Mary Ann was kind enough to allow me to adapt the recipe here. It may seem long, but making this annual treat is not difficult.

Dough

2 cups sifted all-purpose flour
1 cup cake flour
1 1/2 teaspoons salt
2 tablespoons sugar
8 tablespoons (1 stick) cold unsalted butter, cut into bits
1 extra large egg, slightly beaten, plus 1 egg yolk
5 to 6 tablespoons ice water

Filling

1 cup long-grain rice
2 cups whole milk
3-inch piece of vanilla bean, slit lengthwise
1 pound ricotta cheese, well drained
3 large eggs
1/4 cup freshly squeezed orange juice
2 tablespoons grated orange zest
1 cup sugar
1 tablespoon vanilla extract
1 1/2 teaspoons cinnamon

1. Lightly spray a 10-inch tart pan with removable bottom with butter spray. Set aside.

2. To make the dough by hand or in a food processor, mix together the all-purpose and cake flours, salt, and sugar. Work in the butter. Add the whole egg and enough ice water so that the mixture forms a soft dough. It should not be dry. Gather the dough into a ball. Wrap it tightly in plastic wrap, and refrigerate it for 30 minutes.

3. To make the filling, pour the rice and milk into a small saucepan. Scrape the seeds from the vanilla bean into the pan. Cover the pan and bring it to a boil over medium-high heat. Reduce the heat to medium low. Continue barely simmering for about 10 minutes, until all the liquid is absorbed. Set the rice aside to cool.

4. Beat together the ricotta cheese, eggs, orange juice, zest, and sugar in a large bowl. Stir in the vanilla extract and cinnamon. Fold in the cooled rice, and set aside.

5. Preheat the oven to 375°F. Lightly flour a work surface.

6. To assemble the pie, divide the dough in half. Roll it out into two 14-inch circles. Line the tart pan with one circle of dough. Trim the edges even with the top of the pan. Fill this shell with the ricotta and rice filling. There may be more filling than you need.

7. Roll the second circle of dough over the rolling pin and unroll it over the top of the filled tart. Trim off any excess dough and pinch the edges to seal. Use any leftover dough to decorate the top.

8. Brush the top dough with egg yolk.

9. Place the tart on the middle shelf of the oven. Bake for about 40 to 50 minutes. The top will be golden brown and a skewer pierced into the center will be clean.

10. Place on a rack to cool. Remove the sides of the tart pan. Serve cut in wedges.

Italian Ice

Granita di Limone

Serves 8 to 10

You'll always find Italian ice, or "slush," at outdoor festivals like the Topsfield Fair. This authentic recipe uses freshly squeezed lemon juice, which is fairly easy to do with an auto-matic juicer. The slush is just as delicious served in paper cones as in champagne glasses.

4 cups water
2 cups sugar
2 cups freshly squeezed lemon juice
Finely grated zest of 2 lemons

1. Bring the water and the sugar to a boil in a medium saucepan. Cook, stirring constantly, for 5 to 7 minutes. The sugar will be dissolved.

2. Pour the mixture into a glass baking dish. Set it aside to cool to room temperature.

3. Stir in the lemon juice and zest. Freeze for about 30 min-utes. Remove and stir. Return to the freezer, removing and stirring it whenever you think of it, about once an hour for the next 2 hours. Freeze 8 hours or longer.

4. Remove from the freezer, and scrape the frozen mixture out of the dish with the tines of a fork so that it resembles snow. Pile it into paper cones or champagne glasses with a twist of lemon peel and a sprig of mint.

THE JEWISH TRADITION

From Grandma's Chicken Soup to the Deli Counter

Jewish immigrants arrived on the North Shore with people of other faiths from Russia, Poland, Germany, and Eastern Europe throughout the twentieth century. Settling in Lynn, Swampscott, Marblehead, and later Peabody, they nestled homes and cultural centers close around a central temple or synagogue because orthodox Jews do not operate machinery on the Sabbath and therefore walk to religious services. More recent immigrants to the North Shore, having lived in Soviet states, arrived with a different history but similar traditions revolving around their religious beliefs and family life. These priorities intersected with culinary traditions during the Shabbat, or Sabbath, holiday.

Jewish culinary traditions are, first of all, guided by the laws of *kashrut*, known as keeping kosher. People who keep kosher separate meat and dairy for example, and abstain from shellfish and the meat of certain animals. The foods also reflect the country of origin. The most familiar culinary traditions are Ashkenazic, or from Eastern European countries from which Jews immigrated. Familiar dishes from this tradition—such as chopped chicken liver, knishes, latkes, bagels and lox, and pickles—have long been available at delicatessens. Other foods are associated with holidays, such as matzoh with Passover.

More recent immigrants are bringing recipes from the Sephardic traditions of countries in and around the Mediterranean. With them, a whole new palate is beginning to reach the dining room table.

Hanukkah

Hanukkah, the Festival of Lights, is observed during the darkening days of December. The holiday commemorates the 2,000-year-old miracle of oil that burned for eight days when the lamps were relit in the Jerusalem Temple. Each evening, usually before dinner, a candle is lit on the menorah, a candelabra specially designed for the holiday, and children open small gifts. The most well-known course is latkes, potato pancakes cooked in oil, that children relish with applesauce and adults with sour cream. Traditional, seasonal foods surround the latkes to round out a meal, many of the desserts geared to the children's palates and adults' memories.

MENU FOR HANUKKAH

Chicken Soup

Brisket

Potato Latkes with Applesauce

Hanukkah Fritters

Acorn Squash Stuffed with
Dried Winter Fruits

Festive Gelatin Mold

Ice Cream Pie

A North Shore Cook: Barbara Schneider

Anyone who meets Barbara Schneider is attracted to the warmth of her manner—and her perfect smile. Her husband is a dentist, after all. She becomes a second mother to her daughters' friends, staff members, and the college interns who work in her office. Once a full-time mom and homemaker, Barbara focused on her home, family, and community—then her daughters grew up and she went to work on Beacon Hill. The job was something of a homecoming. As a college student, she had interned in the office of Michael Dukakis, then a legislator and later governor and presidential candidate.

On the North Shore, Barbara remains an anchor in the Marblehead Jewish community, active in charitable and cultural events. Family and friends rely on her hospitality at Rosh Hashanah, Yom Kippur, Hanukkah, and Passover.

"The most interesting thing about food is that it's one of the ways we carry on our culture. When I grew up, the holidays were centered around food. My mother was an average cook, but holiday meals were always her best efforts. We looked forward to apples and honey at Rosh Hashanah, latkes at Hanukkah, and flourless chocolate cake at Passover.

"The Sabbath was the holiday of the week. When people were poor, they saved the best meal for the eve of the Sabbath. Friday night dinner was chicken soup, challah, and roasted chicken. Families who didn't keep kosher had *kugel*, noodle pudding, with their chicken. Kosher households saved it for Saturday lunch, traditionally a dairy meal."

Schneider's grandparents' roots were in Eastern Europe, the Ashkenazi tradition. Barbara grew up on dishes characterized by sour cream, smoked fish, and beets. She recalls Friday nights when she and her husband were dating and he had recently been introduced to her family.

"David came to the *Shabbas* meal. It was a formal sit-down dinner, in our dining room with our best china and linens and three or four courses beginning with soup. For the occasion my mother made beet soup, *borscht*, instead of her usual chicken soup, and David commented that he liked it. So borscht became a Friday night staple until we begged her to go back to our favorite chicken soup. But she did that only after David assured her that he liked it just as well as the beet.

"Passover is a difficult menu because you can't use wheat. You know, matzoh comes from our people's suffering in the desert. They made unleavened bread. Today we try to make it taste good, and it's a challenge! The best part of the meal is the *haroset*, a very personal recipe to each household. There are the basic apples, walnuts, and wine, but everyone changes the recipe to suit their family's tastes. I have a friend who adds dates. I try it differently every year.

The flourless chocolate cake from Passover has cut across cultural lines and entered the mainstream. You find it on the menu at upscale restaurants now."

The winter Festival of Lights is Schneider's favorite holiday menu. "Most Christians have been invited to a Passover meal, so they are conversant with that holiday, but no one seems to know about Hanukkah. Everyone knows the latkes, and the candles, but not the rest. If you really want to educate people about Jewish cooking, then tell them about Hanukkah.

"Hanukkah is a children's holiday, so what children like to eat is central to the menu. It runs over eight days, and we choose a weekend night for the most festive dinner, so everyone can relax and enjoy it.

"Brisket is the centerpiece of the meal. I make a stuffed acorn squash based on the ingredients in *tsimmis,* a Rosh Hashanah dish made with dried fruits and winter squash or carrots or sweet potatoes. My kids never liked *tsimmis,* but when I tucked the same dried fruits into an acorn squash, they lit up. It looks beautiful on a platter surrounding the brisket.

"My mother always made a sour cream coffee cake. I make ice cream pie. My kids still like that."

Schneider always expects a crowd at the holiday table. Friends and neighbors who don't have family living nearby are included. She goes to great lengths to make everyone feel welcome and has been known to research guests' family recipes so they appear on the holiday table.

"Today, it's so easy to buy holiday foods. For instance, for the break-the-fast meal on Yom Kippur, I can pick up a platter with the different cold fishes, some white fish, some lox, bagels, and cream cheese. Some one always brings a Jell-O mold. I can spend my time enjoying the company of people I love."

THE RECIPES

Chopped Liver

Chicken Soup with
Matzoh Balls

Shabbat Roasted Chicken

Roasted Brisket

Stuffed Acorn Squash

Winter Fruits

Sweet Potato and
Carrot *Tsimmis*

Potato Latkes

Hanukkah Fritters

Potato Dumplings with Dried
Plums

Challah (Egg Bread)

Pineapple and Cottage
Cheese Noodle Pudding

Butterscotch Noodle Pudding

Ice Cream Pie with
Fudge Topping

Festive Gelatin Mold

Flourless Chocolate Cake

Chopped Liver

Serves 8

Zelda Tasman of Swampscott is fondly remembered by friends and family for her chopped liver. Her daughter, Hope Zabar, carries a vivid recollection: "She had this grinder, the type that clamped onto the kitchen counter—I don't think anyone uses them anymore—and she would grind everything up in it. The texture was particularly creamy. Everyone complimented her on it and asked Mom to bring it for the holidays. Even after she bought a food processor, my mother still made her chopped liver by hand. I always suspected that she had a secret ingredient. I know now that it was just the care that she always took with her best dish."

Zabar thinks that this is a fairly close adaptation of her mother's recipe. A few home cooks incorporate a trace of creamy peanut butter for texture, so it appears as an option here. I resorted to the food processor for ease.

    2 tablespoons vegetable oil
    1 large onion, coarsely chopped
    1 pound chicken livers, cleaned
    3 to 4 large hard-cooked eggs, coarsely chopped
    6 Ritz crackers, crumbled
    1 tablespoon mayonnaise, more or less to taste
    1 teaspoon creamy peanut butter, optional
    Salt and freshly ground black pepper
    Tomatoes, cucumbers, radishes, dill pickles, matzoh
        crackers, cocktail rye bread, for garnish

1. Heat a large skillet over medium heat. Add the oil and warm. Add the onion. Cook, stirring often, 7 to 10 minutes, until the onion is wilted and deeply golden. Remove the onion from the skillet with a slotted spoon, pouring off most of the oil but leaving some to coat the skillet. Set aside.

2. Add the chicken livers to the skillet. Cook, turning often, 5 to 7 minutes. Cut one liver in half to be sure that the interior is cooked. Cool to room temperature.

3. Blend the onion, liver, hard-cooked eggs, and crackers in a food processor or blender. Add half the mayonnaise, peanut butter (if using), salt, and pepper. Continue blending until the mixture is smooth, adding the remaining mayonnaise if you wish. Pile the mixture into the center of a serving plate and surround with tomato and cucumber wedges, radishes, pickles, and matzoh crackers or cocktail rye bread.

Chicken Soup with Matzoh Balls

Serves 8

It seems everyone has heard chicken soup called Jewish penicillin, the cure or at least symptom reliever for colds and flu. In fact, scientists have recently verified that there is some truth to Grandmother's wisdom.

Since this is a clear soup with either egg noodles or matzoh balls, it's best to start with chicken pieces. Wings, backs, and legs have a large amount of bone to add nutrients and body to the stock, and no one feels bad about throwing them out.

The parsnips and dill in the ingredient listing are the clue to this soup's Eastern European, Ashkenazi, heritage. Jewish cooks who have lived in Israel often use different flavorings, such as garlic, tomatoes, cilantro, and cumin.

SCHMALTZ

Vegetable or olive oils were scarce in Eastern Europe, so cooks substituted chicken fat, also called *schmaltz*, as a cooking medium. The fat needed to be cut from several chickens, then rendered by cooking it slowly, with onion for flavor, until it reduced to a liquid. The fat was strained and cooled before using. Because of health concerns and the number of more convenient cooking mediums, schmaltz is rarely used today.

    3 1/2 pounds chicken wings, legs, or backs
    2 parsnips, peeled and cut into large chunks
    2 carrots, peeled and cut into large chunks
    2 ribs celery, cut into 1/2-inch pieces
    1 large onion, quartered
    1 bunch parsley

1 small bunch dill
Kosher salt, to taste
Freshly ground black pepper
Matzoh Balls (recipe follows) or egg noodles

1. Rinse the chicken pieces in cold water and place them in a large soup pot. Pour in cold water to cover. Bring the pot to a boil over high heat. Reduce the heat to medium high and keep the pot at a healthy bubble. With a slotted spoon, skim off the foamy residue that rises to the surface. Cook for 5 to 15 minutes.

2. Add the parsnips, carrots, celery, and onion. Return the soup to a boil. Then turn the heat down to medium. Keep it at a steady simmer.

3. Tie the parsley and dill together. Add them to the soup. Season with salt and pepper. Simmer for 1½ to 2 hours, or until the chicken is tender.

4. Strain the soup, discarding everything but the liquid. Cool and refrigerate for at least 30 minutes.

5. Remove from the refrigerator, and scrape the hardened layer of fat from the surface with a spoon.

6. Bring the soup back to a lively simmer to cook matzoh balls or egg noodles.

Matzoh Balls

Serves 6 to 8

Where you see vegetable oil in the ingredient list, once there was *schmaltz,* rendered chicken fat. Many modern cooks further lighten this recipe by substituting 4 beaten-to-a-froth egg whites for the 2 large eggs.

2 tablespoons vegetable or canola oil
2 tablespoons finely chopped onion
2 large eggs beaten with 1 tablespoon water
3/4 cup fine matzoh meal
3 tablespoons finely chopped fresh parsley
Salt and freshly ground black pepper

1. Heat the oil in a small skillet over medium-high heat. Add the onion, and cook 2 to 3 minutes, until wilted and lightly golden. Take the skillet off the heat and set aside to cool.

2. Stir in the eggs, matzoh meal, parsley, and salt and pepper to taste. Set it aside to rest for 10 minutes. Using wet hands, shape the mixture into balls, about 1½ to 2 inches in diameter.

3. Bring the chicken soup to a boil. Drop the matzoh balls into the boiling soup. Simmer for 20 to 25 minutes. The matzoh balls will float to the top when they are cooked.

STUFFING

If you stuff a chicken, it will need more cooking time. It's easier to cook stuffing alongside the chicken in a separate pan, spooning some of the chicken's cooking juices from the bottom of the roasting pan onto the stuffing.

Shabbat Roasted Chicken

Serves 6 to 8

Roasted chicken is the centerpiece of a typical Friday night, or Sabbath, dinner in Jewish homes. In the 1950s and 1960s, home cooks found that seasoned salt lent a certain sophistication and ease to flavoring food.

> 3½- to 4-pound roasting chicken
> 2 tablespoons vegetable oil
> 1½ teaspoons Lawry's seasoned salt
> Freshly ground black pepper
> Few sprigs fresh sage, rosemary, thyme, optional
> 1 cup chicken stock or water, more if needed

1. Preheat the oven to 375°F. Wash the chicken inside and out. Pat it dry.

2. Rub the oil over the outside of the chicken. Sprinkle with seasoned salt and pepper.

3. Place herbs, if using, on the bottom of a roasting pan. Set the chicken, breast side down, on the herbs. Place the roasting pan in the oven. Immediately turn the heat down to 350°F, and cook for about 30 minutes.

4. Remove the chicken from the oven. Turn it breast side up in the roasting pan. Pour the chicken stock (or water) into the bottom of the pan. Return the pan to the oven for 55 to 60 minutes. An instant-read thermometer pierced into the thickest part of the thigh will read 160°F, and the juices will run clear at the thigh joint.

5. Transfer the chicken to a serving platter and carve it into serving pieces. Juices from the roasting pan may be strained and served alongside.

Roasted Brisket

Serves 8

Brisket, or pot roast, is a staple on the Jewish-American table. The slowly cooked caramelized onions are a traditional flavoring for the meat, but most home cooks put their own signature on this dish, perhaps using a beef broth or spicing homemade or canned stock with wine. Tomato paste is sometimes changed to ketchup; the seasoned salt here might be marjoram to another cook.

    2 to 3 tablespoons vegetable oil
    4 large yellow onions, thinly sliced
    5-pound flat brisket, trimmed
    2 cups chicken stock
    1 pound carrots, thinly sliced
    1 tablespoon tomato paste
    1/2 cup orange juice
    1/4 cup sweet paprika
    1 teaspoon Lawry's Seasoned Salt
    Freshly ground black pepper

1. Warm the vegetable oil in a large, heavy skillet over medium heat. Add the onions and cook for 30 to 35 minutes, stirring from time to time, and turning the heat down if the onions begin to singe. The onions will be deeply colored and very tender, not crispy.

2. Preheat the oven to 350°F.

3. Place the brisket in a deep roasting pan. Pour the stock into the bottom of the pan. Add the carrots, onions, tomato paste, orange juice, paprika, seasoned salt, and pepper to the pan. Cover tightly with aluminum foil. Place in the oven for 2½ to 3 hours.

CUTTING HARD-SHELLED WINTER SQUASH

Barbara Schneider makes quick work of hard-to-peel acorn squash. First she deeply pierces the exterior shell all over with a large cooking fork. A table fork is too delicate. Then she places it in her microwave for as long as it takes to soften the shell without turning the insides mushy. The time in the microwave will vary depending on your model, so start with 10 to 20 seconds and work the time up gradually if you need it.

4. Allow the roast to rest on a cutting board for about 15 minutes.

5. Slice the meat against the grain into ½-inch slices. Return the meat and juices to the pan. Return the pan to the oven and cook, uncovered, for about 30 minutes longer. It will be meltingly tender. Serve hot.

Stuffed Acorn Squash

Serves 6

This is a wonderful recipe to pair with brisket throughout the autumn and winter holidays. Barbara Schneider also makes a "kid-pleasing" version using 3 teaspoons of brown sugar and 1½ cups of applesauce in place of the dried fruits.

3 medium acorn squash
¼ cup maple syrup
1½ teaspoons butter, cut in equal pieces
1½ cups dried pitted plums and apricots, mixed

1. Preheat the oven to 400°F. Slice the squash in half lengthwise. Remove the seeds.

2. Place the squash halves on a baking sheet, cut side up. Drizzle each with 1 teaspoon maple syrup and place ¼ teaspoon butter on each half. Place the baking sheet in the oven for 20 minutes.

3. Remove the squash from the oven. Fill the cavities with the dried plums and apricots. Drizzle the tops evenly with the remaining maply syrup. Bake for 20 minutes longer.

4. Serve the squash on a platter around a brisket.

Sweet Potato and Carrot *Tsimmis*

Serves 6 to 8

The word *tsimmis* translates approximately as "a lot of fuss," but most people who taste it will agree that the fuss is worthwhile.

3 medium sweet potatoes, peeled, and cut into
    1-inch chunks
8 carrots, cut into 1-inch chunks
1 cup mixed dried pitted plums, apricots, and apples,
    plumped in boiling water
$\frac{1}{3}$ cup honey
3 tablespoons butter
$\frac{1}{2}$ cup orange juice
1 tablespoon grated lemon zest
Kosher salt

1. Preheat the oven to 350°F.

2. Combine the potatoes, carrots, dried fruit, honey, butter, orange juice, lemon zest, and salt in a large Dutch oven. Cover. Bake for about 1½ hours, until the potatoes and carrots are tender.

3. Uncover and continue baking for about 20 to 30 minutes, or until the liquid is nearly evaporated. Serve hot.

KOSHER COMMERCIAL PRODUCTS

The circled U on the package of a commercial food product certifies that it has been prepared according to kosher specifications and inspected by the Union of Orthodox Jewish Congregations.

Potato Latkes

Serves 4

Latke is the Yiddish word for pancakes. Latkes are the happily anticipated highlight of a Hanukkah celebration. Traditionally served hot with sour cream or applesauce, today's innovative home cooks also make them from carrots, sweet potatoes, spinach, mushrooms, or any number of vegetables. And toppings can include yogurt, jam, or even salsa.

    4 russet potatoes
    1 tablespoon grated onion
    1 large egg
    1/3 cup all-purpose flour
    3/4 teaspoon salt
    Vegetable oil for frying

1. Peel the potatoes. Grate very finely.

2. Toss the onion, egg, flour, and salt with the grated potatoes until well blended.

3. Heat about ½ inch of vegetable oil in a large skillet over medium-high heat. Place heaping tablespoons of batter into the skillet, gently so the hot oil does not splash. Gently press the batter down to flatten. Cook for 3 to 5 minutes on each side, until the pancakes are crisp and brown.

4. Drain on absorbent paper towels. Serve hot with applesauce, sour cream, or other favorite toppings.

Hanukkah Fritters

Makes 10 to 12 fritters

Liora Kelman speaks four languages, including *Ladino,* a weaving of Mediterranean tongues spoken by Sephardic Jews. The elegant mother of three, a former commandant in the Israeli army, has traveled extensively and is known for her international cooking classes, often taught with her husband, Rabbi Avraham Kelman.

Along with traditional *latke,* the Kelmans make these Sephardic-style fritters, deep-fried in oil, at Hanukkah. The recipe can be doubled easily.

1 package (2 1/2 teaspoons) active dry yeast
1 cup lukewarm water
2 cups all-purpose flour
1 large egg, beaten
2 tablespoons canola oil, plus more oil
    for deep-frying
1 cup water
1/2 cup sugar
3 tablespoons freshly squeezed lemon juice

1. Set the oven at 200°F. Stir the yeast and water together in a large bowl. Gradually add the flour, egg, and 2 tablespoons of oil. Knead the dough right in the bowl. It will be smooth, soft, and elastic.

2. Oil the inside of a bowl. Place the dough in the bowl. Set it in a warm place for 1 hour. It will double in bulk.

3. To make the lemon syrup, bring the water and sugar to a boil in a saucepan. Simmer, stirring, for 5 minutes. The sugar will be dissolved. Pour the syrup into a bowl. Set it aside to cool to room temperature. When the mixture has cooled, stir in the lemon juice.

DRIED PLUMS

If you are no longer able to find a box of prunes in the grocery store, it's because they're going under a new moniker, "dried plums." The California-based industry is glitzing up the product's stodgy image.

4. Fill a large, deep pot about halfway with oil for deep-frying. Heat the oil to 375°F.

5. Scoop up several heaping teaspoonfuls of the dough. Gently slide them, one at a time, into the oil. Do not crowd the pot. The fritters will puff up to nearly double in size. Turn them, after a minute or two, to cook on the other side. Remove the fritters from the pot with a slotted spoon and set them on paper towels to drain. Place the cooked fritters on a baking sheet in the oven while you finish cooking the batch.

6. Place the fritters on a serving platter and drizzle them with the lemon syrup.

Potato Dumplings with Dried Plums

Serves 4 to 6

Liora Kelman never fails to cook this favorite family recipe at Hanukkah.

    1 pound russet potatoes, cooked and peeled
    5 tablespoons butter, at room temperature
    1 large egg, slightly beaten
    1 cup all-purpose flour
    1/2 teaspoon salt
    8 ounces pitted dried plums, chopped
    1/2 cup fresh bread crumbs
    Sugar
    Ground cinnamon

1. Mash the potatoes. Set aside to cool.

2. Mash 3 tablespoons of the butter, the egg, flour, and salt into the potatoes. Work the mixture into a dough. Shape the

dough into a rope about 1 inch in diameter. Cut the rope into pieces about 2 inches long. Poke a hole into each piece of dough with a finger. Stuff a piece of dried plum into the hole, and fold it into the dough.

3. Bring a large pot of water to a boil. Drop a few of the dumplings into the water. Cook for about 30 seconds. The dumplings will float to the surface. Remove them with a slotted spoon and place on a warmed serving plate.

4. Melt the remaining 2 tablespoons of butter in a skillet over medium heat. Add the bread crumbs. Cook for 3 to 5 minutes, until the crumbs are lightly golden. Toss with sugar and cinnamon to taste. Sprinkle over dumplings and serve.

Challah

Egg Bread

Makes 2 loaves

Challah, along with roasted chicken, is a staple at the Friday night meal that brings in the Sabbath. Most families buy their challah; however, from time to time, someone finds a grandmother's dog-eared recipe card tucked in the back of a kitchen drawer.

1 1/2 packages active dry yeast
1/2 cup plus 1 tablespoon sugar
1 3/4 cups lukewarm water
1 3/4 cups vegetable oil
5 large eggs
1 tablespoon salt
8 cups all-purpose flour
Poppy seeds, for top

1. Dissolve the yeast and 1 tablespoon sugar in the luke-warm water. Flour a work surface. Oil the interior of a large bowl.

2. Whisk the oil and yeast mixture together. Gradually beat in 4 of the eggs, then the remaining sugar and the salt. Add flour, about ½ cup at a time. The mixture will form a dough. Shape the dough into a ball. Place it on the work surface and knead until it is smooth.

3. Place the dough in the oiled bowl. Cover with plastic wrap. Set aside to rise in a warm place, about 1 hour. It will nearly double in bulk. Punch down the dough. Cover with a towel. Set aside to rise, about 30 minutes.

4. Use half the dough to form 6 balls. Roll each ball into a rope, about 12 inches long and 1½ inches wide. Place the 6 in a row, parallel to one another. Braid the ropes together, two at a time, until you reach the ends. To make a straight loaf, tuck the ends of the braids underneath. To make a round loaf, twist the braid into a circle and pinch the ends together. Repeat this for the other half of the dough, making a second loaf.

5. Preheat the oven to 375°F. Grease a baking sheet.

6. Place both loaves on the baking sheet, leaving at least 2 inches between them. Make an egg wash by beating the last egg with a drop or two of water. Brush this mixture onto the loaves. Sprinkle the poppy seeds over the wet egg wash so that they stick.

7. Bake for 35 to 40 minutes. The crust will be golden. Cool the bread on a rack before bringing it to the table.

Pineapple and Cottage Cheese Noodle Pudding

Kugel

Serves 10

Barbara Schneider's pineapple and cottage cheese kugel evolved when she inadvertently forgot to buy the sour cream for her mother's original recipe. "At the last minute, all I could do was double the cottage cheese and hope for the best. Everyone liked it so much that I never went back to the original. Then I started using cottage cheese with pineapple already in it. Now I have one less can to open!" she laughs.

1 pound wide egg noodles
1/2 cup (1 stick) butter, melted
1/2 cup sugar
1/2 cup raisins
4 large eggs, beaten
8 ounces low-fat cottage cheese with pineapple
1/2 teaspoon salt
Ground cinnamon
1/2 cup crushed sugar- or honey-coated cornflakes

1. Preheat the oven to 350°F. Butter a 2-quart baking dish.

2. Cook the noodles in a large pot of boiling salted water for 2 to 3 minutes less than directed on the package. They will be tender but still firm. Drain.

3. In a large bowl, toss the noodles with the butter, sugar, raisins, eggs, cottage cheese, salt, and cinnamon to taste. Spread in the baking dish. Scatter the cornflakes evenly over the top.

4. Bake for about 1 hour. The top will be golden. Serve warm in the baking dish.

Butterscotch Noodle Pudding
Kugel

Serves 6 to 8

Kugel brings out the creativity in cooks. I first tasted this noodle pudding at a Superbowl party, where I met Nancy Rozen of Swampscott. Mrs. Rozen's mother created the recipe adapted here many years ago, and it's part of every family celebration. (The New England Patriots didn't win that year, but made up for it at a later Superbowl.)

1 pound wide egg noodles
1/4 cup (1/2 stick) butter, cut into small pieces
3/4 cup sour cream
4 large eggs, beaten
Salt and freshly ground black pepper
1 pound butterscotch chips

1. Preheat the oven to 350°F. Butter a 2-quart oven-to-table baking dish.

2. Cook the noodles in a large pot of boiling water for 2 to 3 minutes less than directed on the package. They will be tender but still firm. Drain.

3. In a large bowl, whisk the butter, sour cream, eggs, and salt and pepper to taste. Toss gently with the noodles and pile into a baking dish. Scatter the butterscotch bits over the top.

4. Bake for about 30 minutes. Remove the baking dish from the oven. Toss the noodles gently. Return the dish to the oven and bake for 30 minutes more. Serve hot right from the baking dish.

Ice Cream Pie with Fudge Topping

Serves 6 to 8

Barbara Schneider's favorite ice cream pie, which I've adapted, leaves plenty of room for improvisation. You can choose any flavor or combination of flavors of ice cream or frozen yogurt to place in the chocolate cookie crust. Barbara recommends Heath Bars, but I'm sure that another favorite candy bar would also be delicious. You can make the pie well in advance and keep it in the freezer.

Crust

3 cups chocolate cookie crumbs
1/2 cup melted butter

Filling

2 quarts any flavor ice cream, or frozen yogurt,
    softened
6 Heath candy bars, coarsely chopped

Topping (Fudge Sauce)

6 squares unsweetened chocolate
2 tablespoons margarine or butter
1 1/2 cups sugar
2 cups evaporated milk
Nuts, jimmies, cherries, etc., for garnish

1. To make the crust, toss together the chocolate cookie crumbs and the melted butter in a bowl. With your fingers, press them into the bottom and up the sides of a springform pan. Place in the freezer for 30 to 60 minutes.

2. To make the filling, smooth 1 quart of the ice cream or frozen yogurt into the pie shell. Sprinkle a layer of chopped Heath Bars over the ice cream. Smooth the remaining quart of softened ice cream over the Heath Bar layer. Wrap in plastic wrap, and freeze at least 2 hours.

UNMOLDING GELATIN

Gelatin molds can be tricky, sometimes sticking so tightly that you wonder if they grew suction cups, other times becoming too slippery to be held. Here are some tips for easy removal:

- Use a little less water, about one-quarter less, than the package directs.
- Spray the mold with cooking spray.
- Fill the mold all the way to the top.
- Be sure the gelatin has completely solidified before unmolding it.
- Dip the mold in warm water for 15 seconds.
- Gently slip a knife between the gelatin and the mold to pop the airlock.

3. To make the topping, melt together the unsweetened chocolate and butter in the top of a double boiler over simmering, not boiling, water. As it melts, stir in the sugar. Gradually add the evaporated milk, stirring constantly. Continue cooking, stirring occasionally, for 10 to 15 minutes. The mixture will thicken. Cool completely and refrigerate.

4. To assemble, spread the fudge sauce over the pie, smoothing it into decorative swirls with a spatula. Scatter nuts, jimmies, or other sprinkles over the top. Place in the freezer and remove about 20 minutes before cutting.

Festive Gelatin Mold

Serves 6 to 10

Fruits and vegetables encased in a shimmering rainbow of colors swept the country starting in the early twentieth century, when Fannie Farmer judged a contest run by Knox Gelatine. The salads became the darling of "domestic scientists" and home cooks. Their popularity reached a peak in the 1950s, cheered on by the manufacturer of Jell-O, which promoted its product with recipes on the back of every box.

Barbara Schneider's favorite gelatin mold was made with blackberry Jell-O. Unfortunately, the company discontinued the blackberry flavor, so I've substituted a raspberry one.

3 (3-ounce) packages raspberry instant gelatin
2½ cups boiling water
2 (10-ounce) packages frozen raspberries, thawed
1 (20-ounce) can pineapple chunks in their own juice
4 large bananas

1. Dissolve the gelatin in the water. Cool to room temperature. Stir in the raspberries and pineapple chunks.

2. Divide the mixture into two portions. Set one half aside at room temperature. Pour the other half into a 2-quart decorative mold. Refrigerate for about 30 minutes. It will be nearly set.

3. Slice the banana into rounds. Layer them on top of the nearly set mixture. Pour the remaining mixture on top. Cover and refrigerate 4 to 8 hours. Unmold shortly before serving.

Flourless Chocolate Cake

Serves 6 to 8

Jewish hostesses brought this luscious chocolate cake to prominence, until it entered the mainstream and became a restaurant staple. Instead of wheat flour, which is not eaten at Passover, the cake uses ground walnuts and potato starch.

  1 cup walnuts
  8 tablespoons sugar
  5 ounces semisweet chocolate, chopped
  2 tablespoons orange juice
  1/2 cup unsalted butter or margarine
  4 large eggs, separated
  1 teaspoon grated orange zest
  2 tablespoons potato starch
  Confectioners' sugar, optional

1. Preheat the oven to 325°F. Grease an 8-inch springform pan. Cut a circle of parchment paper to fit into the bottom of the pan. Grease the paper as well.

2. Grind the walnuts finely in a food processor with 2 tablespoons of the sugar. Set aside.

KOSHER GELATIN

Before the creation of one of America's first con-venience products, Jell-O, making natural gelatin was a time-consuming, messy process involving boiling down animal parts. Calves'-foot jelly, *petcha*, an aspic filled with meat and hard-boiled eggs, was a traditional if labor-intensive dish. Modern cooks have neither time nor access to fresh kosher animal parts to continue making this dish; however, colorful gelatin molds are very much a part of the Jewish-American holiday menu. Orthodox Jews use a kosher gelatin product, Kojel, available in specialty markets and increasingly in supermarkets.

3. Melt chocolate with the orange juice in the top of a double boiler over barely simmering water. Stir until smooth. Add the butter. Stir until blended. Set chocolate mixture aside to cool.

4. Whisk together the egg yolks. Gradually whisk the egg yolks into the chocolate. Stir in 4 tablespoons of the sugar, the orange zest, walnuts, and potato starch.

5. Beat the egg whites until they are softly peaked. Beat in the remaining 2 tablespoons sugar into the egg whites, beating until stiff and shiny. Gently fold the egg whites into the chocolate mixture. There still may be fluffy white patches in the chocolate. That's okay. Spread the batter evenly in the pan.

6. Bake for 40 to 45 minutes, until a knife inserted into the center comes out clean.

7. Cool in the pan for about 10 minutes. Loosen the cake with a knife inserted between the cake and the pan. Gently invert onto a rack and dislodge the pan. Remove the paper. Cool the cake before placing best side up on a platter to serve. It may be dusted lightly with confectioners' sugar.

THE GREEK TRADITION
From Easter Lamb to Summer Picnics

The North Shore was a haven for Greek immigrants throughout the twentieth century. Work in factories and gardens provided a new beginning for many immigrants, but others found more satisfaction in various aspects of the food business, from cooking and serving to manufacturing a variety of food products. Restaurants like the Commodore in Beverly specialized in "continental" fare such as prime rib and baked stuffed shrimp, and homier places—such as Moutsakas in Salem, for example, where Greek owners advertised for "plain Irish cooks"—became fixtures on the North Shore landscape. More and more newcomers opened sandwich shops on busy city corners, where ethnic specialties, such as hot souvlaki wrapped in pita bread and the ubiquitous Greek salad, became staples of carry-out lunches. Larger concerns such as Old Neighborhood Meats, founded by Ephthimios Demakis, were family businesses that prospered as purveyors to the restaurants and markets.

Greek immigrants recalled their native culture through churches and Hellenic societies. Today, North Shore residents of Greek heritage look forward to summer events on the lovely Hellenic Picnic Grounds in Ipswich, especially a three-day festival that attracts people of all heritages for wonderful ethnic specialties prepared by professionals and home cooks.

Greek Easter Dinner

Greek-American families celebrate Easter, *Pascha,* with two dinners. The first is held immediately after the church service at midnight, and another on the following day, Easter Sunday itself. The first course may be *mayeritsa,* a traditional Easter soup made with the offal of the lamb. This is followed by *pastistio,* a layered dish of pasta; homemade braided sweet Easter bread; red dyed eggs; and an array of spiced or honey-coated pastries. Some households roast a whole lamb on outdoor grills specially built for the occasion.

"Greek Orthodox Easter is celebrated in accordance with the ancient Julian calendar," explained Tina Karalekas, who grew up on the North Shore. According to that calendar, Easter falls on the first Sunday following the first full moon after the vernal equinox. "This calls for some explanation to friends who often ask why we don't celebrate the holiday with them."

MENU FOR GREEK EASTER

Egg-Lemon Soup

Green Salad

Roasted Leg of Lamb

Baked Pasta

Spinach or Cheese Pie

Grape Leaves with
Egg-Lemon Sauce

Braided Bread

Phyllo and Nut Pastry

THE PANTRY

- **Cinnamon:** Often used in bark form in Greece, the ground variety can be substituted. It flavors sweets and savories alike.

- **Fats and oils:** Greek olive oil is a deep greenish gold color. The extra-virgin unfiltered oil often comes with tiny bits of flavorful olives still in the oil. Use this for salads or cold dishes. Use refined oil when you apply heat to the food. Imported oils are available at specialty shops.

- **Feta cheese:** A crumbly, white sheep's milk cheese, it is slightly pungent and quite salty. It is widely available at supermarket cheese counters as well as at specialty shops.

- **Honey:** This sweetener goes back to Greek myths as a food of the gods. It is used in desserts and even salad dressings.

- **Rigani:** Also called Greek oregano, this herb is stronger and more pungent than the familiar pizza herb. It is available dried in specialty shops and some supermarkets; you can usually find it fresh only in ethnic markets. Oregano may be substituted, but it does not taste quite the same.

- **Yogurt:** Buy plain yogurt, not vanilla-flavored. Most recipes using yogurt will require strained yogurt. Spoon the yogurt into a fine-mesh sieve and allow it to drain for at least 30 minutes, to thicken.

A North Shore Cook:
Barbara Lazarides

Barbara Lazarides' first business venture was so successful that she has stayed at it for 23 years. Immigrating from Greece as a young mother in the mid-1960s, she and her husband, Harry, saved for their own business. When they bought Maria's Pizza on a busy corner in Beverly, they planned to own it for only five years.

"It was going to be my daugher's college tuition, but we liked it so much that it became the family business."

Over the years, her children, Sophia and Paul, slipped behind the counter. Then daughter-in-law, Jeannie, and now a grandson. The shop does a brisk business throughout the day.

Barbara was born in a small village in northern Greece. Her husband's family had been displaced twice during his childhood, and they were ready for the move. She has fond memories of the welcome to their new country.

The ladies of the Philoptohas Thalia Society had an apartment ready and a job waiting for Harry the following day. They found themselves thrust into the center of community life. "They made us feel as if we had moved to a new neighborhood, not a foreign country. We started, right away, to save for our own home," she says.

A trim, spunky woman, Barbara is at her shop 14 hours a day, greeting customers, taking and filling orders, and baking. Although a pizza is always on tap, savvy customers appreciate the homestyle Greek dishes on her menu. Cubes of chicken marinate in aromatic herbs, while fresh balloons of pita emerge from the oven all day. "Pita can accompany anything," she says. "Anything you can put in a roll can go into a pita."

After school, her 17-year-old grandson often joins her. "He loves the business," she says, "and he's good at it. But we want him to get an education, before he makes a decision, like his father. My son," she says proudly, "can do just about anything."

Over the years, their brothers, sisters, and even Barbara's mother have immigrated and spread out over the New England area. They look forward to holidays, especially Easter, when they can all be together.

Barbara recalls that religious holidays were festive in her village. The girls had new red velvet dresses, to distribute baskets of eggs and the men and boys rolled the colored eggs down hillsides.

"My dad died when I was a baby, so I never got a red dress. When we moved here, we found Greeks from all over Greece. Everyone had customs from their towns and villages, so we melded them together.

"But the eggs were the same. Hard-boiled and dyed red. Some people extracted the color from onion skins. There was a trick to it or you would get brown eggs instead of red.

"During the week leading up to Easter, things were done in a certain way. Each day was reserved for a task."

Barbara keeps many customs, but has adapted others. "I bake breads on Friday, color eggs on Thursday. But we no longer slaughter the lambs our-selves. We don't want the children to see it. We buy newly slaughtered lambs from a farm up north."

Barbara prepares the first festive meal for after the Saturday night resur-rec-tion service, The meal begins after midnight Barbara had the traditional lamb soup from the offal—tripe, intestines, tongue, heart, liver—flavored with dill, parsley, scallions, and fennel - ready when they bring in their candles still lit from church. Before serving, she swirls in her egg-lemon sauce or tomato sauce.

Early Sunday morning, the men start the outdoor grill. As the fire burn, they slowly turn the two lambs on the spit until early afternoon.

"We do two whole lambs, about 38 to 40 pounds, small enough to be tender. We whisk up olive oil seasoned with lemon, salt and pepper, and oregano until it makes a creamy dress-ing to brush over the meat as it turns on the spit. We have an electric rotisserie, so no one needs to stand by and turn it by hand!"

While the cooking goes on, everyone samples the *mezethakia,* bits of cheese, and olives and bread until it is time to spread out the spanakopita and pastitsio and other side dishes.

"And what a pleasure it is to get that first piece of the crackling still hot off the fire!"

THE RECIPES

Marinated Kalamata Olives
Eliés Marinátes

Yogurt and Cucumber Salad
Tsatsíki

Egg and Lemon Chicken Soup
Avgolémono Soupa

Roasted Leg of Lamb
Arnáki

Skewered Lamb
Arní Souvlákia

Rice Pilaf
Piláfi

Spinach Pie
Spanakópitas

Stuffed Grape Leaves
Dolmáthes

Egg-Lemon Sauce
Avgolémono

Eggplant Casserole
Moussakás

Baked Pasta
Pastítsio

Cheese Pie
Tiropita

Green Salad with
Feta Cheese
Salátika me Feta

Braided Easter Bread
Tsoureki

Clove Cookies
Kourabíethes

Phyllo and Nut Pastry
Baklava

Puffed Dough in Honey
Loukoumáthes

Honey Syrup

Marinated Kalamata Olives

Eliés Marinátes

Makes about 3 cups

The flavor of these olives improves with a few days in the refrigerator. Some home cooks like to add tiny niçoise, large Gaeta olives, and whole green olives for a mix of textures and colors.

1 pound kalamata (Greek) olives
3 tablespoons dried oregano
1 tablespoon dried rosemary
$1/2$ tablespoon dried thyme
Grated zest of $1/2$ orange
$1/2$ teaspoon red pepper flakes
2 tablespoons red wine vinegar
Olive oil, to cover

1. Rinse the brine off the olives under running water. Dry on paper towels.

2. Toss olives, oregano, rosemary, thyme, orange zest, and red pepper flakes together in a bowl.

3. Place in a clean jar with the red wine vinegar and enough olive oil to cover. Cover and refrigerate for 48 hours before serving as an appetizer.

SEEDING CUCUMBERS

To seed a cucumber, cut it in half lengthwise. With a teaspoon, scoop out the seeds. Set on paper towels, cut side down, until ready to use.

Yogurt and Cucumber Salad

Tsatsíki

Serves 6

1 large cucumber, peeled, cut in half lengthwise, seeds
    scooped out with a spoon
Salt
1 1/2 cups plain yogurt, drained
2 tablespoons olive oil
1 tablespoon freshly squeezed lemon juice
Freshly ground black pepper
3 cloves garlic, minced
1/4 cup fresh mint leaves

1. Salt the scooped-out sides of the cucumber. Set on paper towels, cut side down, to drain for about 1 hour.

2. Whisk together the yogurt, olive oil, lemon juice, pepper to taste, and garlic. Refrigerate.

3. Rinse the cucumber. Cut it into paper-thin slices. Gently squeeze the cucumber slices in a towel.

4. Chop the mint and whisk into the yogurt mixture. Toss cucumbers and yogurt sauce together and serve.

Egg and Lemon Chicken Soup

Avgolémono Soupa

Serves 6

Tina Karalekas substitutes a version of this soup for a traditional lamb soup at Easter dinner, but it is good year-round, especially steaming hot in the dead of winter. She makes a simple, flavorful stock by boiling a whole chicken with just salt and garlic, often adding pieces of the chicken to the finished soup. Tina says, "The additional egg yolk makes a much richer soup."

> 1/2 cup rice
> 6 cups chicken stock
> Salt to taste
> Juice of 1 1/2 lemons
> 2 whole eggs plus 1 egg yolk

1. Bring the rice and chicken stock to a boil in a heavy pot. Cover and reduce the heat to a low simmer. Cook for about 20 minutes. The rice will be tender and the grains separate. Take the pot off the heat. Set aside to keep warm.

2. While the rice cooks, whisk the lemon juice and eggs together. Lift ¼ cup of the hot stock out of the rice-stock mixture. Slowly drizzle the stock into the egg-lemon mixture, whisking continually.

3. Remove the pot from the heat so the egg mixture does not curdle. Gradually pour all the egg-lemon mixture into rice-stock mixture, whisking continuously. Taste and add salt. Serve immediately.

ENHANCING DRIED OREGANO

Barbara Lazarides rubs dried oregano between her hands to release the natural oils and enhance the flavor.

Roasted Leg of Lamb
Arnáki

Serves 6 to 8

Lamb is a meat that celebrates spring, and it is the center-piece of a Greek-American Easter dinner. If you can get *rigani*, Greek oregano, use it for authentic flavor. The touch of fresh lemon juice at the end brightens the flavor.

Barbara Lazarides whisks up extra marinade "so it makes a creamy dressing." Her husband brushes it over the meat as it is turned on their backyard spit. This recipe is adapted from their method to fit the home kitchen.

Freshly ground black pepper
1 tablespoon dried oregano
1/4 cup olive oil
5- to 7- pound boneless leg of lamb
Juice of 1 lemon
1/2 cup red wine

1. Whisk the pepper to taste with the oregano and olive oil. Taste as you go, and mix it to your liking. Rub it over the whole roast. Wrap tightly in plastic wrap. Refrigerate overnight.

2. Preheat the oven to 425°F. Put the meat on a rack in a roasting pan.

3. Roast for about 15 minutes. Turn the oven temperature down to 350°F. Continue cooking for about 12 minutes per pound, basting every 15 to 20 minutes with pan juices. The roast is done when it registers 140°F on a meat thermometer pierced into the center.

4. Squeeze the lemon to drizzle juice all over the roast. Place the roast on a serving platter. Tent with aluminum foil and leave it to rest for about 20 minutes. The meat continues to cook from residual heat and distributes juices evenly.

5. Pour the wine into the roasting pan. Bring to a boil, stirring up any browned bits from the bottom. Simmer for 3 to 5 minutes.

6. To serve, carve the roast and arrange the meat on a serving platter. Pour the sauce through a fine-mesh strainer to clarify it. Serve the sauce with the roast.

Skewered Lamb

Arní Souvlákia

Serves 6

If you use wooden skewers, soak them for about 30 minutes in a bowl of water so that they do not burn. Cook the lamb outdoors on the grill in summer, or under the broiler in winter. At Maria's Pizza, the Lazarides family cooks chicken cubes this way, and then they stuff them into warm pita bread.

> 1 1/2 pounds lean boneless leg of lamb
> 6 tablespoons freshly squeezed lemon juice
> 1/2 cup olive oil
> 1 clove garlic, crushed
> Salt and freshly ground black pepper
> 1 tablespoon dried oregano
> 2 bay leaves (for indoor cooking only)
> A few branches fresh rosemary, optional
> Zest of 1 lemon
> 3 tablespoons fresh flat-leaf parsley
> Pinch coarse salt

1. Trim the meat and cut into 1-inch cubes.

2. Whisk together lemon juice, olive oil, garlic, salt and pepper to taste, and oregano. Add 2 bay leaves if you plan to cook the meat indoors only. Toss this with the cubes of lamb. Cover and refrigerate overnight.

JUICING A LEMON

To get the maximum amount of juice easily from a fresh lemon, pierce it all over with a sharp knife or fork, then place it in a microwave for 10 seconds. Roll it on a work surface a few times, pressing down on it before cutting it in half and squeezing. An inexpensive plastic or wooden reamer or cup juicer that catches the seeds is a handy tool.

MINCING HERBS AND CITRUS ZEST

A mixture of herbs and citrus zest, chopped nearly as fine as dust, adds an unexpected note to soups, stews, salads, pastas, rice, and meats. Often cooks find the chopping difficult, as the ingredients tend to "hop" all over the cutting board. A sprinkling of coarse salt helps to keep the leaves and peels stable while chopping and sharpens the flavor in the process.

3. Light a charcoal fire, or heat the broiler.

4. Finely chop the lemon zest and parsley together with the coarse salt. Set aside.

5. Remove the meat from the marinade with a slotted spoon. Discard the marinade. Thread the meat onto 6 to 8 skewers. Scatter rosemary branches over the hot coals in an outdoor grill.

6. Grill or broil for 10 to 12 minutes, turning so the meat is browned on all sides. Move the meat to a cooler part of the grill, and leave them for 10 to 12 minutes longer to cook through.

7. Sprinkle the lemon zest–parsley mixture over the meat before serving over the rice pilaf or sandwiched in pita bread.

Rice Pilaf

Piláfi

Serves 6

Never stir rice while it cooks or the grains will become mushy. The trick is to stir once at the beginning of cooking and fluff with a fork at the end.

>   2 tablespoons olive oil
>   1 medium onion, finely chopped
>   1/2 teaspoon salt
>   1 bunch scallions including greens, chopped
>   1 tablespoon chopped fresh mint
>   1/2 cup chopped fresh parsley
>   2/3 cup rice
>   2 cups water or chicken stock
>   Salt and freshly ground black pepper

1. Heat the olive oil in a skillet over medium heat. Add the onion and salt. Cook, stirring, for 5 to 7 minutes. The onion

will be softened and pale gold. Add the scallions and cook, stirring, for 1 minute more. Stir in the mint and parsley.

2. Stir in rice and water or stock. Bring to a boil. Reduce the heat to a simmer. Stir once. Cover, and cook over low heat for 15 to 20 minutes. The rice will be tender and separate and the water will be absorbed. Add salt and pepper to taste and fluff with a fork.

Spinach Pie
Spanakópitas

Serves 6

Nick Xiarhos always uses fresh, not frozen, sheets of phyllo dough. He recommends folding the dough on opposite sides of the baking pan each time, so that one end isn't lopsided.

    2 tablespoons plus 2 tablespoons olive oil
    1 medium onion, finely chopped
    1 (16-ounce) bag spinach or an equivalent amount of
        Swiss chard, washed, stemmed, and chopped into
        1-inch pieces
    Salt and freshly ground black pepper
    Pinch nutmeg
    4 eggs, beaten
    1 pound domestic feta cheese, crumbled
    1/2 cup (1 stick) butter, melted
    1 pound fresh phyllo dough

1. Heat 2 tablespoons of olive oil in a large skillet over medium-high heat. Add the onion and cook for about 3 minutes. When the onion wilts, add the spinach and cook for about 3 minutes longer. The spinach will be wilted. Add salt and pepper to taste, and nutmeg. Cook for about 1 minute more. Set aside to cool.

FETA CHEESE

Retired Salem High School English teacher Nick Xiarhos has been cooking Greek fare for as long as he can remember. Over the years, he perfected a method for making spinach pie so that the feta cheese is spread throughout every bite. "I don't like it when I bite into a clump of cheese and the next bite there's only spinach." He often includes chard, a milder green, in the filling, sometimes substituting it entirely for the spinach. "I think I've improved on a five thousand-year-old recipe!"

PHYLLO DOUGH

When working with phyllo dough, you must remember two things: to keep the sheets of dough moist, and to work quickly. Place the sheets of dough on a kitchen towel and keep the stack covered with a damp—not sopping wet—towel. Take sheets out from under the towel only as you need them. And don't pause until you have used all the dough.

2. Stir the eggs and feta cheese into the spinach mixture. Be sure the mixture is cooled or the eggs will curdle. Add salt and pepper to taste.

3. Combine the butter with the remaining olive oil.

4. Preheat the oven to 350°F. Brush a 9 by 13-inch baking pan lightly with the melted butter mixture.

5. Take up half the sheets of phyllo dough. Brush each sheet, one at a time, with the melted butter mixture. Stack the sheets one on top of another in the baking pan, folding the sheets over to fit inside the pan.

6. Spread the spinach mixture over the phyllo dough in the pan.

7. Brush the remaining phyllo sheets with the melted butter mixture. Fold and layer them over the spinach mixture. Brush the last of the melted butter mixture over the top.

8. Bake for 30 to 35 minutes, until the top crust is golden.

9. Allow to cool slightly before cutting into squares, or halve the squares into triangles, with a sharp knife.

Stuffed Grape Leaves
Dolmáthes

Makes about 3 dozen

Dolmáthes can be eaten as appetizers, side dishes, or the main course. The filling can be rice, fruit, or meat seasoned with fresh herbs, lemon juice, or cinnamon. This recipe calls for rice, perhaps the most familiar Greek-American filling for grape leaves.

    12-ounce jar grape leaves
    1 cup boiling water
    1 recipe Rice Pilaf, cooled (see recipe, page 193)
    Freshly squeezed juice of 1 lemon

1. Separate the grape leaves. Blanch them, a few at a time, in boiling water for 3 to 5 seconds. Drain on paper towels. Trim the stems.

2. Line the bottom of a large pot with a layer of grape leaves, shiny side down.

3. Lay the leaves flat, dull side up, on a work surface. Toss the pilaf filling with half the lemon juice. Place a tablespoon of the filling on each leaf near the lower part. Fold the bottom up to cover the filling. Fold in the sides, and continue to roll toward the leaf point.

4. Place the filled grape leaves closely together in the pot. Drizzle olive oil and the remaining lemon juice over the top. Pour in hot water to barely cover the grape leaves. Bring to a boil. Reduce heat to a simmer. Cover. Cook for 20 to 25 minutes. Serve hot or cold with the Egg-Lemon Sauce.

Egg-Lemon Sauce
Avgolémono

Makes about 1½ cups

Avgolémono sauce is key to Greek-American cooking. Try it with fish or vegetables as well as with the stuffed grape leaves. When cooking, keep the heat low, because the delicate sauce curdles easily. A double boiler works best.

    3 large egg yolks
    ⅓ cup freshly squeezed lemon juice
    1 cup hot chicken stock

1. Heat the water in the bottom of a double boiler to a very low simmer.

2. Whisk the egg yolks in the top of the double boiler for about 2 minutes. When they are pale and foamy, slowly whisk in the lemon juice.

3. Drizzle in ¼ cup of the stock in a slow, steady stream, continually whisking. Whisk in all the remaining stock quickly and steadily.

4. Place the saucepan with the lemon/stock mixture on top of the barely bubbling bottom part of the double boiler. Cook for about 4 minutes, steadily stirring, until it thickens.

5. Remove from the heat and use right away.

Eggplant Casserole

Moussakás

Serves 6 to 8

This recipe looks endless at first glance, but once you read it over, you'll see it's fairly simple. Three components—fried eggplant, cheese sauce, and lamb cooked in tomato sauce—are layered and baked. You can cook the meat a day ahead. I've oven-fried the eggplant for health and time reasons.

SWEATING EGGPLANT

To remove bitter juices from large globe eggplants, cut them into slices, salt heavily, and set aside for 20 to 30 minutes. The salt draws out beads of dark, bitter juice. Rinse the eggplant slices quickly under cold running water and pat dry.

2/3 cup olive oil
1 onion, finely chopped
2 pounds lean ground lamb
1/2 cup red wine
1 (32-ounce) can tomato purée
1 cup chopped fresh flat-leaf parsley
1 cup chicken stock
1 tablespoon dried oregano, crumbled
1 tablespoon ground cinnamon
1/2 teaspoon ground allspice
Salt and freshly ground black pepper
2 large eggplants, sliced 1/2-inch thick, salted, and
     rinsed
2 tablespoons (1/4 stick) butter
1/4 cup all-purpose flour
2 cups milk
1 cup small-curd cottage cheese, drained in a
     fine-mesh sieve for 1 hour
1/4 cup crumbled feta cheese
1/2 teaspoon grated nutmeg
5 large eggs
1 cup fresh bread crumbs
1 cup grated Parmesan

1. To cook the meat, warm 2 tablespoons of the olive oil in a skillet over medium heat. Add the onion and cook for about 5 minutes, stirring often. The onion will be wilted.

EGGPLANT GENDER

Food folklorists have a knack for always finding the nearly seedless globe eggplant: Turn the eggplant on its head, stem side down. Check the bottom. If the indented flower end is circular, the eggplant is a "girl" and will be full of seeds; if it is oval, it will be a nearly seedless "boy." The seeds in the female are bitter. Many cooks dispute this method, but it always works for me.

2. Add the ground lamb to the pan. Cook, breaking up lumps, for 5 to 7 minutes. It will be lightly browned. Pour in the wine. Bring to a boil. Reduce the heat to a simmer and cook for about 3 minutes. Add the tomato purée. Simmer for about 10 minutes longer. Stir in all but 1 tablespoon of the parsley, chicken stock, oregano, cinnamon, allspice, and salt and pepper to taste. Simmer for 15 to 20 minutes. Most of the liquid will be absorbed. Set aside. (You can cook the recipe ahead to this point.)

3. To cook the eggplant, preheat the oven to 400°F. Brush the eggplant slices with olive oil. Oil several baking sheets. Place the eggplant on the baking sheets. Bake for 2 to 3 minutes on each side. The slices will be golden brown. Drain on paper towels. Reduce the oven temperature to 350°F.

4. To make the white sauce, melt the butter in a saucepan over low heat. Whisk in the flour. Cook, whisking constantly, for 1 to 2 minutes, until the mixture is a pale gold. Pour in the milk very slowly, whisking constantly. Bring to a boil while whisking. Remove the saucepan from the heat.

5. Gently whisk the cottage cheese, feta, and nutmeg into the saucepan. Whisk the eggs until foamy, and gently stir them into the saucepan.

6. To assemble the casserole, butter a 9 by 13-inch baking dish. Begin layering the ingredients in this order—eggplant, meat, sauce—ending with a layer of cheese sauce. Scatter the bread crumbs and grated cheese over the top. Cover with aluminum foil.

7. Bake for about 30 minutes. Remove the foil. Bake for about 30 minutes longer. The casserole will be bubbling and golden brown. Serve hot.

Baked Pasta

Pastítsio

Serves 10 to 12

Pastítsio, sometimes called Greek macaroni and cheese, is a feature of the Easter dinner table. Barbara Lazarides spices hers with just enough cinnamon. She makes it so expertly that she no longer needs measuring equipment.

Semolina and farina (fine-milled flours) and #6 spaghetti (a very thick noodle) are found in specialty shops and increasingly in large city supermarkets.

> 2 boxes of #6 spaghetti
> 1 1/2 cups (3 sticks) butter, additional for pan
> 1 small onion, finely grated
> 1 1/2 pounds lean ground beef
> 2 1/2 cups grated Parmesan or Romano cheese
> 1/4 cup finely chopped parsley
> 2 tablespoons tomato puree
> salt and freshly ground black pepper
> 1/2 gallon milk
> 1 teaspoon sugar
> 1 cup fine semolina or fine farina
> 6 large eggs

1. Preheat the oven to 350 F.

2. Cook the pasta. Drain. Set aside. Butter a large deep baking dish, such as one used for lasagna.

3. Melt 1/2 stick butter in a skillet over medium-high heat. Add the onion and cook, stirring, for 1 to 2 minutes. The onion will wilt. Add the ground beef. Cook, breaking up clumps, for 5 minutes. It will be lightly brown, no longer red. Add 1/2 cup of the grated cheese, the parsley, and tomato puree. Season with salt and pepper. Simmer for 3 to 4 minutes. Set aside.

4. To layer the pasta, sprinkle ½ cup grated cheese over the bottom of the baking dish. Spread half the pasta into the dish and sprinkle ½ cup of grated cheese over it. Cut ½ stick butter into bits and scatter it over the cheese. Layer on the ground beef mixture. Sprinkle ½ cup of grated cheese over the beef. Cut another ½ stick butter into bits, scattering it over the cheese. Layer on the remaining pasta and sprinkle on ½ cup of grated cheese. Scatter ½ stick of butter cut into bits over this layer of cheese also. Set aside.

5. Melt the remaining stick of butter in a large saucepan over low heat. Add the milk and sugar. Bring the mixture to a boil. Slowly pour in the semolina (or farina), whisking constantly. The mixture will thicken. Remove the pan from the heat.

6. Lightly whisk the eggs and cinnamon in a bowl. Whisk the eggs into the milk and pour the mixture evenly over the contents of the baking pan.

7. Transfer the pan to the oven. Bake for 35 to 45 minutes. The top will be golden brown. Let it sit for 15 minutes before cutting it into squares.

Cheese Pie

Tiropita

Serves 10 to 12

When thawing filo dough, Barbara Lazarides advises leaving it a full 8 hours or overnight in the refrigerator. She buys her filo in a market that sells a lot of it, so she knows it hasn't been in the freezer or refrigerator case for long. Barbara prefers using whipped cream cheese in her tiropita, but says that ricotta works as well.

    1 package phyllo dough
    1 1/2 cups (3 sticks) butter, melted and kept warm
    1 1/2 pounds feta cheese
    1 pound whipped cream cheese, or whole milk ricotta
    6 large eggs
    1/4 teaspoon freshly ground black pepper

1. Preheat the oven to 350°F. Butter a baking dish, such as one used to make lasagna. Spread the phyllo dough on a work surface and cover with a lightly moist kitchen towel.

2. Blend together the feta and cream cheeses (or ricotta, if using), the eggs, and black pepper in a bowl.

3. Place four pieces of phyllo dough in the baking dish so that they drape outside the each of the four sides. They should extend far enough out of the pan to reach the center when folded back. Leave the ends outside the pan and brush each sheet generously with melted butter. Now layer half the remaining phyllo dough, one piece at a time, flat into the bottom of the pan, brushing each piece with melted butter.

4. Spread the cheese mixture evenly over the sheets of phyllo. Now fold the dough sheets that are draped outside the pan over the cheese mixture creating a pocket or envelope for the cheese. Layer all the remaining phyllo sheets flat on top, brushing each one with butter. Do not butter the top sheet. Instead, score it with a knife into squares or triangles to

PITTING OLIVES

You can buy a gadget that pits olives or cherries, or you can pit them the way professionals do: Place two or three olives on a cutting board, place the flat of a large knife over them, and smack the knife soundly with your hand. The olives will split and the pits will shoot out (or at least loosen).

mark the servings. Then brush butter over it. At this point, you can freeze the pie and later take it directly from the freezer to the oven to finish cooking.

5. Transfer the baking sheet to the oven. Bake for 30 minutes. The top will be golden brown.

Green Salad with Feta Cheese

Salátika me Feta

Serves 6

No Greek-American meal is complete without salad. If you are able to get Greek olive oil, it will certainly enhance the salad. Otherwise, use your favorite brand. Have this Greek sandwich shop specialty as a main course lunch, a side salad, or stuff it with souvlaki into a pita bread. Be sure to pit the olives if you're making a sandwich.

1/3 cup olive oil
2 teaspoons wine vinegar
Freshly squeezed juice of 1 lemon
1 clove garlic, peeled and left whole
Leaves from a few sprigs of fresh oregano,
    or 1/4 teaspoon dried oregano
Salt and freshly ground black pepper
1 large head iceberg lettuce, torn into bite-size pieces
1 head of romaine lettuce, torn into bite-size pieces
6 tomatoes, quartered
2 cucumbers, peeled, seeded, and sliced crosswise
3 scallions, white and 2 inches of greens, thinly
    sliced crosswise
1 small red onion, thinly sliced
1 cup kalamata olives
2 green peppers, seeded and thinly sliced
1 cup (1/4 pound) feta cheese, crumbled

1. To make the dressing, place the oil, vinegar, lemon juice, garlic, oregano, salt, and pepper in a jar with a tightly fitting lid. Shake and refrigerate. Remove the garlic before using.

2. Toss together the lettuces, tomatoes, cucumber, and scallions in a salad bowl. Pour on the dressing. Toss to coat the vegetables. Scatter the olives, green pepper rings, and feta over the top.

Braided Easter Bread
Tsoureki

Makes one 9-inch braided wreath

Barbara Lazarides is fortunate to be able to mix up large quantities of dough using professional kitchen equipment. She devotes a full day to baking her Easter breads, which she braids in a variety of ways. This recipe, which I've adapted to make one loaf in the home kitchen, gives directions for a circular wreath. The eggs that are nestled into Easter bread are first hard-cooked and dyed red.

    1 cup milk
    1 package (2 1/2 teaspoons active dry yeast)
    1 cup sugar
    5 1/2 to 6 cups all-purpose flour
    2 cups (4 sticks) butter
    6 large eggs, beaten
    Grated zest of 1 lemon
    1 teaspoon salt
    1/2 teaspoon almond extract
    1 to 5 hard-cooked, colored eggs
    1 egg yolk
    2 teaspoons water

1. Flour a work surface.

2. Combine the milk, yeast and 2 tablespoons of sugar in a large bowl. Set aside for 15 minutes. The mixture will bubble.

3. Stir in 2 cups of flour, the butter, the eggs, lemon zest, salt, almond extract, and the remaining sugar. Add the remaining flour, ½ cup at a time, until a soft dough forms. Turn the dough onto the floured surface and knead until smooth. Add flour, if required, to prevent the dough from sticking.

4. Place the dough in a bowl. Cover with a kitchen towel. Set in a warm place for 1½ hours. The dough will double in bulk.

5. Preheat the oven to 350°F. Grease a baking sheet.

6. Divide the dough into three equal pieces. On the floured surface, roll each piece into a 30-inch-long rope. Braid the pieces together and form into a circle, pinching the ends together. Place on the baking sheet. Set the loaf aside, covered, to rise, for 30 minutes.

7. Carefully nestle the egg(s) into the dough between the braiding. The eggs will be only partially covered.

8. Make an egg wash by whisking the egg yolk with 2 teaspoons water. Brush it over the loaf.

9. Transfer the baking sheet to the oven. Bake for 35 to 45 minutes. A knife piercing the bread will come out clean.

Clove Cookies

Kourabíethes

Makes 3 to 4 dozen cookies

When pediatric nurse Doreen Kent, of English-Irish heritage, married Nick Xiarhos, she learned to cook the Greek dishes he loved. At Easter, she loves baking these powdered-sugar cookies with a whole clove hidden in the center. Doreen cautions bakers to "be sure to warn guests to remove the cloves before eating." Some home cooks substitute a generous pinch of ground cloves in the batter.

Mrs. Xiarhos uses chopped walnuts, but some cooks eliminate them altogether because of allergies.

- 2 cups (4 sticks) unsalted butter
- 2 tablespoons vegetable shortening
- 3 egg yolks
- 1/4 cup powdered (confectioners') sugar, plus additional for dusting baked cookies
- 3 to 4 dozen whole cloves, *or* a large pinch ground cloves
- 5 cups flour
- 3/4 cup walnuts, finely ground

1. Beat the butter and vegetable shortening together with a hand mixer, making sure they are thoroughly incorporated. Beat in the egg yolks, sugar, and ground cloves, if using. Gradually add the flour until it forms a dough. Knead in the nuts. Set aside to rest for about 1 hour.

2. Preheat the oven to 350°F. Grease several baking sheets.

3. Break off grape-size pieces of dough and roll them into balls or crescents. (Stuff a whole clove, if using, into the center of each.) Line up the cookies on a baking sheet, with a small space between each one. Bake for 8 to 10 minutes. Be careful not to overbake. The cookies will be very pale gold.

Transfer them to a rack to cool. Dust generously with more powdered sugar. To store, layer the cookies in a tin with waxed paper between layers, sifting a little more powdered sugar over each layer.

Phyllo and Nut Pastry
Baklava

Makes 12 to 14

You can cut the *baklava* into smaller, bite-size pastries for a larger yield.

> 1 pound walnuts, finely chopped
> 1/4 cup sugar
> 1 teaspoon ground cinnamon
> 1 pound phyllo pastry sheets
> 2 cups (4 sticks) unsalted butter, melted
> 2 cups Honey Syrup (recipe follows)

1. Preheat the oven to 300°F.

2. Combine the nuts, sugar, and cinnamon.

3. One at a time, brush eight sheets of phyllo with butter, layering them on a 10 by 15-inch baking sheet. Sprinkle every other sheet of phyllo generously with the nut mixture in between the layers until the mixture is used. Brush two more phyllo sheets and place on top for the final layer. Use a sharp knife to cut the pastry into diamond-shaped pieces.

4. Place an empty baking pan on the bottom shelf of the oven. Pour 2 inches of hot water into the pan. Place the pastry on the center shelf. Bake for about 2 hours. Check the water every 30 minutes and replenish as needed.

5. Remove the baked baklava from the oven. Drizzle the honey syrup over it. Cool before serving.

Puffed Dough

Loukoumáthes

Makes about 3 dozen

I first tasted these pastries at a picnic, on the beautiful grounds of the Hellenic Center in Ipswich. Lines form while the sweet clouds of dough are deep-fried, and at least half a dozen of them are piled on each napkin to take away. I've also seen them served in paper cones.

    2 teaspoons active dry yeast
    3 tablespoons plus 1 teaspoon sugar
    1 cup lukewarm water
    2 cups all-purpose flour, or more as needed
    Pinch salt
    2 tablespoons olive oil
    Vegetable or canola oil for frying
    2 cups Honey Syrup (see recipe, page 209)
    Powdered (confectioners') sugar for dusting

WORKING WITH HOT OIL

To add dough to a pot of hot oil without splashing, coat a spoon with oil by dipping it into the pot. Then scoop some dough. The dough will slip right off the spoon into the pot. Remove the cooked dough with a separate, slotted spoon.

1. Dissolve the yeast and 1 teaspoon of the sugar in ¼ cup warm water. Set aside for about 10 minutes.

2. Mix the flour and salt together in a large bowl. Add the yeast mixture, olive oil, and ½ cup warm water. Mix to form a soft dough. Cover with plastic wrap. Set aside for about 2½ hours, to rise. It will be bubbling on the surface. If the dough seems too thin, beat in more flour. Knead it right in the bowl for 2 minutes. Set aside.

3. In a heavy pot, heat oil to about 375°F for deep-frying. Place a few tablespoon-size dollops of dough in the pot. Cook, a few at a time, turning, for about 3 minutes. They will puff up and turn golden. Remove from the pot with a slotted spoon. Drain in a colander lined with paper towels.

4. Dunk the still-hot dough puffs into honey syrup to coat. Dust with powdered sugar before eating hot, out of hand.

Honey Syrup

Makes about 2 cups

Use this syrup for *baklava* and *loukoumáthes*.

2 cups honey
1/4 cup sugar
1 cup water
2 tablespoons freshly squeezed lemon juice

1. Bring the honey, sugar, and water to a boil in a saucepan. Turn down the heat and simmer for 7 to 10 minutes. The syrup should coat a spoon.

2. Cool. Stir in the lemon juice.

THE DINER
Home Cooking on the Road

Diners are the American bistro. New Englanders take special pride that this natural outgrowth of the Industrial Revolution originated here, in Providence, Rhode Island, when entrepreneurs carried sandwiches, pie, and coffee to workers in the newly opened factories in their horse-drawn "lunch wagons." Within twenty years, the idea was widespread. The wagons grew kitchens, counters, and stools, and put down roots within walking distance of those factories. New industries specialized in outfitting the eateries from windows to wall clocks. The streamlined results looked like railroad dining cars and were nicknamed "diners." Their popularity was due as much to the easy camaraderie as to the rib-sticking sustenance: everyone from hard hats to sailors to musicians lined the counters or snuggled into neon-lit booths.

The North Shore's fast-growing textile, leather, and jet-engine plants were fertile ground for diner development in the early twentieth century. By the 1930s and 1940s, seventy-four diners had sprung up between Saugus and Salisbury, most serving plant workers on the day, swing, and graveyard shifts. As the cars grew jet-age stainless-steel exteriors, they welcomed new families with their boomer babies at weekend breakfasts and teens munching burgers and fries in the late-afternoon blare of the jukebox. But the rise of suburbs, shopping malls, and fast-food chains sounded the diner's death knell. The abandoned remains were gradually dismantled until the economic boom of the 1980s invited a short revival. For a few years a Danvers diner was resurrected with an updated interior and menu, but true to its new name, Flash in the Pan, it was quickly gone, bought by a European collector.

Today a handful of diehards remain open for business. Each has a story to tell. In Lynn, the Full Moon, in nearly pristine condition, is owned and operated by Southeast Asian immigrants who serve up Cambodian, Vietnamese, and Thai home cooking, a true representation of the modern American dream. On these same busy city streets, traffic screeches to a halt at the sight of live chickens strutting around in front of the Capitol Diner. The Agawam Diner in Rowley, owned by the same family since 1940, is famed for home-baked pies, and the Fishtale Diner, hauled from town to town for decades, has finally settled in Salisbury. Viewed in a romantic haze by historians, pilgrims, and photographers, diners are still a respite for regular customers content to grab a decent meal in a place where no one minds if you want pie for breakfast.

BLUE PLATE SPECIAL

Beef and Barley Soup

Old-Fashioned Meatloaf
with Milk Gravy

Potatoes O'Brien

Glazed Carrots

Mile-High Lemon
Meringue Pie

THE NORTH SHORE'S DINERS

- Agawam Diner, 167 Newburyport Tpke., Rowley
  978-948-7780
- Capitol Diner, 431 Union St., Lynn
  781-595-9314
- Chubby's Diner, 72 Main St., Salisbury
  978-462-3332
- Fishtale Diner, 420 Bridge Rd., Salisbury
  978-465-1674
- Foster Street Diner, 94 Foster St., Peabody
  978-532-0935
- Full Moon Restaurant, 38 Bennett St., Lynn
  781-596-3860
- Pilgrim Diner, 4 Boston St., Salem
  978-745-2348
- Portside Diner, 2 River St., Danvers
  978-777-1437
- Salem Diner, 70 Loring Ave., Salem
  978-741-7918

North Shore Cooks: The Galanis Family of the Agawam Diner

It's 3:30 P.M. and John W. Galanis is fielding orders at the grill of the Agawam Diner in Rowley. The tall 40-something-year-old has one ear on the waitresses and another on the kitchen crew as he breads order after order of fish fillets and places them in the deep-fryer, managing to keep his apron spotless in the process. He plates them with fries and coleslaw and sends them out front to a hungry "four-top" (table for four), not missing an incoming order for two hamburgers, medium rare.

"It slows down around this time, in the winter," he says, looking out at the nearly full dining room. "There's no line at the door."

Galanis worked in the diner through his teenage years at Ipswich High School and college years at Suffolk University. After a stint in Boston restaurants, he returned to the business that his grandfather, John Galanis, the family patriarch, established in

1940 with the rest of his extended family. The diner is not a one-person operation; it's a true family business with all the bustle and banter that come with close relatives. Brothers, uncles, aunts, cousins, and children—from Grandma Georgia Galanis on down—all have washed dishes, pared vegetables, and wiped down tables here.

Andy Galanis, age undisclosed, holds court at the front door. He is the keeper of the flame. He knows the history of this place and has the sense of humor to usher in the long lines of customers daily.

"I see a free table over there with a lovely view of the dumpster. Why don't you ladies have a seat there?" he asks. And they do, gratefully, because everything is delicious here. Everything is homemade.

John's cousin, Jim Pappas, age 65, is the baker. He comes in every night at ten or eleven and works until nine the following morning. He works alone in the basement bakery, except for a helper on two mornings a week.

According to John, "Jim's always been the baker. He went to school in Oklahoma as a young man. He bakes all the rolls and pies. We have maybe twelve to fifteen different pies out there every day, six of them cream pies. He used to take special orders for Thanksgiving, but it got to be too much. Two years ago, he did more than six hundred pies. Now people have to come here to taste them."

As John works, other relatives pop into the kitchen to say hello on their way in or out for the day. He tries to count the number of family members involved in the business and takes three tries to get to ten. Or was it eleven?

"I guess that's it approximately. Did I mention Aunt Jennie? She was one of my dad's sisters."

Uncle John enters by a back door. He does the bookkeeping. He also does some of the prep work. "It's relaxing chopping the vegetables and making the chicken pies. I started here as a dishwasher. My mother was in the kitchen then. She'd say to me, 'Go bring that guy a cup of coffee,' or 'Here, bring this sandwich out to the counter.'

"I started off gradually, I never noticed. I really don't know anything else," he says a little wistfully, then quickly changes the subject.

"Hey, did you know my nephew here makes great chili? Ten gallons at a time. And American chop suey. They just fly out of here."

"He's the peacekeeper in the family," chuckles his nephew, pausing a minute at the grill.

"I don't have recipes. I know what I put in, but only in large amounts. I couldn't tell you how to cook for six or eight people. That's what I like about cooking," he says. "You can do it by feel. I tried baking for a short time, hated it. If you're off by just a little bit, you ruin the whole thing!"

The dining room is starting to pick up again. A waitress calls in an order. No orders are written down. They are called through the gleaming stainless-steel kitchen as they were in 1940 and through the 1950s and 1960s when the family owned three diners. One of the originals sat across the street many years ago. Sold now, it's in Salisbury operating under a new name.

The Agawam is booming enough from 5:30 A.M. through 11:00 P.M. 364 days a year, to keep the whole family busy.

The Portside Diner in Danvers was called the Cape Ann Diner when it sat on Main Street in Gloucester. You can see the words still painted on its side. The present owners have added Greek specialties to the menu.

Beef and Barley Soup

Serves 6 to 8

2 tablespoons vegetable oil
1 small onion, chopped
1 cup chopped celery
8 cups Beef Stock (recipe follows)
1/2 cup pearl barley
2 cups peeled and cubed potatoes
1 cup cubed carrots
Beef from ribs (see Beef Stock, recipe follows),
    cut into pieces
2 cups canned tomatoes, drained
1 cup frozen peas
Salt and freshly ground black pepper
2 tablespoons chopped fresh parsley

1. Heat the vegetable oil in a heavy soup pot over medium-high heat. Add the onion and celery. Cook, stirring for 3 to 5 minutes. The vegetables will be softened.

2. Add the beef stock. Bring to a boil. Add the barley. Reduce the heat to a simmer. Cover and cook for about 20 minutes.

3. Add the potatoes, carrots, beef, and tomatoes. Simmer gently for about 20 minutes.

4. Add the peas. Simmer for about 10 minutes. The vegetables and barley will be tender. Add salt and pepper to taste. Sprinkle with parsley before serving.

Beef Stock

Makes about 8 cups

Diner cooks often left a pot of stock bubbling on the back of a big eight-burner stove. That was the secret to delicious soups. Make the stock ahead and freeze it for real old-fashioned soup. It doesn't take much tending, bubbling away happily while you forget it for up to five hours.

2 tablespoons vegetable oil
2 pounds beef bones, such as short ribs, with some
    meat still attached
12 cups water, or more as needed
Tops of 1 bunch celery
5 carrots, trimmed and cut into large chunks
1 large onion, cut in quarters
2 tablespoons tomato paste
Salt and freshly ground black pepper
2 bay leaves

1. Preheat the oven to 425°F. Pour the oil into a shallow baking pan. Add the bones, turn them in the oil to coat lightly, and spread them in a single layer on the baking sheet. (Use a second sheet if necessary.) Roast for 20 to 25 minutes. They will be browned on the outside. Remove the meat from the bones and set it aside for the soup.

2. Bring the water, celery, carrots, and onion to a boil in a large soup pot. Add the bones. Scrape any browned bits from the baking pan into the pot. Add the tomato paste, salt, pepper, and bay leaves. Bring the pot back to a boil. Reduce to a healthy simmer. Cook, partly covered, for 3 to 5 hours. Check the pot every hour or so to add water, if needed.

3. Strain the stock through a sieve, keeping the liquid and discarding the solids. Chill for at least 2 hours. Scrape and discard the layer of fat that forms on the top before using the stock.

Old-Fashioned Meatloaf

Serves 6 to 8

Authentic diner meatloaf is tasty but not gussied up. Look for a ground tomato product labeled "kitchen ready," or whirl canned tomatoes in the blender.

If you want real mashed potatoes to go with the meatloaf, turn to the chapter on Irish-Americans and check the recipe for Champ (page 105).

1 1/2 pounds ground beef
8 ounces ground pork
3 tablespoons grated onion
Salt and freshly ground black pepper
1 tablespoon Worcestershire sauce
1/4 cup ketchup
1 cup ground tomatoes
1 large egg, beaten with 2 teaspoons water
2 cups fresh bread crumbs
4 to 6 slices bacon

1. Preheat the oven to 350°F. Grease a 5 by 9-inch pan.

2. Mix together the beef, pork, onion, salt and pepper to taste, Worcestershire sauce, ketchup, and tomatoes. Blend the egg mixture and bread crumbs into the meat mixture. Pack into the loaf pan. Cover the top with the bacon slices.

3. Bake for 50 to 60 minutes. The loaf will be browned on top and the edges bubbling. Let the meatloaf sit for 10 minutes before serving.

Milk Gravy

Makes about 3 cups

This is a gravy to make when there isn't a roast in sight.

    ¹/₄ cup (¹/₂ stick) butter
    ¹/₄ cup all-purpose flour
    ¹/₄ cup Beef Stock (page 216)
    2 cups milk
    Salt and freshly ground black pepper

THE CAPITOL DINER, LYNN

Located in Central Square, Lynn, the Capitol Diner fortuitously sits in the shadow of the city newspaper offices. This makes for some tasty conversation with morning bacon and eggs.

1. Melt the butter in a nonstick skillet over medium heat. Whisk in the flour and cook, whisking, for 3 to 5 minutes. The flour will become light tan. (Do not raise the temperature or tiny black flecks will appear in the flour, meaning it has burned.)

2. Gradually add the stock, then the milk, whisking constantly. Bring to a simmer. Cook, stirring, for 3 to 4 minutes. The liquid will thicken. Season to taste with salt and pepper before serving.

Potatoes O'Brien

Serves 6

This change from mashed potatoes is a staple with bacon and eggs as well as meatloaf. The potatoes can be baked or boiled a day ahead and refrigerated until needed for this recipe.

2 tablespoons vegetable oil
4 large russet potatoes, cooked and cut into
    $1/2$-inch dice
1 medium onion, chopped
1 large green bell pepper, chopped
1 red bell pepper, chopped
Salt and freshly ground black pepper

1. Preheat the oven to 400°F. Film a baking sheet with vegetable oil.

2. Gently toss the potatoes, onion, and bell pepper in the oil in a bowl to coat them lightly. Spread in a single layer on the baking sheet. Sprinkle with salt and pepper.

3. Bake for 10 to 15 minutes. Check to see if the potatoes are browned before serving hot.

Glazed Carrots

Serves 6 to 8

The amount of carrots is not exact—you can't guess in advance how many carrots will be in a bunch. The parsley here is optional, but it adds a punch of color. Maple syrup is a hallmark of a New England diner.

2 bunches carrots, trimmed, peeled, and sliced
　　into rounds
6 tablespoons (3/4 stick) butter
2 tablespoons pure maple syrup
Salt and freshly ground black pepper
Chopped fresh parsley

1. Combine the carrots with water to cover in a saucepan and bring to a boil. Add the butter, maple syrup, and salt and pepper to taste. Reduce the heat to a simmer. Cook, uncovered, over low heat for 12 to 15 minutes. The liquid will be thick and nearly evaporated.

2. Toss the carrots so that the liquid glaze coats them evenly before serving, sprinkling the top with parsley.

THE FISHTALE DINER

The Fishtale Diner in Salisbury, a 1940 Worcester Lunch Car, is the North Shore's best-traveled diner, having lived in Ipswich, Cook's Corner, Maine, and finally Salisbury. It also had a face-lift: The original stainless-steel exterior was replaced with porcelain enamel.

Mile-High Lemon Meringue Pie

Makes one 9-inch pie

The pie stores well in the refrigerator, uncovered, for a day or two. Any longer and the meringue separates and flattens.

9-inch piecrust, prebaked and cooled
1 1/2 cups sugar
6 tablespoons cornstarch

DINER-SPEAK, ALPHABETICALLY

Here is a glossary of the verbal shorthand wait-staff once shouted at cooks to facilitate orders. It's a language rarely spoken these days, but some of the words have entered our everyday speech. Some of my students assembled this list when they did a special project on diner food.

- A: Adam and Eve on a raft—poached eggs on toast
- B: Bow-wow—hot dog
- C: Clean the kitchen—hash
- D: Deadeye—poached egg
- E: Eighty-six—the kitchen's run out
- H: Houseboat—banana split
- J: Joe—coffee
- L: Lumber—toothpick
- M: Mud—black coffee
- N: Nervous pudding—Jell-O
- P: Put out the lights and cry—liver and onions
- S: Squeeze one—orange juice
- T: Take it for a walk—to go
- W: Wrecked hen—scrambled eggs

¼ teaspoon salt, plus a pinch for the meringue
2 cups water
4 egg yolks, beaten
2 tablespoons unsalted butter
½ cup freshly squeezed lemon juice, strained through a fine-mesh sieve
¼ teaspoon finely grated lemon zest
5 egg whites
¼ teaspoon cream of tartar

1. Preheat the oven to 300°F. Have a baked piecrust ready.

2. Pour 1 cup of the sugar, the cornstarch, and ¼ teaspoon salt into a saucepan. Place the pan over very low heat. Gradually stir in the water and egg yolks. Increase the heat to medium, and bring the mixture to a simmer, stirring constantly. Cook for about 1 minute longer. Remove the pan from the heat.

3. Whisk in the butter until it melts. Gradually whisk in the lemon juice and gently stir in the lemon zest. Pour this mixture into the piecrust.

4. Use an electric mixer or large wire whisk to beat the egg whites, cream of tartar, and pinch of salt until they are creamy. Gradually add the remaining ½ cup sugar, continuing to whisk or beat until stiff peaks form. Pile this onto the lemon filling, pulling it up into peaks.

5. Bake for 12 to 15 minutes. The peaks will be lightly golden on top.

6. Cool on a rack before serving at room temperature.

THE GLOBAL TABLE
From Melting Pot to Salsa

From all corners of the world, they still arrive on the North Shore, seeking the freedom and prosperity of the American dream, and still settle into this diverse little pocket north of Boston, to spice our melting pot. Today new immigrants make their homes beside families whose ancestors arrived generations ago. Culinary philosopher Joe Carlin (whose profile appears in the opening chapter) thinks that the blend of nationalities and their foods is no longer a melded stew, but rather a salsa or stir-fry in which each component adds its unique flavors to the whole while retaining its own separate character. Food is key to the lively mix.

Americans of French ancestry trickled south onto these shores from Canadian provinces from before the American Revolution. When the Industrial Revolution affected the region north of Boston, it brought a new influx of French heritage from Canada. The new factories also drew immigrants from Eastern Europe, most notably Poland, Germany, Hungary, and Ukraine. They clustered around their churches and social clubs, climbed the political and economic ladder in Ipswich, Salem, Peabody, and Lynn, and added piquant and sturdy ingredients to the melting pot. Polish-American cabbage rolls and Franco-American pork pie were already familiar when the newest arrivals found themselves homesick for the flavors of annatto or lemongrass.

In recent years, immigrants from the Caribbean and South America brought sparkling culinary accents to the small cities strung along the coast. Vietnamese, Thai, and Cambodian immigrants now add their stamp with storefront eateries. In tiny Dracut, Cambodian and Polish-American farmers forged a partnership to grow exotic ingredients for Boston and New York restaurants. Pulling all these groups together at one table, North Shore Community College's annual Intercultural Fair and Peabody's International Fair annually highlight home cooks who share dishes from Bosnia to Brazil, from Ukraine to Guatemala.

A North Shore Cook: Nikki Louk

Monsophanna "Nikki" Louk's gleaming white chef's coat sets off a lovely dark complexion that doesn't need makeup to glow. Just out of culinary school, she laughs easily with her co-workers, but maintains a purposeful manner about work.

She loves pretty clothes and gold jewelry. She wears the jewelry sparingly; there are health codes to consider.

A short while ago, Nikki was just another freshman in Culinary Techniques 101. If she worked at her *mis en place* and knife skills a little more intensely than other students, her quick laughter made her popular with classmates. But those dark eyes sometimes look away a beat too soon, perhaps because of a lingering memory of the refugee camp where she was born in 1980.

"My parents were arranged. In the camp," she says, by way of explanation. the words come out haltingly.

Her mother, Ya Dong, and father, Neang Louk, were still teenagers when they were separated from their families escaping the "killing fields" of Cambodia in the late 1970s. Their union has endured, but neither ever saw their families again.

"They got some stories. I don't want to hear them," she says, waving her hand as if to brush them away. "All are very sad. I can't believe what my mom and dad have been through."

Nikki was born while they waited to get to the United States. Once more, she looks away, down at neatly manicured hands. "We went from Thailand to Revere. I'm not sure how we got there. I was too young to understand, and we don't look back on sad times or talk about them a lot. We all became citizens."

Neang Louk now works at a Boston newspaper and Ya Dong at a plastics company. Their son Santdaro "Ro" Louk was born shortly after they arrived in 1982. He enrolled in culinary school with his sister, but later he set out to explore other options. Nikki herself experienced one false start in her education.

"I always loved cooking, but never thought it was something to study in school. I got good grades in high school, and my guidance counselors thought I should go to college and that psychology was a good field. I was very unhappy. So I left college. Culinary school gave me an opportunity to do what I really love."

Nikki enjoys cooking "real American" entrées like steak and potatoes. In fact, she found her way to culinary school when she and brother Ro worked at Kelly's Roast Beef in Saugus and she served up huge sandwiches and ample sides of onion rings, and fries. She's also discovered an itnernational flair. Working as assistant kitchen manager at Carrabba's Italian Grill, she's training to step up to full kitchen manager.

The family recently moved into a split-level ranch house in a residential neighborhood complete with front lawn and trees. Nikki was swept away by the warm welcome and their first Fourth of July block party complete with hot dogs, burgers, and potato salad. In their bright, new kitchen, Ya Dong is teaching native Cambodian dishes, and Nikki applies her professional techniques to them.

"I love the smell of lemongrass. And I just learned how to make my mother's spicy chicken stew with peanuts. Some of the vegetables I know by sight and in Cambodian only. To learn their names in English, I have to look them up in my textbooks," says Nikki, with that quick laugh.

"I'm really proud of my parents. They've been through a lot. They really worked hard to give us opportunities." This time she doesn't look away.

THE PANTRY

- **Annatto:** Delicately flavored, brick-red seeds used in Caribbean cooking to create a golden-yellow color in rice dishes. The seeds must first be steeped in hot oil, then strained out, and the oil used in cooking.
- **Caraway seeds:** Aromatic seeds used whole, ground, or crushed in Eastern European cooking; often a component of rye bread, sauerkraut, and pork dishes, and even used to flavor vodka.
- **Chayote:** A one-seeded squash. Chayote is used in Caribbean, Mexican, and Southeast Asian soups and stews. It has the texture of a potato and is treated similarly in the kitchen. You can find it in small ethnic markets or in the produce sections of large urban supermarkets.
- **Cilantro:** An aromatic herb that closely resembles flat-leaf or Italian parsley. The bright green, delicately outlined leaves have a mild lemon-lime scent and flavor. Used in Asian, Mexican, and Caribbean cooking, cilantro is generally available in supermarkets. Smell the leaves before buying it because it is often confused with parsley.

- **Dill:** A popular herb in Eastern European cookery, which adds color, flavor, and aroma to soups and salads. The leaves and seeds are also used dried.
- **Horseradish:** Pungent, flavorful root used grated or prepared (grated and marinated). It is used in sauces, salads, butters, and pickles.
- **Lemongrass**: Tall stalks of aromatic grass, crushed for the sweet lemon flavor and used in Asian cooking. Sold in bunches at Asian specialty grocers or large supermarkets in urban areas.
- **Paprika:** A dried red spice made from red peppers. Paprika, which can be either hot or sweet, is a staple of Eastern European cooking. The mild, sweet version of paprika entered the mainstream as a garnish for potato salad.
- **Poppy seeds:** Used crushed with honey, raisins, and nuts to flavor cakes and desserts, especially during the Christmas season; also used whole in breads, rolls, and cakes.

THE RECIPES

Armenian Ground
Meat Kebabs
Losh Kebab

Hungarian Cold
Sour Cherry Soup
Meggyleves

Russian Beet Soup
Borscht

Vietnamese Rice Noodles
in Spicy Broth
Bahn Pho

Caribbean Rice and Chicken
Arroz con Pollo

Hungarian Chicken Paprikash
Csirkepaprikas

Holiday Pork Pie
Tourtière

Polish Braised Cabbage Rolls
Golabki

Cambodian Lemon Chicken
Muan Croat Tchmaa

Colombian Chicken
Potato Stew
Ajiaco

German Rolled Stuffed Steak
Rouladen

Polish Filled Dumplings
Pierogi

Savory Potato and Cream
Cheese Filling
Kartoflami

Hungarian Cucumber Salad
Tejfeles Uborkasalata

Asian Peanut Noodles
Pad Thai

Vegetables Polonaise
Jarzyny po Polsku

Polish Lover's Knot Cookies
Chrusciki

Nana's Chocolate Cake
Gateau au Chocolat

Puerto Rican Rum Cake
Sopa Borracha

Maple-Walnut Pie

WOODEN SKEWERS

When cooking food on wooden skewers, first soak them in water for 20 to 30 minutes to keep them from charring on the grill or under the broiler.

Armenian Ground Meat Kebabs

Losh Kebab

Serves 6 to 8

A popular dish in the Armenian neighborhoods of Methuen, these kebabs make wonderful appetizers or a great main course served over rice pilaf. They are delicious cooked indoors under the broiler or outdoors on the grill.

1 pound ground beef
1 pound ground lamb
1 medium onion, grated
$1/4$ cup chopped fresh flat-leaf parsley
1 (6-ounce) can tomato paste
$1/2$ cup fresh bread crumbs
1 large egg, beaten
$1/4$ teaspoon ground allspice
Salt and freshly ground black pepper

1. Blend together the beef, lamb, onion, parsley, tomato paste, bread crumbs, egg, allspice, and salt and pepper to taste. Chill in the refrigerator for at least 2 hours.

2. Preheat the broiler. Form the meat into 2-inch football shapes around the skewers.

3. Place the skewered meat on a baking sheet about 3 inches from the broiler. Broil for 3 to 5 minutes on each side. The meat will be browned. Serve hot as an appetizer or over rice pilaf as a main course.

Hungarian Cold Sour Cherry Soup

Meggyleves

Serves 4 to 6

Bill Sano teaches symphonic analysis at Marian Court College. Most people assume his family name is Italian, but the name was originally Hungarian—Sanyo, pronounced *shanyo*. When Sano took one of my classes, he wrote on a questionnaire that he had enrolled, "Because the title, Autumn Soups, sounded so romantic." This soup, a Hungarian heirloom, certainly has an aura of romance. It comes from his mother, Irma Bickel Sano.

LEMON JUICE

A tablespoon of freshly squeezed lemon juice will brighten the flavor of any vegetable stock of fruit soup.

    1 tablespoon all-purpose flour
    1 cup sour cream
    2 teaspoons confectioners' sugar
    3 cups sour cherries, pits removed
    6 cups water
    ¾ cup granulated sugar

1. Gently whisk together the flour, sour cream, and confectioners' sugar.

2. Combine the cherries, water, and granulated sugar in a large saucepan and bring to a boil. Lower the heat to a simmer. Cook for 15 to 20 minutes. The cherries will be very tender.

3. Slowly stir ½ cup of the cooking liquid from the pot into the flour mixture. Pour this mixture back into the pot. Bring the soup just to a boil. Lower the heat to a slow simmer. Cook for about 5 minutes.

4. Cover and cool in the refrigerator before serving chilled or at room temperature.

Russian Beet Soup

Borscht

Serves 6 to 8

Rebecca Brown and I tested dozens of beet soups before we found this meatless borscht with Ukrainian roots made by families who settled the neighborhood around St. Nicholas Church. The church is a Salem landmark topped with striking blue onion domes.

3 to 4 fresh beets, trimmed
Water
1 medium onion, diced
1 carrot, cut into thin strips
1 rib celery, diced
1 medium leek, trimmed and minced
Salt and freshly ground black pepper
1/4 cup minced fresh dill, plus extra for garnish
Sour cream

1. Bring the beets, with water to cover, to a boil over high heat. Lower the heat to a simmer. Cook for about 40 minutes. Strain the beet stock through a fine-mesh strainer. Set aside. Cool the beets. Peel and cut them into matchsticks. Set aside.

2. Bring 4 cups cold water, the onion, carrot, celery, leek, and salt and pepper to taste in a large soup pot and bring to a boil. Lower the heat to a simmer. Cook for about 20 minutes. The vegetables will be tender.

3. Add the cooked beets to the pot. Pour 1 cup of the beet stock into the pot. Bring to a boil. Reduce the heat to a simmer. Cook for about 5 minutes. Stir in the 1/4 cup dill. Add more beet stock, if the soup needs thinning. Add more seasoning, if needed. Serve garnished with a dollop of sour cream and a sprig of fresh dill.

Vietnamese Rice Noodles in Spicy Broth

Bahn Pho

Serves 6 to 8

COLD WATER

Always begin a pot of soup with cold water. Hot water will bring the flavor of the water pipes to the soup.

Bahn, or *bun,* are dried rice noodles, often called rice sticks. They must be soaked in hot tap water for about 20 minutes to soften them before using. Make the initial stock with either beef or chicken.

3 pounds beef bones (with some meat attached) or
    whole chicken breast
2 quarts cold water
1 whole yellow onion, peeled
2 cloves garlic, peeled
2 stalks lemongrass, thinly sliced
2-inch piece fresh ginger, crushed
3/4 teaspoon red pepper flakes
2 tablespoons Asian fish sauce
2 medium carrots, thinly sliced in rounds
Dried rice noodles
1 cup shredded spinach
2 scallions, finely chopped
Fresh sweet basil leaves, finely chopped
Fresh cilantro leaves, finely chopped
2 to 3 limes, cut in wedges

1. Bring the beef bones or chicken breast, water, onion, garlic, lemongrass, and ginger to a boil in a large soup pot. If using beef, simmer for 2 hours; if using chicken, simmer for 1 hour. Strain the stock and return it to the pot. Remove the meat from the bones and cut it into thin strips. Set it aside.

2. Bring the stock, red pepper flakes, fish sauce, and carrots to a boil over high heat. Reduce the heat to medium-high

ANNATO OIL

To extract the color from annato seeds to use in Caribbean rice dishes, heat $1/2$ cup vegetable oil in a small saucepan over low heat. Add the annato seeds and cook, stirring, for 5 minutes. The oil will turn a rich, deep orange. Strain out the seeds, cool, and store, tightly covered, in the refrigerator, up to one week.

and simmer for 10 minutes. The carrots will be tender when pierced with a fork.

3. Soak the noodles in a bowl of boiling water for 20 minutes.

4. Add the cooked meat, noodles, and spinach to the pot. Simmer for 3 to 5 minutes. The greens will be just wilted.

5. Ladle the soup into serving bowls. Scatter some chopped scallions, basil, and cilantro over the top. Pass a bowl of lime wedges for seasoning.

Caribbean Rice and Chicken

Arroz con Pollo

Serves 6 to 8

Marisol Navas has lived and traveled throughout the Caribbean islands and is an expert on Caribbean art and traditions. Growing up in Puerto Rico, she was intrigued to watch cooks in her mother's kitchen prepare *soffrito*, the gently simmered mixture of chopped vegetables, fat, and pork that is the key to truly delicious rice and chicken.

> 3 tablespoons vegetable oil
> 3- to 3$1/2$-pound chicken, cut into 8 serving pieces
> Salt and freshly ground black pepper
> 3 tablespoons finely chopped pork product,
>   such as ham, salt pork, or bacon
> 2 cloves garlic, minced
> 1 medium yellow onion, finely chopped
> 1 red bell pepper, finely chopped
> 2 large green bell peppers, finely chopped
> 1 bay leaf
> 8 plum tomatoes, seeded and chopped

1 1/2 cups converted white rice
1/4 cup white wine
4 1/2 cups canned or homemade Chicken Stock
    (see recipe, page 139)
1 tablespoon annato oil
1/4 cup chopped fresh cilantro leaves

1. Preheat the oven to 350°F.

2. Heat 2 tablespoons of the vegetable oil in a large oven-proof casserole over medium-high heat. Season the chicken pieces on both sides with salt and pepper. Cook the chicken in batches, turning, for 5 to 7 minutes. The skin will be golden. Remove the chicken pieces from the pan and set them aside to drain on brown paper.

3. To make the soffrito, heat 1 tablespoon of vegetable oil and the chopped pork product in the pan over medium-high heat. Add the garlic and onion and cook, stirring, for 2 to 3 minutes, until they begin to wilt. Add the red and green bell peppers and bay leaf. Cook for 3 minutes more, until they soften. Add the tomatoes. Cook, stirring, for another 2 minutes.

4. Add the rice, wine, and chicken stock. Bring the mixture to a boil. Stir in the annato oil. Place the chicken on top of the rice. Cover, and cook over low heat for 30 to 40 minutes. There will be no liquid. The rice will be tender and the grains separate. Remove the chicken. Discard the bay leaf. Fluff the rice, stirring in half the cilantro. Place the rice on a serving platter and the chicken pieces on top. Scatter the remaining cilantro over the top.

SOFFRITO

Caribbean cooks take pride in their personal soffrito mixes. Aromatic vegetables such as onion, celery, garlic, and green bell peppers are diced and simmered gently along with cured ham, bacon, or salt pork in lard or vegetable oil. Then the mixture is seasoned with herbs such as cilantro or oregano. The best cooks make a large batch and freeze it, thawing small amounts as needed. You can also purchase jars of soffrito ready-made in Caribbean markets.

Hungarian Chicken Paprikash

Csirkepaprikas

Serves 6

Bill Sano says, "There are two million versions of chicken paprikash, but this is the one my mother, a home economics teacher and an excellent cook, made for my father. His family was from Hungary." Sano is an entertainer who understands that this dish has the presence to occupy center stage.

2 tablespoons vegetable oil
1 medium onion, chopped
Salt and freshly ground black pepper
2 tablespoons sweet paprika
4 pounds chicken, cut into serving pieces
1 1/2 cups water
2 cups sour cream
Buttered noodles for serving

1. Heat the oil in a deep skillet over medium-high heat. Add the onion and cook, stirring for about 2 minutes. Sprinkle in the salt, pepper, and paprika. Continue cooking for 4 to 5 minutes longer. The onion will be golden and wilted.

2. Add the chicken to the pan. Work in batches, leaving space between the chicken pieces so that they brown. Cook for 4 to 5 minutes on each side.

3. Pour in the water. Bring the liquid just to the simmering point. Cover the pan. Turn the heat to medium-low. Cook slowly for 50 to 60 minutes. The chicken will be tender.

4. Remove the chicken from the pan. Set aside. Whisk the sour cream into the pan juices. Bring the mixture to a low simmer; do not boil.

5. Return the chicken to the pan and spoon the sauce over it before serving over buttered noodles.

Holiday Pork Pie

Tourtière

Serves 6 to 8

A winter holiday recipe offered on the eves of Christmas and the New Year, this is a sustaining winter dish of Franco-American descent. Kim Lyons prepares this simply, as her mother taught her, in a deep-dish pie plate, to be served hot or at room temperature. Use a basic mashed potato recipe, such as the one on page 104, minus the scallions.

 2 tablespoons butter
 1 small onion, chopped
 1 1/2 pounds lean ground pork
 Salt and freshly ground black pepper
 1/4 teaspoon ground cloves
 1/2 teaspoon ground cinnamon
 1/4 teaspoon grated nutmeg
 1 teaspoon Bell's seasoning
 1 cup water
 1 cup mashed potatoes
 Favorite pie crust for two-crust deep-dish pie

1. To make the filling, melt the butter in a large skillet over medium-high heat. Add the onion and cook, stirring, for 2 to 3 minutes, until the onion is softened and lightly golden. Add the pork and cook, breaking it up with a spoon as it cooks. Add salt and pepper to taste, the cloves, cinnamon, nutmeg, and Bell's seasoning. Continue to cook for 4 to 5 minutes. Add the water. Continue cooking for about 5 minutes longer. Set aside to cool, about 15 minutes.

2. Fold the mashed potatoes into the pork mixture. Set aside.

3. Preheat the oven to 350°F.

CLEANING GREENS

To clean any leafy greens—beet, cabbage, lettuce, herbs, and so on—swirl them in a sink filled with cold water. Lift the greens out of the water before draining the sink. If there is grit at the bottom of the sink, repeat the process until the greens are thoroughly cleaned.

4. Roll out two crusts to fit a deep-dish pie pan with some overhang.

5. Fit one pie dough circle in the pan. Pour in the pork-potato mixture. Cover with the second circle of dough. Fold under the edges of the dough and crimp. Pierce the top dough a few times with a fork or cut small slashes to vent steam.

6. Bake for about 30 minutes. The crust will be golden brown.

Polish Braised Cabbage Rolls
Golabki

Serves 8

Jennie Lojko immigrated from Poland in the early part of the twentieth century and married Joh Klus in Salem in 1933. She passed her recipe for stuffed cabbage rolls to her daughter Dolores Klus Lohring, then to her granddaughter, Suzanne Lohring. Suzanne swears by her grandmother's technique for parcooking the cabbage leaves. She cuts out the core at the bottom of the cabbage, leaving the head whole. Then she places it, cored side down, to blanch in a pot of boiling water, for about 2 minutes. She takes it out of the pot and places it in a colander, again cored side down, to drain. She leaves it there to pull the leaves off, one by one, as needed. Suzanne trims the cabbage leaves by cutting a V into the thickest part of the stem. She uses the outer leaves, and any that tear, to line the bottom of the casserole where the *golabki* will finish cooking.

There are between 20 and 30 leaves on a head of cabbage, so the serving amount here is approximate, based on two cabbage rolls per serving. Home cooks moisten the filling with diluted tomato soup. The filling is also good stuffed into green peppers for a satisfying meal.

1 head green cabbage
1/4 cup (1/2 stick) butter
2 tablespoons vegetable oil
1 onion, finely chopped
2 pounds lean ground beef
1 1/2 cups cooked rice
1 teaspoon salt
1 teaspoon freshly ground black pepper
1/4 teaspoon Bell's seasoning
2 tablespoons ketchup
1 large egg, beaten
2 cans (10-ounce) tomato soup
2 1/2 cans water

**WIGILIA,
POLISH-AMERICAN
CHRISTMAS EVE**

Once the sun sets on Christmas Eve, Polish-Americans usher in the holiday with a festive table. In a slower-paced past, the dinner consisted of twelve dishes. Although they may not keep this custom, many Polish-American families still keep the tradition of setting an extra place at the table to welcome an unexpected guest.

1. Core the cabbage. Bring a large pot of water to a boil. Add the cabbage, cored side down. Cook for 2 to 3 minutes, just until the cabbage is bright green. Place cored side down in a colander to drain.

2. Melt the butter and vegetable oil in a skillet over medium-high heat. Add the onion and cook for about 5 minutes. The onion will be wilted. Add the beef to the skillet. Continue cooking for about 15 minutes. Mix the cooked rice with the beef. Add the salt, pepper, Bell's seasoning, and ketchup. Set aside.

3. Blend the egg into the cooled meat mixture.

4. Separate 16 to 20 whole cabbage leaves from the head. Pat the leaves dry with paper towels. Trim out the toughest part of the ribs.

5. Preheat the oven to 350°F. Line the bottom of a large heavy casserole with the outer cabbage leaves. If any leaves are torn, also use them to line the casserole.

6. Place a cabbage leaf flat on a work surface. Place 2 tablespoons of the beef-and-rice mixture at the bottom center of the leaf. Fold the leaf upward, once. Then fold the sides to

DOUGHNUTS

Salem, Massachusetts, known for witchcraft, has more doughnut shops per capita than anywhere else in the United States. The reason is linked to the Polish immigrants who settled there at the turn of the twentieth century. Until about 1980, dozens of competing small coffee shops, owned and operated by Polish-American families, perfumed the early morning air with freshly made doughnuts. The favorite was, and still is, jelly doughnuts, direct descendants of *paczki*, the jelly-filled deep-fried pastries made in Polish homes. Today, most of the independent shops are gone, but Ziggy's Donuts and Coffee Time still make authentic *paczki* at certain times of the year and by special order.

meet in the center, and roll the leaf all the way upward from the bottom. Place the rolls, open edge down, in layers in the casserole dish.

7. Whisk the tomato soup with the water. Pour the mixture over the cabbage rolls. Bake for about 1½ hours, until the cabbage leaves are slightly browned and wilted. Serve with the sauce poured over them.

Cambodian Lemon Chicken

Muan Croat Tchmaa

Serves 6

In less than a generation, this dish has become Cambodian-American.

    3 pounds skinless, boneless chicken breast
    Grated zest of 1 lemon
    3 scallions, chopped
    1 onion, sliced
    1/4 cup soy sauce
    1 teaspoon sugar
    1/4 cup sherry
    3 tablespoons peanut or canola oil
    Hot steamed rice for serving

1. Cut the chicken into 2-inch cubes and place in a bowl.

2. Combine the lemon zest, scallions, onion, soy sauce, sugar, sherry, and oil. Whisk together. Reserve ½ cup of the mixture. Pour the remainder over the chicken pieces. Cover and refrigerate for 2 hours, or overnight.

3. Soak 12 bamboo skewers in water for at least 30 minutes. Preheat the oven to 300°F. Drain the chicken, discarding the marinade.

4. Thread the chicken onto the skewers. Place on a baking sheet and bake for about 20 to 25 minutes, turning and basting once or twice with the reserved marinade. Serve over rice.

Colombian Chicken Potato Stew

Ajiaco

Serves 6 to 8

Potatoes are a New World food, native to South America, although most people associate them with other countries. Guidance counselor Luz Baretto-Longus grew up in Colombia, where this colorful stew of yellow and orange vegetables flecked with bright green cilantro is a family staple.

2 tablespoons vegetable oil
3-pound chicken, cut into serving pieces
5 cups canned or homemade Chicken Stock
   (see recipe, page 139)
1/4 teaspoon red pepper flakes
3 red-skinned potatoes, skin on, cut into 2-inch chunks
3 Yukon gold potatoes, skin on, cut into 2-inch chunks
1 large sweet potato, peeled and cut into 2-inch chunks
1 medium onion, cut into wedges
1/2 pound baby carrots
Salt and freshly ground black pepper
2 ears corn, shucked and each cut into 4 pieces
1/3 cup whipping cream
1/4 cup minced fresh cilantro
1 avocado, peeled and diced

1. Heat the oil in a heavy casserole over medium-high heat. Add the chicken pieces. Cook in batches for 7 to 10 minutes. Do not crowd the pan. The chicken will be golden on the outside. Remove the chicken and set aside.

2. Add the stock to the casserole and bring to a boil over medium-high heat. Add the red pepper flakes; red, gold, and sweet potatoes; onion; and carrots. Season with salt and pepper to taste. Bring the mixture back to a boil. Lower the heat

to a simmer. Add the chicken. Cook for about 20 minutes.

3. Add the corn to the casserole. Cook for 5 to 7 minutes longer. The potatoes will be tender.

4. Stir in cream and cilantro just before serving garnished with the avocado.

German Rolled Stuffed Steak
Rouladen

Serves 6

Annette Popp left East Germany shortly after the Berlin Wall came down. Here she met and fell in love with a Baltimore chef-turned-musician, Jeff Austraw. Now settled on the North Shore, this busy mother and architect admits that her husband does most of the cooking, but she cleans! He has learned this recipe, which Annette calls "regular mom food."

Artha Gerland, a German language instructor at North Andover High School, hosts a dinner for her students each spring. They prepare the *rouladen,* and as the meat simmers, they prepare *spaetzle* to accompany it. Artha suggests hot buttered noodles as an alternate accompaniment. I've added their recipes here.

2 to 2¹/₂ pounds top round, cut into half-inch-thick
    slices measuring 4 by 6 inches
5 tablespoons Dijon-style mustard
Freshly ground black pepper
3 strips bacon, finely chopped
1 small onion, finely chopped, plus 1 small onion,
    quartered
1 clove garlic, finely chopped
1 pound lean ground beef
1 large dill pickle, finely chopped

2 tablespoons vegetable oil
2$^1/_2$ cups canned or homemade beef stock
$^3/_4$ cup red wine
1 tablespoon tomato paste
$^1/_2$ cup sour cream

1. Place the slices of beef between pieces of waxed paper. Pound gently with a flat surface of a meat mallet or the back of a small skillet until the slices are about ¼ inch thick. Be careful not to tear the meat. Spread one side of each slice with mustard and sprinkle with black pepper. Set aside.

2. To make the filling, sauté the bacon in a skillet, for about 2 minutes, to render the fat. Add the chopped small onion. Cook, stirring, for 5 to 7 minutes. The onion will be wilted. Add the garlic. Cook, stirring for about 2 minutes. Add the ground beef and cook, stirring, for 5 minutes. Set aside to cool. Stir in the chopped pickle.

3. To stuff the steaks, place them flat on a work surface, mustard side up. Spread a tablespoon of the filling evenly over each steak. Roll the steaks. Fasten each end with a toothpick.

4. To cook the *rouladen,* heat the vegetable oil in a deep skillet over medium-high heat. Add the beef rolls in batches, turning them so they brown on all sides. Reduce the heat to medium-low. Add the quartered onion and the stock. Simmer very gently for 1 hour. The beef will be tender when pierced with a fork. Remove the rouladen from the skillet. Set aside.

5. To make the gravy, bring the liquid in the skillet to a boil. Add the wine and tomato paste. Cook, bubbling madly, over high heat. The liquid will reduce by a third. Bring the heat down to a gentle simmer. Stir in the sour cream. Return the beef to the skillet, turning to heat through for 5 minutes. Serve with *spaetzle* or hot buttered egg noodles.

Polish Filled Dumplings

Pierogi

Serves 6 to 8

These tender dumplings are a part of every Polish-American celebration. Suzanne Lohring often fills hers with a creamy savory potato mixture. This recipe is an adaptation using Suzanne's techiques.

    2 cups all-purpose flour, sifted
    1 large egg
    ½ cup warm water
    1 teaspoon salt
    2 tablespoons melted butter

1. Heap the flour on a work surface. Make a well in the center. Put the egg, water, salt, and melted butter into the well. Blend until the mixture forms a dough. Knead, about 2 minutes. Form the dough into a ball. Set aside in a bowl, covered tightly with plastic wrap, about 30 minutes.

2. Flour a work surface. Knead the dough for about 15 minutes. It will be soft and smooth.

3. Roll out the dough to ½-inch thickness. Cut circles from the dough using a 4- to 5-inch-diameter cookie cutter.

4. Place a teaspoon of the filling (recipe follows) in the center of each circle. Fold the dough circles in half. Lightly moisten the inner edges with water and press them together to seal in the filling.

5. Bring a large pot of water to a slow, steady simmer. Gently slide the dumplings into the pot in small batches so that the water temperature is not lowered. The dumplings will rise to the top. Continue to simmer for 7 to 8 minutes. The dumplings will be tender.

PERFECT *PIEROGI* DOUGH

Pierogi are dumplings filled with sweet or savory ingredients, including creamy cheeses, potatoes, ground meat, cabbage, or fruit jams. The secret to perfect *pierogi* is a smooth, tender dough. A 1975 community cookbook printed in Salem offered the following tips:

- Knead the dough in small batches.
- Cover the dough that is set aside to keep it from drying out.
- Let the dough rest at least 30 minutes before forming the dumplings.

6. Remove the dumplings from the pot with a slotted spoon. Drain in a colander. Put them on a warm serving platter. Cover and keep them warm in a 200°F oven until ready to serve.

Savory Potato and Cream Cheese Filling

Kartoflami

Makes approximately 1 cup

This is one of many fillings for pierogi.

> 3 medium potatoes, peeled and cubed
> Water
> 1/2 cup (1 stick) butter
> 1 small onion, finely chopped
> 3 ounces cream cheese, softened at room temperature
> Salt and freshly ground black pepper

1. Bring the potatoes, with water to cover, to a boil in a large saucepan. Cook for about 10 minutes. The potatoes will be tender when pierced with a fork. Mash the potatoes or put them through a potato ricer, and set them aside to cool.

2. Melt the butter in a skillet over medium heat. Add the onion and cook for 5 to 7 minutes. The onion will be softened. Set aside to cool.

3. Mix the mashed potatoes, onion, and cream cheese together in a bowl. Season to taste with salt and pepper. Cool the mixture before filling the pierogi.

Hungarian Cucumber Salad

Tejfeles Uborkasalata

Serves 6

Bill Sano pulled this cooling salad from the family recipe box. I've tried the recipe with the recently available European cucumbers, with great results.

2 large cucumbers
2 teaspoons salt
3 tablespoons cider vinegar
3 tablespoons water
$1/2$ teaspoon sugar
Pinch freshly ground black pepper
1 cup sour cream
Paprika for garnish

1. Peel the cucumbers and thinly slice. Sprinkle with salt and toss in a bowl. Set aside for 30 to 60 minutes.

2. Whisk together the vinegar, water, sugar, pepper, and sour cream for a dressing.

3. Wrap the cucumber slices in cheesecloth and gently wring the moisture from them.

4. Lightly toss cucumbers with the sour cream dressing. Garnish with paprika. Chill for at least 4 hours before serving.

Asian Peanut Noodles
Pad Thai

Serves 6

When I first encountered this recipe, I was surprised at the ketchup in the ingredients list, but its inclusion is just the newest example of the resourcefulness of cooks who have been transplanted to a new place on the planet. Some cooks use lime juice instead.

3 tablespoons peanut or canola oil
1 pound medium shrimp, peeled and cleaned
6 ounces flat rice stick noodles (*bahn pho*)
1/3 cup fish sauce
3 tablespoons ketchup
1 tablespoon sugar
3 tablespoons water
3 large eggs, lightly beaten
2 tablespoons minced garlic
2 cups bean sprouts, well rinsed
2 tablespoons chopped fresh cilantro leaves
3 tablespoons finely chopped scallions, green part only
1/4 cup finely chopped roasted peanuts
1/2 teaspoon crushed red pepper flakes
2 limes, cut into 6 wedges each

1. Heat 1 tablespoon of oil in a large nonstick skillet over high heat. Add the shrimp. Cook, stirring constantly, for 1 to 2 minutes. The shrimp will turn pink and begin to curl. Remove them from the skillet. Drain on paper towels. Set aside. Dry the inside of the skillet.

2. Place the noodles in a large bowl. Pour very hot tap water over them to cover. Let them soak for 15 minutes. Drain.

3. Meanwhile, whisk together the fish sauce, ketchup, sugar, and water. Pour this mixture over the noodles. Toss together gently so the noodles do not break.

4. Heat the remaining oil in the skillet over medium-high heat. Add the eggs. Cook, stirring constantly. When the eggs are set, add the garlic. Cook, stirring constantly, for 8 to 10 seconds longer. The garlic will be fragrant.

5. Add the noodle mixture to the skillet. Gently toss for about 2 minutes. The noodles will be tender. Keep the skillet on the heat. Toss the noodles with the shrimp, bean sprouts, and cilantro before serving surrounded by small bowls of the scallions, peanuts, red pepper flakes, and lime wedges for individual flavoring.

POLONAISE TOPPING

Use the Polonaise bread crumb topping on the following vegetables:

- whole asparagus spears
- brussels sprouts
- green or wax beans
- Savoy cabbage
- carrots
- whole leeks

Vegetables Polonaise

Jarzyny po Polsku

Serves 4 to 6

This method of presenting a single boiled or steamed vegetables from Poland's royal kitchens was adopted in "continental" restaurants for its striking appearance. Anthony Graffeo of Saugus, a professional chef, told me of the preparation of a whole cauliflower crowned with the golden crumbs. He adds chopped, hard-cooked eggs to his Polonaise for green vegetables. The vegetables should be properly trimmed, even when cooked whole.

1 1/2 pounds fresh vegetable of your choice, trimmed
1/4 teaspoon sugar
2 tablespoons butter
Salt and freshly ground black pepper
2 tablespoons fine dry bread crumbs

1. Bring a large pot of water to a boil. Add ½ teaspoon salt and ¼ teaspoon sugar. Add the vegetables. Be sure they are covered by the water. Reduce the heat. Simmer until the vegetables are tender. The cooking times will vary with the vegetable used, so pierce with a fork to check for tenderness. Drain.

2. Meanwhile, melt the butter in a small skillet. Stir in salt and pepper to taste. Add the bread crumbs. Cook, stirring, for 2 to 3 minutes. They will be golden.

3. Arrange the vegetables on a serving platter and sprinkle the bread crumbs. Serve hot.

Polish Lover's Knot Cookies
Chrusciki

Makes 60 to 80 cookies

These ruffled cookies are also known as *chrust, chruscik,* bowties, and myriad other names. Made with ribbons of dough shaped into bows, their edges are sometimes trimmed with pinking shears. They are traditional at weddings. The best home cooks at St. John the Baptist parish in Salem gather each September to make more than two thousand of the delicate cookies in one evening for their annual picnic.

    4 cups all-purpose flour
    1/3 cup granulated sugar
    1/2 cup (1 stick) butter
    3 large eggs, beaten
    1 teaspoon ground cardamom
    1 tablespoon cognac
    1/4 cup heavy cream
    Vegetable or canola oil for frying
    Confectioners' sugar

1. Sift together the flour and sugar.

2. In a large bowl, beat the butter until light and fluffy. Gradually add the flour mixture, beating until well mixed. Beat in the eggs. Add the cardamom, cognac, and heavy cream. Beat well until the mixture forms a smooth dough.

Roll it into a ball. Wrap the dough in plastic wrap. Refrigerate for about 1 hour. It will be well chilled and easy to roll out.

3. Divide the dough into four pieces. Roll each piece lightly into a ball. Work with one dough ball at a time, rewrapping and refrigerating the rest to keep them moist and easy to use. Flour a work surface. Roll out the dough until it is paper-thin. Cut the dough into 1½-inch-wide strips. (Use pinking shears if you want the ruffled edge.) Cut each strip so that it is 5 inches in length. Cut a 1-inch slash through the center of each piece. To form each cookie, push one end of the dough ribbon part way through the slit to make a loop. Set aside on a floured baking sheet until all the cookies are formed.

4. Pour 2 to 3 inches of oil into a deep skillet or pan. Heat to 365°F. Gently lower in the ribbons so they do not splash, a few at a time. Cook until they are lightly golden, watching carefully so they do not burn.

5. Remove them from the pan with a slotted spoon. Drain on paper towels. Cool. Sprinkle with confectioners' sugar. Cookies can be stored in airtight containers separated in layers by waxed paper.

Nana's Chocolate Cake

Gateau au Chocolat

Makes one 2-layer cake

Mike Frechette owns the Red Raven Restaurant in Salem, where his tongue-in-cheek paintings decorate the walls. From time to time, his Franco-American grandmother's chocolate cake is a featured special on the dessert menu. Nana Frechette changed the fillings each time, spreading seedless raspberry preserves, peanut butter, or pureed banana between the layers before frosting them.

   1 3/4 cups all-purpose flour
   1 cup plus 1/4 cup unsweetened cocoa powder
   2 teaspoons baking soda
   1 teaspoon baking powder
   1 teaspoon salt
   2 cups sugar
   3 eggs
   1 cup vegetable oil or unsalted butter
   1 1/4 cups sour cream
   1 cup very strong warm brewed coffee
   2 tablespoons plus 2 tablespoons vanilla extract
   3 cups confectioners' sugar
   1/2 cup (1 stick) unsalted butter, at room temperature
   12 ounces cream cheese, at room temperature

1. To make the cake, preheat the oven to 350°F. Grease two 9-inch round cake pans.

2. Sift the flour, cocoa, baking soda, baking powder, and salt into a large mixing bowl.

3. Cream together the sugar, eggs, and oil. Blend in the sour cream, coffee, and vanilla.

4. Combine the wet and dry ingredients, blending until just smooth. Pour the batter into the cake pans.

5. Bake for 25 to 35 minutes, until the center springs back when touched. Cool on a rack before frosting.

6. To make the frosting, beat together the confectioners' sugar, cocoa, butter, cream cheese, and vanilla. Spread lavishly between the layers and over the top and sides of the cake.

Puerto Rican Rum Cake

Sopa Borracha

Serves about 8

Yes, the recipe name does translate as "drunken soup," referring to the amount of rum poured over the cake. Just pick up a supermarket angel food cake for a cool and easy Caribbean-style dessert on a blistering August day.

Because of health concerns, modern cooks place the finished cake under a broiler for 2 to 3 minutes to brown the meringue. You can also use a blow torch specially designed for home use and available at specialty stores.

> 3 cups sugar
> 1 1/2 cups water
> 1 cup Puerto Rican light rum
> 1-pound sponge or angel food cake
> 2 egg whites
> 8 to 10 maraschino cherries

1. Combine 2½ cups of the sugar and the water in a heavy saucepan and bring to a boil over high heat. Cook, stirring, for about 5 minutes, until the sugar is dissolved. Reduce the heat to a simmer. Continue to cook an additional 5 to 7 minutes, until you have a heavy syrup. Remove the pan from the heat. Stir in the rum.

2. Pour the sugar syrup over the cake. Set aside to absorb the syrup.

3. Beat together the egg whites and remaining ½ cup sugar until it forms a meringue of stiff peaks.

4. Dollop the top with the meringue and place it in the refrigerator until set. Decorate with maraschino cherries before serving.

Maple-Walnut Pie

Makes one 9-inch pie

Maple syrup–based pie has a lot in common with Southern pecan pie. Both originated with French-speaking settlers from Canada; both have a sweet syrup base and a nut topping.

1/4 stick (2 tablespoons) butter
1 cup all-purpose flour
1 cup maple syrup
1 cup water
9-inch unbaked pie shell
1/3 cup chopped walnuts
Whipped cream, optional

1. Preheat the oven to 425°F.

2. Melt the butter over medium heat. Stir in the flour. Cook, stirring for 3 to 4 minutes, until the mixture is golden. Slowly whisk in the maple syrup and water. Cook, stirring, a few minutes longer. The mixture will thicken. Remove from the heat to cool.

3. Pour the cooled maple syrup mixture into the pie shell. Top with the walnuts.

4. Bake for 10 minutes. Turn the oven temperature down to 350°F. Continue baking for another 20 minutes, until the crust is golden and the filling brown.

5. Cool on a wire rack before serving, dolloped with whipped cream, if desired.

REAL MAPLE SYRUP

Maple syrup is produced throughout the northeastern United States and Canada. Massachusetts maple syrup is available in four grades, the depth of color and flavor determined by the season of production (early spring to late summer).

- Grade A Light Amber: delicately flavored, used for making maple cream and candy
- Grade A Medium Amber: popular table syrup
- Grade A Dark Amber
- Grade B: also known as cooking syrup, used in cooking and baking

RESOURCES

A North Shore Resource: Nancy Matheson-Burns

It's Monday night. Every table in the dining room of a popular eatery is filled, although tonight the restaurant is closed to the public. Instead it is crowded with food professionals sampling an array of products from

Dole & Bailey, Inc., a company known for custom cut meats, seafood, and "Chef's Signature" products. The company's president and CEO is introduced and Nancy Matheson-Burns steps to the podium.

Matheson-Burns's company is the resource for many of the products found in chefs' kitchens and supermarket shelves. Known for her dynamic personality and boundless energy, this lady grew up in the family business. During every school vacation, her father saw to it that she worked in every corner of the plant.

"I cleaned the plant that first summer," she says, "scrubbing and sweeping floors. Then I moved up to packing meat. Eventually I got to work in an office, but because I was the boss's daughter, I had to prove myself in every corner of the company."

Loving children, she enrolled in college as an education major, but one summer spent in sales ignited her passion for the inner workings of the professional kitchen. She made friends with the chefs and found her niche. Over the years, Nancy moved on from seafood operations to general manager, and to vice president of sales. Before she stepped up to the top job, she started to think once more about children.

"Bill and I had been married ten years without children. One morning we noticed a piece in the sports section of the paper, of all places. It was the story of a 12-year-old who was looking for a family. We knew in a glance, and we set off on this wonderful adventure.

Over the next few years, she and husband Bill "adopted five beautiful children"—Elise, Billyran, Joshua, Aaron, and Angel. She credits their deep faith for starting on that path.

"Then, at 39, I found I was pregnant and we had Matti! Matti is a beautiful gift, full of life, energy, and love."

The Burns family lives in Boxford on a four-acre farm that wraps around a duck pond. The children have grown up there surrounded by free-roaming animals.

"Besides chickens, ducks, geese, sheep, and bunnies, we have six horses, ponies, and three pygmy goats. And there's the pigs, Wilbur and Clementine. We feel the animals teach the kids about giving of yourself to the care of something else. The kids always find room in their hearts and time in their lives to care for an injured wild creature."

Matheson-Burns admits that she doesn't cook, but her respect for those who do and her impressive list of commitments have placed her into the forefront of the food industry on a national level. The first woman to chair the National Association of Meat Processors, she also advises the U.S. Department of Agriculture and past chair of the Marketing Advisory Council for Certified Angus Beef. Merging her interests in food and family, she also serves on the advisory council of Heifer Project International, a foundation that assists families in developing nations in attaining economic freedom by buying and raising livestock, one animal at a time. She's garnered armloads of awards, but she downplays her role, preferring the spotlight be focused elsewhere.

At Dole & Bailey, which she fondly calls "the plant," she is credited with creating an upbeat atmosphere. She has a particular talent for spotting, tapping, and nurturing talent, often hiring college students and guiding them up the ladder, much as her career evolved.

Back at the restaurant, Matheson-Burns is working the room, charming current and prospective clients. She talks with the owner, dining room manager, and executive chef, then stops for a word with the bus boy as she grabs her coat, before "heading back to Boxford to check on homework assignments before bedtime prayers."

RESOURCES

Specialty Markets and Shops

Brazilian specialties
Bonao Market
312 Union Street
Lynn, MA
781-599-8860

Cambodian products
Paylin Market
865 Western Avenue
Lynn, MA
781-598-8225

Caribbean specialty products
Santo Domingo Grocery
158 Chestnut Street
Lynn, MA
781-592-2260

Jimenez Market
201 Union Street
Lynn, MA
781-598-5999

Jewish delicatessen
Grossman's Market
252 Humphrey Street
Marblehead, MA
781-639-4448

Jewish kosher meats and specialty products
Levine's Kosher Meat Market
474 Lowell Street
Peabody, MA
978-535-6449

Italian specialty foods
J. Pace & Sons
Village Park Shopping Plaza
325 Main Street
Saugus, MA
781-231-9599

Polish pastries
Coffee Time Bake Shop
96 Bridge Street
Salem, MA
978-744-0995

Ziggy & Sons Donuts
2 Essex Street
Salem, MA
978-744-9605

Portuguese cookware and pottery
Casa Portugal
96 Tremont Street
Peabody, MA
978-531-5525

Portuguese specialty breads and pastries
Central Bakery
48 Walnut Street
Peabody, MA
978-531-2101

Portuguese and Greek sausage and meats
New England Meat Market
62 Walnut Street
Peabody, MA
978-531-0846

Russian specialty products
Foods of Europe
28 State Street
Lynn, MA 01901
781-599-4779

Russian specialty products
Ocean International
132 Lewis Street
Lynn, MA 01902
781-599-1167

Fine meats and seafood to the industry
Dole & Bailey, Iinc.
16 Conn Street
Woburn, MA
800-777-2648

Farm-Grown Products

**Farm-fresh turkeys, turkey pies,
and trimmings**
Raymond's Turkey Farm
163 Hamstead Street
Methuen, MA
978-686-4075

Fresh-grown herbs
The HERB FARM-acy
30 Elmwood
Salisbury, MA
978-834-7879

Farmer's Markets

Amesbury
Municipal Parking Lot at Friend Street
Amesbury, MA
978-388-8661

Groveland
Friend's Landing Parking Lot
85 Walter Street
Groveland, MA
978-374-1709

Lynn
Olympia Square (Washington Street
    and Central Avenue)
Lynn, MA
781-586-6764

Marblehead
Marblehead Middle School
89 Village Street
Marblehead, MA
781-631-1243

Saugus
Cliftondale Square exit from Route 1
Cliftondale Square
Saugus, MA
781-231-4142

Topsfield
Topsfield Fair Grounds
207 Boston Road (Route 1)
Topsfield, MA
978-887-5000

West Newbury
Laurel Grange
Grange Hall
21 Garden Street
West Newbury, MA
978-352-2986

Farm Stands and "Pick-your-own" Farms

Cider Hill Farm
45 Fern Avenue
Amesbury, MA
978-388-5525
www.ciderhill.com

Clark Farm
163 Hobart Street
Danvers, MA
978-774-0550

Connors Farm
30 Valley Road (Route 35)
Danvers, MA
978-777-1245
www.connorfarm.com

Ingaldsby Farm
14 Washington Street
Boxford, MA
978-352-2813

Marini Farm
259 Linebrook Road
Ipswich, MA
978-356-0430

Meadowbrook Farm
247 Essex Street
Hamilton, MA
978-468-3030

Russell Orchards
(formerly Goodale Orchards)
143 Argilla Road
Ipswich, MA 01938
978-356-5366
www.russellorchardsma.com

Fairs and Festivals

Memorial Day Weekend
Spring Planting Moon (Native American)
Native American food, music, and crafts
Topsfield Fair Grounds
207 Boston Road (Route 1)
Topsfield, MA
617-884-4227

June
Feast of the Holy Ghost (Portuguese)
Procession and traditional dinner
Our Lady of Fatima Church
50 Walsh Avenue
Peabody, MA
978-531-9819

St. Peter's Fiesta (Italian)
Calamari, the blessing of the fleet,
and a greased pole contest
St. Peter's Square
Gloucester, MA
www.stpetersfiesta.org

July
Ipswich Clambake and Greek Festival
Clams and wonderful Greek specialties
from stuffed grape leaves to
Greek fried dough
Ipswich Hellenic Center
117 County Road (Route 1A)
Ipswich, MA
978-356-4742

July-August
Yankee Homecoming
Music, parades, fireworks, and
great food
Newburyport, MA
www.yankeehomecoming.com

August
Southeast Asian Water Festival
The Mekong Delta on the Merrimack
    River
Lowell Heritage State Park
Lowell, MA
978-454-4286

September/October
Peabody International Fair
Multiethnic flavors and culture
    in Peabody Square
Mayer's Office, City of Peabody
978-532-3000

Polish Festival
Enough ethnic pastries to blow
    an artery!
St. John the Baptist Church
St. Peter Street
Salem, MA
978-744-1278

Early October
Topsfield Fair
Harvest fair with agricultural exhibits,
    including the largest pumpkin, a
    midway, and rides
Topsfield Fair Grounds
207 Boston Road (Route 1)
Topsfield, MA
978-887-5000
www.topsfieldfair.org

Higher Learning

North Shore Community College
1 Ferncroft Road
Danvers, MA
978-762-4000
www.nsc.mass.edu

Endicott College
376 Hale Street
Beverly, MA
978-927-0585
www.endicott.edu

Salem State College
352 Lafayette Street
Salem, MA
978-542-6000
www.salem.mass.edu

Marian Court College
35 Littles Point Road
Swampscott, MA
781-595-6868
www.mariancourt.edu

INDEX

Walnut
  -gorgonzola tart, 124–25
  and phyllo pastry, 207–8
Ward's Greenhouse Apple Pie Contest, 29
Welch, Fraffie, 13
Welsh rarebit, 17
Whiskey cake, 111–12
White Star Fish Market, 132
Wigilia (Polish-American Christmas Eve), 236
Wollmering, Rita, 32, 33
Woodman's (restaurant), 15

Xiarhos, Doreen Kent, 206
Xiarhos, Nick, 194, 206

Yogurt and cucumber salad, 189

Zabar, Hope, 163
Zeppole con alici, 136–37
Ziggy's Donuts, 237